OLIVER BERRY, HELENA SMITH, NEIL WILSON

Contents

Northern Islands

Unst
Yell · Fetlar
Hillswick · Ulsta · Toft
SHETLAND
Foula · Lerwick
· Mousa

ORKNEY · Fair Isle
Westray · North Ronaldsay
Rousay · Sanday
· Stronsay
N O R T H
Hoy · Kirkwall
Stromness *S E A*
South
Ronaldsay
· John O'Groats

0   100 km
0   50 miles

---

0   200 km
0   100 miles

Stornoway
Lewis
Tarbert
St Kilda *Harris*
North Uist
South Uist
Barra
Sea of the Hebrides
Mallaig
Kyle of Lochalsh
Inverness *Loch Ness*
Aviemore
Elgin · Fraserburgh
Aberdeen
Stonehaven
Montrose
SCOTLAND
Fort William
Glencoe
Oban *Mull*
Perth
Dundee
St Andrews
Stirling
Dumbarton
Glasgow · **EDINBURGH**
Kilmarnock
Ayr · Berwick-upon-Tweed

Helmsdale
John O'Groats
See Northern Islands inset

Ullapool
The Minch

A T L A N T I C
O C E A N

Jura
Islay
Arran

SCOTLAND p181

Dumfries
Stranraer
NORTHERN IRELAND
BELFAST ✪
Keswick
Carlisle
N O R T H
S E A
Newcastle-upon-Tyne
Durham
Middlesbrough

CUMBRIA & THE LAKES p27

Isle of Man
Irish Sea
IRELAND
Blackpool
Harrogate
Leeds
York
Hull
NORTHERN ENGLAND p97
Scarborough
Darlington

DUBLIN ✪
Llandudno
Liverpool
Manchester
Sheffield
Skegness
ENGLAND
Caernarfon
Stoke-on-Trent
Lincoln
Nottingham

CENTRAL ENGLAND p121
Shrewsbury
Leicester
Birmingham
GREAT BRITAIN
Norwich
SOUTHEAST & EAST ENGLAND p141
WALES p209
Aberystwyth
Stratford-upon-Avon
Northampton
Cambridge
Ipswich
Colchester
St George's Channel
WALES
Cheltenham
Gloucester
Swindon
Oxford
Luton
LONDON
Pembroke
Swansea
Bristol Channel
CARDIFF ✪
Bristol
Bath
Reading
Windsor
LONDON p163
Canterbury
Strait of Dover
BELGIUM
DEVON & CORNWALL p53
Ilfracombe
Barnstaple
Salisbury
Southampton
Brighton
Dover
Portsmouth
Eastbourne
Exeter
Bournemouth
ENGLISH CHANNEL
FRANCE
Plymouth
Torquay
Land's End
Penzance
SOUTHWEST ENGLAND p75
See Channel Islands inset

Channel Islands
0   50 km
Alderney
Guernsey
FRANCE
St-Peter Port
Jersey
St Helier
Isles of Scilly

Call it a hike, a stroll, a toddle or a ramble – there really is nothing that the British like better than a jolly good walk in the countryside.

Since ancient times, people have been exploring every last inch of this old island on foot, leaving behind a great web of byways, bridleways, lanes, tracks and footpaths covering practically every corner of the British landscape. And what a landscape it is: wild moors, green dales, medieval fields, heather-topped fells, gorse-covered clifftops, weird stone circles and snow-blown glens that have inspired some of the greatest poems, paintings and symphonies the world has ever known. William Wordsworth, Edward Elgar, JMW Turner, Dylan Thomas and Winston Churchill are just a few of the greats who have sought solace and inspiration tramping along Britain's valleys and hilltops, and every day, no matter what the weather brings, thousands of walkers continue to follow in their footsteps.

Walking is, quite simply, in the British blood. Just remember to pack the brolly (umbrella).

Highlights

HELVELLYN & STRIDING EDGE, CUMBRIA & THE LAKES

Few walks in Britain offer the heart-in-the-mouth, seat-of-the-pants thrills of Helvellyn and its twin arête ridges, Striding and Swirral Edge. p42

HADRIAN'S WALL, NORTHERN ENGLAND

Walk in the footsteps of the Romans along the famous Anglo-Scottish barrier, ticking off forts and watchtowers as you go. **p108**

PORTHCURNO TO LAND'S END, DEVON & CORNWALL

Last stop Britain: views of the Scilly Isles and Longships Lighthouse unfurl from Cornwall's western tip. **p68**

THE RIDGEWAY, SOUTHWEST ENGLAND

Tramped since ancient times, the 87-mile Ridgeway is often called Britain's oldest road – but you don't need to do the whole thing to experience its magic. **p90**

THE SEVEN SISTERS, SOUTHEAST & EAST ENGLAND

Gleaming white chalk cliffs form the centrepiece of England's most celebrated stretch of coastal scenery. **p144**

HAMPSTEAD HEATH, LONDON

London's grandest green space offers the kind of woodlands, lakes and wildlife habitats you wouldn't expect to find in the middle of the UK's capital city. **p174**

LOCH AFFRIC CIRCUIT, SCOTLAND

For quintessential Highland scenery – lochs, woodlands, snowy mountains and all – Glen Affric steals the show. **p188**

HAYSTACKS, CUMBRIA & THE LAKES

It's far from the highest Lakeland fell, but the views over Buttermere are hard to better. No wonder it was Alfred Wainwright's favourite. **p38**

PEN Y FAN, CORN DU & CRIBYN, WALES

This trio of peaks make up the finest ridge walk anywhere in the Brecon Beacons – and some would say in all of Wales. **p220**

THE MALVERN HILLS, CENTRAL ENGLAND

Edward Elgar found his musical muse stalking the Malvern Hills, and it's hard not to feel inspired by the rolling countryside. p132

Best For...

ANDREW KEARTON/ALAMY STOCK PHOTO ©

BILLY STOCK/SHUTTERSTOCK ©

👀 WILD VIEWS

It's far from a wilderness, but Britain still has some surprisingly wild corners.

KINDER SCOUT, CENTRAL ENGLAND
The highest point in the Peak District, Kinder Scout (pictured) feels wild in a way few areas of Britain do. **p124**

STANAGE EDGE, CENTRAL ENGLAND
This stark gritstone escarpment broods over the Dark Peak moorlands and the Hope Valley. **p130**

LANGDALE PIKES, CUMBRIA & THE LAKES
The peak-bagger's route par excellence, with a sky-top view over Great Langdale towards Bowfell and Crinkle Crags. **p30**

INGLEBOROUGH, NORTHERN ENGLAND
This lonely mountain forms part of the Three Peaks circuit. For us, it has the grandest views. **p100**

THE QUIRAING, SCOTLAND
The peaks and pinnacles of Skye's northern peninsula are a draw for landscape photographers. **p202**

🗼 COASTAL SCENERY

Surrounded by sea, Britain's epic coastline is home to some of its most unforgettable walks.

PORTHCURNO TO LAND'S END, DEVON & CORNWALL
Ignore the rubbish theme park: Land's End is still the femme fatale of Cornwall's coastal drama. **p68**

RHOSSILI BAY, WALES
The jewel of the Gower: a crescent of golden sand backed by a great grassy down (pictured). **p218**

STACKS OF DUNCANSBY, SCOTLAND
Head north – way north – to see pyramid-shaped sea stacks rising out of the North Sea. **p194**

RYE TO WINCHELSEA, SOUTHEAST & EAST ENGLAND
These sprawling golden sands comprise East Sussex's only dune system. **p154**

ROBIN HOOD'S BAY, NORTHERN ENGLAND
Ancient fossils, grassy cliffs and fishing villages straight off a postcard – Yorkshire's coastline is all about breezy beauty. **p114**

STEVE ADAMS/GETTY IMAGES ©   MATTHEW MICAH WRIGHT/GETTY IMAGES ©   LOOP IMAGES/GETTY IMAGES ©

WILDLIFE

Pack the binoculars and bring out your inner David Attenborough.

THE NEW FOREST, SOUTHWEST ENGLAND
Free-roaming ponies, snuffling pigs and wild deer. **p88**

KYNANCE COVE & LIZARD POINT, DEVON & CORNWALL
Spot seals, choughs and basking sharks off Lizard Point. **p62**

LOCH AFFRIC CIRCUIT, SCOTLAND
Golden eagles and ospreys soar over this Highland glen. **p188**

RICHMOND PARK, LONDON
Autumn is peak season for the red deer rut. **p176**

CATBELLS, CUMBRIA & THE LAKES
Derwentwater is a refuge for Britain's native red squirrel (pictured). **p34**

ANCIENT HISTORY

Littered with henges, dolmens and hillforts, Britain is an archaeologist's textbook.

AVEBURY & SILBURY HILL, SOUTHWEST ENGLAND
Mysterious monuments pepper the plains around Avebury (pictured. **p82**

HADRIAN'S WALL, NORTHERN ENGLAND
Roman legionnaries patrolled this Anglo-Scottish frontier. **p108**

CAER CARADOC, CENTRAL ENGLAND
The hillfort where the Celtic Catuvellauni made their last stand. **p134**

ST ALBANS, SOUTHEAST & EAST ENGLAND
Visit the remains of a Romano-British town. **p158**

A POST-HIKE PINT

Have a post-ramble ale by a roaring log fire.

SCAFELL PIKE, CUMBRIA & THE LAKES
Hiking heritage abounds at the Wasdale Head Inn. **p46**

THAMES PATH, LONDON
Stop for a snifter at the Mayflower, where the Pilgrim Fathers sailed for the New World. **p170**

THE BACKS, SOUTHEAST & EAST ENGLAND
Join students at the Mill, full of 19th-century atmosphere. **p150**

TEIGN GORGE, DEVON & CORNWALL
Watch the river flow by from the Fingle Bridge Inn. **p56**

MALHAM LANDSCAPE TRAIL, NORTHERN ENGLAND
The Lister Arms (pictured) welcomes weary Malham hikers. **p112**

With Kids

Britain is a fantastic place to get out and about in the great outdoors with the kids. With its varied landscape and centuries of historical interest, from ruined castles to spooky abbeys, you'll be surprised at how much enthusiasm – and stamina – they can muster.

BEST REGIONS

Many of the walks in this book, especially the ones rated as Easy or Moderate, will be just as good for children as for adults, but there are a few regions that are especially suited to family hikes.

Devon & Cornwall Best for coastal scenery, along with the potential for seaside swims and beach paddling.

Southwest England The New Forest is ideal for wildlife-spotting, with plenty of deer and wild ponies.

Cumbria & the Lakes Excellent for longer hill walks packed with real drama.

Scotland Wild mountain scenery that's guaranteed to keep young minds interested.

WHAT TO TAKE

• A decent (waterproof) pair of shoes/boots is essential, along with waterproof coat and trousers to match. Spare socks and thermal layers are recommended.

• Get the kids to pack their own kit (and carry their own rucksack) – it gets them involved, and sets them up well later for when they might want to strike out on their own.

• Take plenty of trail snacks to avoid any hangry hiccups – something sweet and chocolatey is a good reward at the end of a long walk.

• Encourage kids to carry their own water, and make sure they learn to drink small amounts at regular intervals – again, it's a good way to instil lessons that'll stand them in good stead later on.

• Don't forget to pack a sunhat and suncream – sunburn can happen quickly out in the open, even on cloudy days.

PLANNING

In order to avoid those mid-hike blow-ups, it's important to choose walks that have something to offer kids. The most essential thing is not to be too ambitious with times and distances. Take things slow, build in plenty of snack breaks, and consider doing just a section of the walk rather than insisting on the full circuit.

Geocaching

Rather like a supersized treasure hunt, geocaching is a fantastic way of keeping the kids engaged on a walk. Using your mobile phone and an associated app, or a dedicated GPS unit along with coordinates downloaded from geocaching websites, kids can track down the secret stashes, which usually contain a logbook for recording your find, and sometimes small items to swap (it's worth packing a few little trinkets just in case). You can also record your experiences online. The major player is geocaching.com, which also has its own app for Apple and Android phones.

The caches are everywhere – urban, rural, mountain, city or country-side, there's pretty much bound to be a cache nearby. There's even one on the top of Mt Snowdon. The best thing about it is that the kids will be exercising without even realising it – and once you've found a few, it starts to become seriously addictive.

 ## Best Walks for Kids

Cat Bells The Lake District fell for all ages. p34

The New Forest Wildlife galore, including ponies, deer and pigs. p88

Dunstanburgh Castle No hills, a ruined castle (pictured) and a sandy beach to go wild on. p106

Hadrian's Wall Relive history along the Roman wall. p108

The Four Falls Walk Four waterfalls, including a magical one you can disappear behind. p216

• Relentless uphill slogs or flat, featureless landscapes are likely to bore them pretty quickly, so choose a walk with a good hit of scenery: ruined castles, lonely lighthouses, big hilltop views and interesting kinds of wildlife are all surefire winners. Wiggly, windy routes with lots of varied scenery tend to be better than long, straight ones.

• Take binoculars and a wildlife guide for identification.

• Get them to plot the route on a map as you go (ideally a paper one, not a digital download), which helps teach some basic navigation skills.

• Ask them to record the journey with a camera, capturing points of interest such as noteworthy plants, trees, animals and flowers.

GETTING AROUND

Travelling by car is often the most sensible option for families, especially for more remote areas: there's plenty of room for luggage, and zero potential for lengthy waits for trains or buses in the middle of a downpour. And it often works out cheaper than buying multiple train and bus tickets. Broker sites make it easy to compare car-rental rates online. Most rental agencies will provide child car seats, although you may have to pay extra and book these in advance.

Having said that, many trails are accessible by public transport – which means you won't have to worry about parking problems.

• The Family & Friends Railcard (£30, www.railcards.co.uk) covers up to four adults and four children travelling together; adults get 33% and children get 60% discounts, so the fee is easily recouped in a couple of journeys.

• If you're concentrating your travels on southeast England, a Network Railcard (per year £30) covers up to four adults and up to four children travelling together outside peak times.

• Many local bus services offer discounted tickets for children, or family travel passes that also include adults.

Accessible Trails

Britain's countryside is undeniably glorious, but enjoying its full potential isn't always that easy for people with access needs. Things are slowly changing, however, and with a bit of online research, it should be more than possible to find a walk that matches your individual needs.

ACCESSIBLE PATHS

There's no getting around it: for the most part, hiking routes in Britain still tend to be geared towards fully able walkers. Many country paths involve rugged terrain, muddy paths, stiles, kissing gates and other obstacles that make them unsuitable for wheelchair users and walkers with other forms of limited mobility.

But being a slower walker or wheelchair user shouldn't deter you from getting out into nature and enjoying its beauty and benefits. There are now lots of excellent websites which can help you find a walk suited to your ability – from specially designed walks for hikers with visual impairments to sensory walks for people with reduced hearing. There are also a growing number of locations that offer special all-terrain mobility scooters or off-road wheelchairs for hire; **Countryside Mobility South West** (www.countryside mobility.org) covers a large area of the southwest.

All the UK's 15 **national parks** now have dedicated pages on their websites covering accessibility issues, with information on suitable trails, access, mobility assistance and other resources. The main visitor centres in each national park can also provide detailed on-the-ground information.

The **National Trust** (www. nationaltrust.co.uk) is leading the way in providing access to some of its most popular sites: many of its most prominent gardens, beauty spots and areas of coast now have sections of paved or hard trails suitable for wheelchairs and mobility scooters; some sites also offer enhanced interpretation tools such as audioguides or braille sheets. You can download an accessibility guide from its website at www.nationaltrust.org.uk/features/access-for-everyone.

The Ramblers (www. ramblers.org.uk/advice/walking-with-a-disability-or-health-issue.aspx) provides a wealth of information on walking for people with disabilities. It also organises regular guided walks for lesser-abled hikers, and can put you in touch

Useful Resources

Walks with Wheelchairs (www.walkswithwheelchairs.com) Walks filtered by location, distance and terrain.

Ramblers Routes (www.ramblers.org.uk) Offers searchable walks with tags for 'easy access'.

Phototrails (www.phototrails.org) Detailed route database with a full photo slideshow for assessing difficulty and terrain.

Accessible Countryside for Everyone (www.accessiblecountryside.org.uk) Listings of accessible walks across the UK.

Disabled Ramblers (www.disabledramblers.co.uk) Rambles for people who use mobility scooters and off-road wheelchairs.

GPS Cycle and Walking Routes (www.gps-routes.co.uk) Trails built on disused railway lines.

The Outdoor Guide (www.theoutdoorguide.co.uk/walks/wheelchair-friendly-walks) Wheelchair-friendly walks, browsable by name, image or map location.

Best Accessible Walks

Thames Path Much of the path (pictured) is paved with no gates. **p170**

St Albans A section along an old railway line is perfect for wheelchairs and pushchairs. **p158**

The Backs A civilised and scholarly route along streets and paved paths. **p150**

Porthcurno to Land's End Paved paths lead from the visitor centre out to the headland. **p68**

Malham Landscape Trail The stretch from Malham village to Malham Cove is wheelchair friendly. **p112**

with local walking groups who can help you get out on the trail.

Regent's Canal towpath walk (p166) should offer no obstacles for people with mobility issues, while **Tarn Hows** (p51) consists of hard trails circling the scenic lakeside spot.

If you have reduced mobility, remember it's not just the walk you need to think about – other factors are also important to consider, such as accessible toilets, disabled-friendly parking spaces, access by public transport and whether or not that cosy pub or cafe at the end of the route is wheelchair-friendly. As with more able walkers, know your limits, be prepared, and let someone know where

you are going and when you are planning to return. Wheelchair users should take a companion unless they're already familiar with the route.

OLDER WALKERS

Hiking is a popular activity for all ages in Britain, and for many people, it develops into a lifelong love affair. Most of the hikes in this book should be suitable for moderately fit hikers of all ages, although some of the harder walks involve more unstable terrain and cover considerable distances, so it's important to be realistic about your own ability.

Age UK (www.ageukmobility. co.uk/mobility-news/article/the-uk-s-best-walks-for-older-people)

has lots of useful background information and advice on how to choose the right walk for your age and ability.

• Hiking poles are a very handy accessory for older walkers, as they give you a firm platform when covering unstable terrain.

• Hilly or rocky trails can be very hard on the hips and knees, so choose level routes if you have those problems.

• When you're doing your research and planning, remember to think about issues such as building in regular rest stops, access to toilets, location of car parks and so on.

Essentials

BRITAIN'S FOOTPATH NETWORK

Britain has a long-standing tradition of open access to the countryside (underpinned by 'right to roam' laws), which means much of the coastline and countryside is open to walkers. For a more detailed explanation of Britain's rights of way, see p20.

WHEN TO GO

• The best time of year for walking is usually from April to October, although at lower elevations you can walk most of the year round.

• Late spring (May) and early autumn (September) equal fewer crowds; the weather is usually settled, and in Scotland, there's drier weather and far fewer midges than in high summer.

• From June to August the weather is generally warm and dry, and long evenings mean plenty of daylight – but the best-known routes are likely to be crowded, parking can be difficult, and as always in Britain, you should never underestimate the possibility of a midsummer downpour.

• High-level winter walking is for experienced mountaineers only, as it often requires crampons and ice axes. At higher elevations – including the mountains of Wales, the Lake District, Scotland and parts of northern England – snowfall is usually guaranteed between November and March.

WHAT TO TAKE

For most of the walks in this book, you won't need any special equipment or expertise. We've concentrated mostly on day rambles designed for the average walker (often with a rewarding pint at the end). A good, breathable waterproof jacket (and perhaps a pair of waterproof trousers or gaiters), plus a daypack stuffed with a map, a couple of warm layers, trail snacks and plenty of water, should be all you really need for most of our walks. A mobile phone is useful for emergencies, but don't rely on it for navigation.

One item you should definitely invest in, however, is a high-quality, sturdy pair of boots. Britain's fickle weather means that trails can often be boggy and slippery, and having decent support means you're much less likely to twist or sprain an ankle. It's up to you whether you go for fabric or leather – the key thing is that they've been properly fitted by a professional, have

Safety Tips

- Check the weather forecast before you go with the Met Office (www.metoffice.gov.uk) or BBC Weather (www.bbc.co.uk/weather).
- Pack for all weathers, even if the forecast looks favourable: a breathable weatherproof jacket and warm layers are essential.
- On harder walks, leave a note with someone detailing your route and expected time of return.
- Set your pace and objective to suit the slowest member of your party.
- Carry a mobile for emergencies, but don't rely on it for navigation.
- If in trouble, call 999 and ask for Mountain Rescue.

Resources

Ramblers (www.ramblers.org.uk) The UK's leading organisation for walkers.

National Trails (www.nationaltrail.co.uk) Route planning for long-distance paths.

Scotland's Great Trails (www.scotlandsgreattrails.com) Route planning for Scotland.

Walk Highlands (www.walkhighlands.co.uk) Database for walks of all lengths in Scotland.

Walking Englishman (www.walkingenglishman.com) Short walks in England and Wales.

plenty of tread and have been thoroughly broken in *before* you set out. A blister on the trail is a guaranteed way to ruin a nice day out.

For a few of our harder walks – especially the ones that tackle the mountains of Scotland, Wales and the Lake District, and the more remote parts of Dartmoor and Exmoor – you'll need a bit more gear. Trails here can be indistinct and hard to follow in bad weather, so you should always be properly prepared. Ideally, you should carry a compass, full waterproofs and insulation layers, a head torch, a whistle and perhaps even a bivvy bag. The Scottish Highlands are not a place to spend an unplanned night in the open.

MAPS

The UK's national mapping agency is the **Ordnance Survey** (www.ordnancesurvey.co.uk, often abbreviated to OS), whose maps have been the official point of reference for generations of British walkers.

By far the most useful are the 1:25,000 Explorer series, with their distinctive orange jackets. They're fantastically detailed, covering every contour, fence, bridleway, cattle-grid and trig point (although deciphering the map legend is a lifetime's work in itself). If you know how to use a compass, they can also be used for navigation, a skill well worth acquiring if you're walking off the beaten track. The laminated waterproof versions are worth the extra cost.

They have two drawbacks. Firstly, the size: they're enormous (refolding an Explorer map in the teeth of a howling gale is an ordeal familiar to every seasoned British rambler).

Secondly, the boundaries can seem rather arbitrary, meaning you'll often require several maps to cover a particular route.

Alternatively, the entire OS catalogue can now be downloaded to your mobile device. They're the same as the printed versions, with added benefits like 3D route visualisation and topographical feature finders, and are fully downloadable, meaning you don't need a signal to use them. But – and this is a big but – you should *always* carry a paper backup. Paper maps will never run out of battery, and won't stop working if you drop them in a puddle.

Many hikers swear by 1:25,000 **Harvey Superwalker Maps** (www.harveymaps.co.uk), which are specifically aimed at hikers. They sacrifice a bit of topographical detail for clarity and ease of use.

Walking in
Great Britain

Many of Britain's footpaths are centuries old, dating from the days when walking was the only way to get from A to B. No matter where you walk, you'll likely be following one of these historic paths – making a walk in Britain a journey through history as much as geography.

HISTORY

For much of its history, the only practical way to get around in Britain was on foot. A number of truly ancient paths have been found by archaeologists, some dating back millennia: among the very oldest is the Sweet Track, a 1.2-mile-long causeway across the Somerset Levels that's believed to date from 3807 BC (amazingly, it's now thought that it sits on top of an even older path, the Post Track, built in 3838 BC). There are numerous others – the Icknield Way, the Derbyshire Portway, the Ridgeway, Offa's Dyke – not to mention countless bridleways, byways, corpse roads and mule tracks, many of which have been tramped for millennia, suggesting that the British fondness for walking is definitely not a modern phenomenon.

These ancient paths developed into a network criss-crossing much of the British countryside. In many cases, however, these old routes were not officially recorded, and instead were passed down through a combination of local folklore, word-of-mouth, unofficial parish records and so on. Often, this informal arrangement led to conflict between landowners and walkers – a situation epitomised by the famous Kinder Mass Trespass in 1932, in which hundreds of walkers deliberately trespassed on the Peak District hill of Kinder Scout, which had been declared off-limits to the public by its owner. This act of mass civil disobedience was instrumental in the National Parks and Access to the Countryside Act 1949, which led to the first official register of public rights of way in England and Wales. This was later expanded under the Countryside and Rights of Way Act 2000, which permitted walkers the 'right to roam' on designated areas of 'access land', opening up much of the countryside for the first time.

RIGHTS OF WAY

Even though most land in Britain is privately owned, 'rights of way' ensure much of Britain remains accessible. If a right of way exists, access to it cannot be restricted by the owner, even if it crosses private property. In England and Wales, this means you have a legal right to follow these paths through fields, woods, pastures, paddocks, farmyards and even, very occasionally, people's back gardens. They are officially recorded on Ordnance Survey maps (www.ordnancesurvey.co.uk), and often signposted.

A couple of minor caveats: firstly, you must stick to the correct route, and do no damage (not always straightforward when crossing a farmer's field

through head-high wheat). Secondly, just because they're marked on a map doesn't mean they're maintained – unless they're regularly used, paths quickly become overgrown. As such, sticking to well-established routes is prudent. For more information see the Access pages on **Natural England** (www.naturalengland.org.uk).

In some mountain and moorland areas, walkers can move beyond the rights of way, and explore at will. Known as 'freedom to roam', where permitted it's clearly advertised with markers on gates and signposts. If you come from Australia, America or a country where a lot of land is jealously guarded with padlocked gates and barbed-wire fences, this can be a major revelation.

In Scotland, there is a similar tradition of access to open country. The **Scottish Outdoor Access Code** (www.outdooraccess-scotland.scot) states that everyone has the right to be on most land and inland waters, providing they act responsibly. There are restrictions during lambing time, bird-nesting periods and the grouse- and deer-hunting seasons. Local authorities aren't required to list and map rights of way, so they're not shown on Ordnance Survey (OS) maps of Scotland, as they are in England and Wales. However, the **Scottish Rights of Way & Access Society** (www.scotways.com) keeps records of these routes, provides and maintains signposting, and publicises routes in its guidebook, *Scottish Hill Tracks*.

LONG-DISTANCE TRAILS

For hardcore hikers, there's a formidable choice of long-distance routes criss-crossing Britain's highlands and islands.

The most high-profile of these are England and Wales' **National Trails** (www.nationaltrail.co.uk) and **Scotland's Great Trails** (www.scotlandsgreat trails.com). These are very clearly marked, both on the ground and on maps. Most routes take around one to two weeks to complete, although some are substantially longer: if time is short, you can always just choose to do a section of the route rather than tackling the whole thing.

PREVIOUS PAGE: HADRIAN'S WALL (P108)
ON THIS PAGE: (TOP) OFFA'S DYKE (P212)
(BOTTOM) BROADWAY TOWER (P137), COTSWOLD WAY

The **Long Distance Walkers Association** (www.lwda.org. uk) is a good place to start your research. It also holds organised walking events throughout the year.

CLASSIC LONG-DISTANCE TRAILS

Pennine Way (www.national trail.co.uk/pennine-way, 268 miles) Wild walking across the northern Pennines.

Hadrian's Wall Path (www. nationaltrail.co.uk/hadrians-wall-path, 84 miles) See 2000-year-old forts along the great Roman barrier.

Cotswold Way (www.national trail.co.uk/cotswold-way, 100 miles) Quintessential English rambling: cottages and fields galore.

Pembrokeshire Coast Path (www.nationaltrail.co.uk/pemb rokeshire-coast-path, 186 miles) Access some of Wales' most glorious coastal scenery.

The Ridgeway (www.national trail.co.uk/ridgeway, 87 miles) An ancient way used by Britons for countless centuries.

Offa's Dyke Path (www.national trail.co.uk/offas-dyke-path, 177 miles) Castles and hills line the Anglo-Welsh border.

South West Coast Path (www. southwestcoastpath.org.uk, 630 miles) A coastal epic, stretching from Minehead in Somerset to Poole in Dorset.

Coast to Coast (www.wain wright.org.uk/coasttocoast. html, 190 miles) The Lake District's most famous fellwalker, Alfred Wainwright, devised this cross-England route.

Great Glen Way (www.scotlands greattrails.com/trail/great-glen -way, 78 miles) Glens galore on the way from Fort William to Inverness.

West Highland Way (www. scotlandsgreattrails.com/trail/ west-highland-way, 96 miles) The classic Highland hike. Established in 1980, this is Scotland's first (and still its most popular) long-distance route.

BRITAIN'S COAST PATHS

Trails encompass much of the UK coastline. including the 870-mile **Wales Coast Path** (www.walescoastpath.gov.uk) and the 630-mile **South West Coast Path** (www.southwest coastpath.org.uk), which in 2020 became part of the much larger 2795-mile **England Coast Path** (www.nationaltrail.co.uk/ england-coast-path).

Much – but sadly not yet all – of Scotland's coastline is also accessible; **Scotland's Great Trails** (www.scotlandsgreat trails.com) has advice on coastal walks, including the Ayrshire Coastal Path, Berwickshire Coastal Path, Fife Coastal Path and Moray Coast Trail.

WALKING BY REGION

SOUTHERN ENGLAND

The chalky hills of the South Downs stride across the counties of West Sussex and East Sussex, while the New Forest in Hampshire is great for easy strolls and the nearby Isle of Wight has excellent walking options. The highest and wildest area in southern England is Dartmoor, dotted with Bronze Age remains and granite outcrops called 'tors' – looking for all the world

 Rambling

If you hear someone in the UK refer to themselves as a rambler, they're not passing comment on their muddled train of thought. What they actually mean is that they're a walker – and a keen one at that.

Founded in 1931, the Ramblers Association (now abbreviated to just the Ramblers, www.ramblers.org. uk) is a registered charity that was established to champion the benefits of walking to the British public.

The organisation has several aims: to protect paths and increase access for walkers; to provide support and facilities for walkers; and to promote the benefits of walking for people of all ages. The charity has more than 123,000 members and 25,000 volunteers, divided into local Ramblers groups across the country. It publishes a regular magazine and has several apps to download, including Pathwatch, which allows users to report problems they encounter on footpaths.

like abstract sculptures. Exmoor has heather-covered hills cut by deep valleys and a lovely stretch of coastline, while the entire coast of the southwest peninsula from Dorset to Somerset offers dramatic walking conditions – especially along the beautiful cliff-lined shore of Cornwall.

CENTRAL ENGLAND

The gem of central England is the Cotswolds, classic English countryside with gentle paths through neat fields, mature woodland and pretty villages of honey-coloured stone. The Marches, where England borders Wales, are similarly bucolic with more good walking options. For something higher, aim for the Peak District, divided into two distinct areas: the White Peak, characterised by limestone, farmland and verdant dales, ideal for gentle strolls; and the Dark Peak, with high peaty moorlands, heather and gritstone outcrops, for more serious hikes.

NORTHERN ENGLAND

The Lake District is the heart and soul of walking in England, a wonderful area of soaring peaks, endless views, deep valleys and, of course, beautiful lakes. On the other side of the country, the rolling hills of the Yorkshire Dales make it another very popular walking area. Further north, keen walkers love the starkly beautiful hills of Northumberland National Park, while the nearby coast is less daunting but just as dramatic – perfect for wild seaside strolls.

WALES

For walkers, North Wales *is* Snowdonia, where the remains of ancient volcanoes bequeath a striking landscape of jagged peaks, sharp ridges and steep cliffs. There are challenging walks on Snowdon itself – at 1085m, the highest peak in Wales – and many more on the nearby Glyderau and Carneddau ranges, or further south around Cader Idris. The Brecon Beacons is a large range of gigantic rolling whaleback hills with broad ridges and tabletop summits, while out in the west is Pembrokeshire, a wonderful array of beaches, cliffs, islands, coves and harbours, with a hinterland of tranquil farmland and secret waterways, and a relatively mild climate year-round.

SOUTHERN & CENTRAL SCOTLAND

This extensive region embraces several areas just perfect for keen walkers, including Ben Lomond, the best-known peak in the area, and the nearby hills of the Trossachs, lying within the Loch Lomond and The Trossachs National Park. Also here is the splendid Isle of Arran, with a great choice of coastal rambles and high-mountain hikes.

NORTHERN & WESTERN SCOTLAND

For serious walkers, heaven is the northern and western parts of Scotland, where the forces of nature have created a mountainous landscape of utter grandeur, including two of Scotland's most famous place names, Glen Coe and Ben Nevis (Britain's highest mountain at 1345m). Off the west coast lie the dramatic mountains of the Isle of Skye. Keep going north along the western coast, and things just keep getting better: it's a remote and beautiful area, sparsely populated, with scenic glens and lochs, and some of the largest, wildest and finest mountains in Britain.

SUGGESTED READING

• *The Grasmere and Alfoxden Journals* (Dorothy Wordsworth) William Wordsworth's beloved sister documents her life alongside the poet in the Lake District and the Quantocks.

• *Memoirs of a Fellwanderer* (Alfred Wainwright) The Bard of Lakeland reflects on a lifetime of fellwalking – the perfect companion piece to his *Pictorial Guides*.

• *The Old Ways: A Journey on Foot* (Robert Macfarlane) Lyrical journey along some of Britain's ancient network of paths, byways, tracks and bridleways.

• *The Living Mountain* (Nan Shepherd) This wonderful journal of life in the Cairngorms lay forgotten for many years, but is now regarded as a classic of British nature writing.

• *The Salt Path* (Raynor Winn) Set against the backdrop of the South West Coast Path, the author comes to terms with illness, homelessness and the travails of life.

• *Nightwalk* (Chris Yates) A profound and poetic meditation on the pleasures of walking in the British countryside after dark.

PEAK BAGGING

'Peak bagging' or 'hill bagging' is a term used to refer to walkers who aim to tick off all the summits in a list. The most popular collection for UK peak baggers is probably the Munros – all the Scottish mountains over 3000ft, named after Sir Hugh Munro, who produced the first list in 1891. But there's now a huge number of other lists to tackle: the Wainwrights, County Tops, Birketts, Deweys, Marilyns, Simms, Dodds, Humps, Tumps and Highland Fives, to name but a few.

OPPOSITE PAGE: PEMBROKESHIRE COAST

You can check out a fairly comprehensive database at **Hill Bagging** (www.hill-bagging. co.uk), along with all kinds of stats, league tables and records.

THE THREE PEAKS CHALLENGE
The gruelling Three Peaks Challenge involves reaching the three highest points of the British mainland – Ben Nevis (1345m/4409ft) in Scotland, Snowdon (1085m/3560ft) in Wales and Scafell Pike (978m/3209ft) in England – in under 24 hours. The standard route starts in the late afternoon with the ascent of Ben Nevis, followed by a six-hour overnight dash to scale Scafell Pike before breakfast, topped off by another three-hour drive and then the climb to the top of Snowdon. To successfully complete the challenge, participants have to make it back to the bottom of Snowdon before the clock ticks round to the 24-hour mark. An alternative Three Peaks Challenge traverses three famous Yorkshire peaks – see p101.

WALKERS' GLOSSARY

Byway Rural, usually unsurfaced road.

Bridleway Track where horse riders have right of way.

Cairn Pile of rock or stones, often used to mark paths.

Fell Dialect word for hill, especially used in Cumbria and areas of northwest England, deriving from Norse *fjall*.

Kissing gate Enclosed U- or V-shaped gate that allows one person to pass through at a time.

Munro Mountain in Scotland over 3000 feet.

Scramble Cross between a walk and a climb, graded accorded to difficulty.

Scree Steep, sloping area composed of small, loose stones.

Shanks' pony Old English term for walking.

Stile Wooden or stone steps, used for crossing walls.

Tor Dialect word for a rocky (usually granite) outcrop.

Trig point Triangulation pillar used by cartographers for calculating distances and elevations.

Wainwright One of the 214 hills in the Lake District covered by Alfred Wainwright in his seven-volume series, *A Pictorial Guide to the Lakeland Fells*.

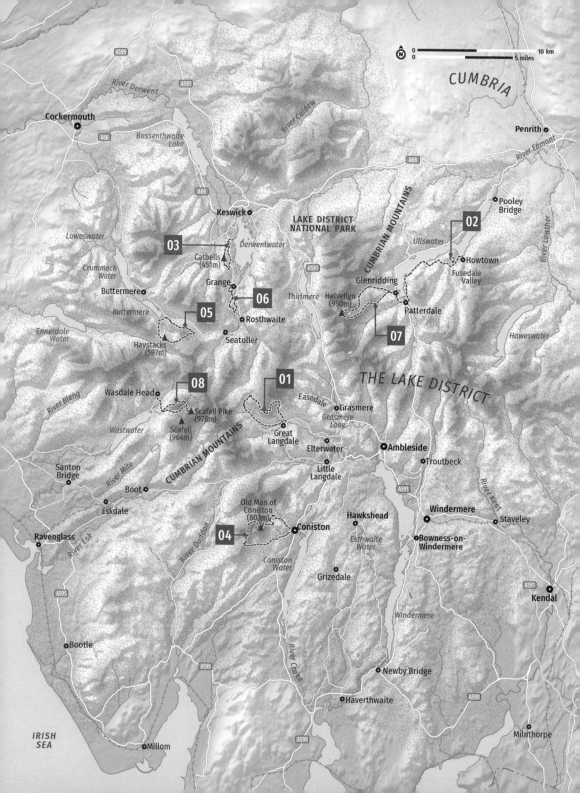

CUMBRIA

Cockermouth

Penrith

River Derwent

A595

A66

A591

River Caldew

River Eamont

River Lowther

Bassenthwaite
Lake

Pooley
Bridge

Keswick

A66

CUMBRIAN MOUNTAINS

02

Ullswater

Loweswater

LAKE DISTRICT
NATIONAL PARK

Howtown

03

Derwentwater

Catbells
(451m)

Glenridding

Fusedale
Valley

Crummock
Water

Grange

06

A591

Helvellyn
(950m)

Patterdale

Buttermere

Thirlmere

Haweswater

Buttermere

05

Rosthwaite

07

Ennerdale
Water

Haystacks
(597m)

Seatoller

THE LAKE DISTRICT

River Bleng

08

Wasdale Head

01

Easedale

Grasmere

River Mite

Scafell Pike
(978m)

Great
Langdale

Grasmere
Lake

Scafell
(964m)

Wastwater

CUMBRIAN MOUNTAINS

Elterwater

Ambleside

Troutbeck

Santon
Bridge

Little
Langdale

River Esk

Boot

A591

River Kent

Eskdale

Old Man of
Coniston
(803m)

Hawkshead

Windermere

Staveley

Ravenglass

04

Coniston

Esthwaite
Water

Bowness-on-
Windermere

River Duddon

Coniston
Water

Grizedale

A595

River Crake

Windermere

A591

Kendal

Bootle

Newby Bridge

IRISH
SEA

Haverthwaite

Milnthorpe

Millom

A590

0   10 km
0   5 miles
N

CUMBRIA & THE LAKES

Explore
CUMBRIA & THE LAKES

If England has a hiking heartland, it's here. Since the days of the Romantic poets, people have been tramping the fells in search of inspiration and escape – although with an annual tally of around 15 million visitors, that Wordsworthian cloud-like feeling is a little harder to come by these days. Nevertheless, with its sheep-scoured hilltops, mountain tarns and glacial lakes, it's home to some of the nation's greatest walks. Little wonder, then, that it's also the UK's most popular national park.

WINDERMERE

Stretching for 10.5 miles between Ambleside and Newby Bridge, Windermere isn't just the queen of Lake District lakes – it's also the largest body of water anywhere in England, closer in stature to a Scottish loch. It's been a centre for tourism since the first trains chugged into town in 1847 and it's still one of the national park's busiest spots. The town is actually split in two: Windermere Town is 1.5 miles from the lake, at the top of a steep hill, while touristy, overdeveloped Bowness-on-Windermere (usually shortened just to Bowness) sits on the lake's eastern shore. Accommodation (and parking) can be hard to come by during holidays and busy periods, so plan accordingly.

AMBLESIDE

Once a busy mill and textile centre at Windermere's northern tip, Ambleside is an attractive little town, built from the same slate and stern grey stone that's so characteristic of the rest of Lakeland. Ringed by fells, it's a favourite base for hikers, with a cluster of outdoors shops and plenty of cosy pubs and cafes providing fuel for adventures. It's in a prime spot for exploring the central fells and the famous valley of Great Langdale.

KESWICK

The most northerly of the Lake District's major towns, Keswick has perhaps the most beautiful location of all: encircled by cloud-capped fells and nestled alongside the idyllic, island-studded lake of Derwentwater, a silvery curve criss-crossed by puttering cruise boats. It's brilliantly positioned for further adventures into the nearby valleys of Borrowdale and Buttermere, and a great base for walking – the hefty fells of Skiddaw, Blencathra and the Fairfield Range rise nearby.

WHEN TO GO

The Lake District is by far the UK's most popular national park, so expect big crowds and traffic jams in summer, especially in August and around bank holiday weekends. The Lakeland weather is notoriously fickle – showers can strike at any time of year, so bring wet-weather gear just in case. Visit in early spring and late autumn for lighter

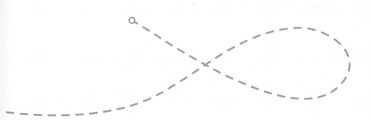

crowds; September and October are wonderful for autumnal colours, while daffodils line the lakeshores in March and April.

Snow usually covers the fell-tops between November and April, closing off the summits of the higher fells to most average hikers, as crampons and ice-axes become mandatory, and experience is required to navigate the fells safely without being able to discern the paths. At lower elevations, however, many trails remain open: it's best to check with local visitor centres or national park staff if you're unsure.

TRANSPORT

The vast majority of people visit the Lake District by car, but it is entirely possible to explore by public transport. To get here via the main West Coast train line (eg from Glasgow or Manchester), you need to change at Oxenholme for connecting trains to Kendal and Windermere.

National Express (www. nationalexpress.com) coaches run direct from London Victoria and Glasgow to Windermere and Kendal, and there is a good network of local buses, mainly operated by Stagecoach (www. stagecoachbus.com). You can download timetables from the Stagecoach website or the Cumbria County Council website (www.cumbria.gov.uk).

There are round-the-lake ferry services on Windermere, Coniston Water, Ullswater and Derwentwater. Windermere also has cruises and a cross-lake ferry service.

If you do drive, be prepared for heavy traffic during peak season and holiday weekends. Many Cumbrian towns use timed parking permits for on-street parking, which you can pick up for free from local shops and tourist offices. National Trust membership is a good idea, as it means you can park for free at all of the National Trust's car parks (which otherwise charge extortionately high rates).

WHERE TO STAY

There's an enormous range of places to stay in the Lake District: grand country hotels, country inns and boutique B&Bs are all covered here, and budget travellers have a superb choice of hostels (both YHA and independent) and campsites. There are also several remote bothies that allow walkers to experience a night well off the beaten track.

Prices tend to be higher inside the national park's boundaries, however, and there are premiums in peak seasons such as Easter and summer school holidays.

WHAT'S ON

Dalemain Marmalade Festival (wwwdalemain.com; ⊘Feb) Where marmalade-making becomes an art form.

Keswick Mountain Festival (www.kes wickmountainfestival.co.uk; ⊘May) This festival celebrates all things mountainous.

Great North Swim (www.greatrun. org/greatswim/great-north-swim; ⊘Jun) The waters of Windermere become a gigantic swimming pool.

Borrowdale Fell Race (www.borrow dalefellrunners.co.uk; ⊘Aug) Fell-runners tackle 6500ft of ascent.

Grasmere Sports Day (www.gras meresports.com; ⊘Aug) Guides racing, Cumbrian wrestling and hound trailing.

World's Biggest Liar Championships (www.santonbridgeinn.com/the-worlds-bigest-liar; ⊘Nov) Fibbers exchange tall tales.

01

LANGDALE PIKES

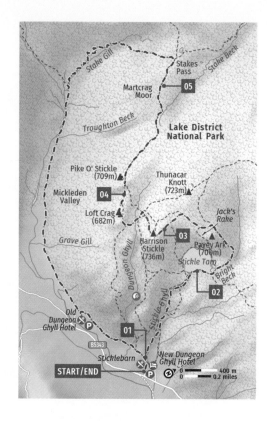

DURATION	DIFFICULTY	DISTANCE	START/END
5-6hr	Hard	7 miles/ 11.5km	New Dungeon Ghyll Hotel

TERRAIN	Rocky, high fells

The classic circuit of Great Langdale ticks off between three and five Wainwrights depending on your route. It covers some steep, hard-going miles, but the stirring views over the Langdale and Mickleden Valleys are worth the effort.

GETTING HERE

Parking spaces in Langdale can be scarce in summer. There are National Trust car parks at Stickle Ghyll and the Old Dungeon Ghyll hotel (free for NT members), plus an NPA car park opposite the New Dungeon Ghyll, but all are often full by 10am. Local farmers often open fields to act as an overflow. Bus 516 (six daily) from Ambleside stops at Skelwith Bridge, Elterwater and the Old Dungeon Ghyll.

STARTING POINT

Hikers gather in the car park beside the New Dun-

geon Ghyll Hotel; the nearby Sticklebarn is a good place for a pre-hike snack.

01 **Langdale** (from the old Norse for 'long valley') is a classic u-shaped glacial valley, but it's unusual in that it doesn't have a lake at the bottom. The summits along its northern edge, known as the Pikes, are a favourite of fellwalkers. You'll be covering seven steep, hard-going miles, and several thousand feet of ascent, so it would be sensible not to make this your first fell walk. The trail starts behind the New Dungeon Ghyll Hotel, leading steeply up the ravine of Stickle Ghyll. The easiest path starts on the beck's left bank, then crosses over stepping stones halfway up, climbing sharply to **Stickle Tarn** (pictured).

02 Take a breather at the tarn and admire the craggy views of your next target, **Pavey Ark** (700m). There are several routes to the summit, including the treacherous scramble up the face

Langdale Axe Factory

On the scree slopes beneath Pike O' Stickle and Harrison Stickle in Great Langdale is one of the largest Neolithic axe factories in Britain. The area has rich deposits of a form of greenstone, a hard form of volcanic stone which can be worked to a fine, sharp edge. Hundreds of 'reject' axe heads still litter the quarry site. Amazingly, around 27% of the Neolithic axes discovered in Britain originate from Langdale, with examples found as far afield as Ireland and Cornwall.

Best for

WILD VIEWS

OLIVER BERRY/LONELY PLANET ©

of Pavey Ark known as 'Jack's Rake'. A much more achievable ascent is the route dubbed by Wainwright as North Rake. The trail leads up Bright Beck, and climbs a scree gully to the summit; take care near the edge. Pavey Ark is actually an outlying peak of Thunacar Knott, so peak-bagging purists will want to head northwest for 500m to the summit. There's no path; just head across the grass for the highest point.

03 From here, pick up the well-worn trail along the cliff from Pavey Ark, and follow it to the top of **Harrison Stickle**, at 736m the highest of the Pikes.

04 The path drops down the fell's west side and climbs over the rubbly ridge of **Loft Crag** (682m), leading northwest to the distinctive hump of **Pike O' Stickle** (709m). There's some scrambling involved in getting to the top – the drops are daunting but the views are worth it, so take your time and be sure of your footholds.

05 Once you've conquered the Pikes, follow the faint path across the grassy slopes of Martcrag Moor to the junction at **Stakes Pass**; the trail isn't always distinct here. When you reach the pass, turn south and follow the zigzagging trail downhill for

around 3 miles into the Mickleden Valley, ending at the Old Dungeon Ghyll Hotel. From here it's an easy amble back along the road to the car park at New Dungeon Ghyll.

TAKE A BREAK

The **Old Dungeon Ghyll** (☏ 015394-37272; www.odg.co.uk; Great Langdale; s £58, d £116-132; P 🛜 🐾) – affectionately known as the ODG – is awash with Lakeland heritage: many famous walkers have stayed here, including Prince Charles and mountaineer Chris Bonington. The slate-floored, fire-warmed Hiker's Bar is a must for a posthike pint.

02

HALLIN FELL

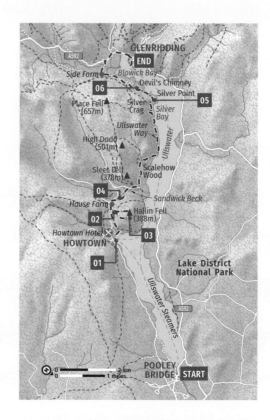

DURATION	DIFFICULTY	DISTANCE	START/END
3½-4hr	Moderate	7½ miles/ 12.2km	Howtown Pier/ Glenridding

TERRAIN	Grassy fell and lake shore

Like Catbells (p43), Hallin Fell might be little compared to many Lakeland fells, but it offers one of the best bang-for-buck views in the national park – an Ullswater show-stopper.

GETTING HERE

By far the best way to get to the trailhead at Howtown is aboard the handsome Ullswater Steamers, either from Glenridding or Pooley Bridge.

STARTING POINT

From the steamer jetty in Pooley Bridge, you'll have a grand view south across Ullswater. Hallin Fell is on the lake's west side, dwarfed by much higher peaks behind.

01 Hop off the steamer at Howtown Pier. Cross over the bridge and follow wooden signs pointing to Sandwick. You'll go through a couple of swing gates, then start to climb up the fell following the line of an old **drystone wall**. The path tracks roughly along the roadside to begin with, so it's hard to get lost. Then it bears right and begins to climb gently up the fell's southern side.

02 Continue uphill. It's a fairly straightforward climb of about 20 minutes to the top at 388m. When you take a breather, remember to turn round and admire the views down into the neighbouring valleys of Boredale and Martindale, which is home to a beautiful 16th-century church.

03 There are several rocky humps dotted around the fell's top; the true summit is marked by a **stone trig point**. The view from here is really quite something: a bird's-eye perspective looking north across Ullswater all the way to Pooley Bridge (you might be able to spy one of the lake steamers beetling

Ullswater Steamers

Ullswater's historic **steamers** (017684-82229; www. ullswater-steamers.co.uk; cruise all piers pass adult/child £15.95/6.95) are a memorable way to explore the lake (although strictly speaking they haven't actually 'steamed' for decades). The various vessels include the stately *Lady of the Lake*, launched in 1877 and supposedly the world's oldest working passenger boat. The boats run east–west from Pooley Bridge to Glenridding via Howtown; there are nine daily sailings in summer, three in winter.

OLIVER BERRY/LONELY PLANET ©

along far below). To the north, you should be able to see right across to the Helvellyn range. Take your time up here – it's a real corker of a lunch spot.

04 Backtrack down the fellside. When you reach the road, turn west past Hause Farm, crossing the fields as you follow the course of Sandwick Beck. The path skirts around the northern side of Sleet Fell through Scalehow Wood, then loops southwest along the wooded shores of Ullswater (pictured). You're now following the **Ullswater Way** (www.ullswa ter.com/the-ullswater-way), a newly established route that circumnavigates the whole lakeshore. Ullswater is famous for its displays of springtime daffodils – they inspired Wordsworth's best-known poem (you know the one – it begins 'I wandered lonely as a cloud...').

05 After a while you'll reach the distinctive headland of **Silver Point**, overlooked by the imposing face of Silver Crag, an outlying peak of nearby Place Fell. This was a favourite beauty spot of Alfred Wainwright's, with an amazing view up the lake and across towards the Helvellyn massif. There is a route up to the top of the crag, but it's scrambly.

06 Continue south past the rock formation known as the **Devil's Chimney** and the inlet of Blowick Bay, rounding the lake's southernmost point through Side Farm. The route then follows the main road back to Glenridding, where you can catch the return ferry back to Pooley Bridge.

TAKE A BREAK

The endearingly old-fashioned **Howtown Hotel** (www.howtown-hotel. co.uk) is a cosy place for a pre-hike lunch, with a small cafe on the side serving hot soup, sandwiches and snacks. Otherwise there are pubs and cafes in Patterdale and Glenridding.

03

CATBELLS

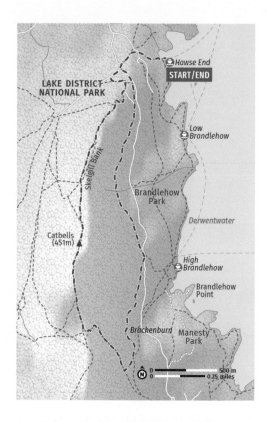

DURATION	DIFFICULTY	DISTANCE	START/END
1½hr	Easy	3.8 miles/ 6.2km	Hawse End jetty

TERRAIN	Grassy fell

Though it's only 451m in height, the mini-mountain of Catbells packs a photogenic punch despite its modest dimensions, with sweeping views over dreamy Derwentwater.

Lakeland's most famous hillwalker described the mini-mountain of **Catbells** as 'one of the great favourites, a family fell where grandmothers and infants can climb the heights together, a place beloved'. Alfred Wainwright's words in *Book Six: The Northwestern Fells* may certainly be true, but the family will still need to be fit. This is a brilliant first-timer fell, and for many a walker, it's served as the gateway to a lifetime of Lakeland walking.

The classic path starts near the **Hawse End jetty** on Derwentwater's west side; the best way to get there is aboard the Keswick Launch. From Hawse End,

the path rises steeply for around 1.5 miles to the summit, which gives a really fine panorama over Skiddaw, the Newlands Valley and Derwentwater. The route then drops down the fell's southern flank to **Brackenburn** and **Manesty Park**.

From here, you can either choose to continue along the fellside path, or follow a lower path through the woods of **Brandlehow Park** back to the jetty. If you're lucky, you might spot a red squirrel darting through the treetops; Beatrix Potter is said to have had the idea for *The Tale of Squirrel Nutkin* while she was wandering in the woods around Derwentwater.

In case you're wondering about the fell's rather curious name, Catbells probably derives from 'cat's bield', a wild cat's shelter – a handy factoid with which to impress your fellow walkers.

04

OLD MAN OF CONISTON

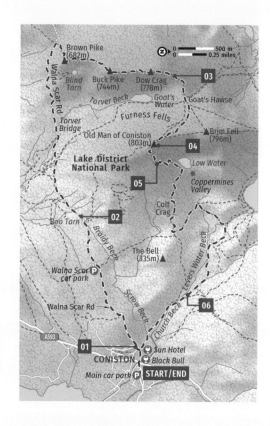

DURATION	DIFFICULTY	DISTANCE	START/END
4-5hr	Moderate	7.1 miles/ 11.4km	Coniston

TERRAIN	Rocky fells, old mine workings

Hunkering above Coniston like a benevolent giant, the Old Man (803m) presents an irresistible challenge. The most popular route shoots straight up from the village, but it's a leg-shredding slog – a much more rewarding route circles round behind the Old Man via Brown Pike and Dow Crag.

GETTING HERE

Coniston is 8 miles from Ambleside. Bus 505 runs hourly. The Coniston Bus-and-Boat ticket (www. golakes.co.uk/Windermere-Coniston-Bus-and-Boat) includes a return ticket on the 505, a trip on the Coniston Launch (www.conistonlaunch.co.uk) and entry to John Ruskin's house at Brantwood (www. brantwood.org.uk).

STARTING POINT

There is a large car park in the centre of Coniston. Alternatively, you can cut off a bit of the walk by parking at the end of Walna Scar Rd.

01 Follow the road past the Sun Hotel for half a mile to the start of Walna Scar Rd. Go through the gate and head west along the track, admiring the view across the barren expanse of **Torver High Common**.

02 The path leads west, passing the tiny pond of Boo Tarn after about a mile. Ignore the side-trail on your right that leads north towards the pool of Goat's Water. Instead, continue west, following the trail as it climbs the south flank of **Brown Pike** (682m) and traces the ridgeline across **Buck Pike** (744m) and **Dow Crag** (778m). The views east across Goat's Water to the Old Man are superb, but the drop is severe; take care near the edge, especially when it's windy.

Steam Yacht Gondola

Built in 1859 and restored in the 1980s by the National Trust, this wonderful **steam yacht** (📞015394-63850; www.nationaltrust.org.uk/steam-yacht-gondola; Coniston Jetty; adult/child/family half lake £11/6/25, full lake £21/10/48) **looks like a cross between a Venetian vaporetto and an English houseboat, complete with cushioned saloons and polished wood seats. It's a stately way to see the lake, especially if you're visiting Brantwood, and it's ecofriendly – since 2008 it's been powered by waste wood.

EDUCATION IMAGES/GETTY IMAGES ©

03 From Dow Crag, the trail circles round **Goat's Water**, dropping into the saddle of Goat's Hause before ascending the calf-testing incline up the Old Man's west side. This is the toughest part of the day, a real stamina-sapper, but eventually you'll find yourself standing on the Old Man's head.

04 At 803m, the **summit** is the highest of the Furness Fells. The panorama extends east over Coniston Water, north towards Swirl How and Wetherlam, and west towards Dow Crag and the Seathwaite Fells beyond. If you're lucky, you may see Morecambe Bay glinting away.

05 From the cairn at the top, a zigzag trail tracks sharply down the mountain's northern side into **Coppermines Valley** (pictured). The side of the hill is littered with spoil heaps, and the rocks can be quite slippy, so watch your step. Follow the slip-slidy path down to Low Water, then east through the abandoned slate quarries beneath Colt Crag; a stone staircase has been cut out at points, but it's steep. Mining remains are scattered all around: ruined buildings, old tram lines, winding engines, winches and steel cables, a reminder that the Lake District was an industrial centre long before it became a beauty spot.

06 The path winds down the valley along the southern bank of Levers Water Beck and Church Beck, then descends back to the village.

 **TAKE A BREAK**

The **Sun Hotel** (📞015394-41248; www.thesunconiston.com; ⏰10am-11pm) has a fell-view beer garden and serves decent grub. A little further into the village, the **Black Bull** (📞015394-41335; www.conistonbrewery.com/black-bull-coniston.htm; Yewdale Rd; ⏰10am-11pm) brews its own ales, including Bluebird Bitter and Old Man Ale.

05
HAYSTACKS

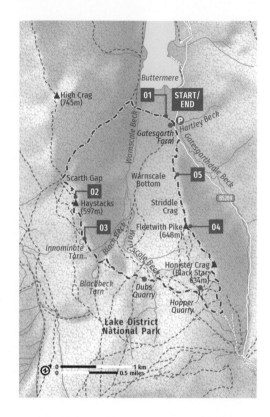

DURATION	DIFFICULTY	DISTANCE	START/END
4-5hr	Moderate	5.5 miles/ 8.8km	Gatesgarth Farm

TERRAIN	Rocky fells, quarry paths

'For a man trying to get a persistent worry out of his mind, the top of Haystacks is a wonderful cure.' So said Alfred Wainwright in Book 7 of his *Pictorial Guides*, and if anywhere sums up what he loved about the Lakeland fells, it's Haystacks, his favourite mountain and final resting place.

GETTING HERE

Buttermere is 9 miles drive from Keswick via Whinlatter Pass. The valley has an excellent bus service: the 77/77A (seven daily Monday to Saturday, five Sunday) makes a circular route from Keswick via Portinscale, Borrowdale, Honister Pass, Lorton and Whinlatter.

STARTING POINT

The walk begins in the heart of Buttermere, surrounded by magnificent fells on every side; there is a small car park near Gatesgarth Farm.

01 This route follows Wainwright's preferred ascent from Gatesgarth, and descends via the arête of Fleetwith Pike. As always, a map is helpful as the paths can be confusing. Park at Gatesgarth Farm (or better still, catch the 77 bus from Buttermere). Head southeast across Peggy's Bridge, and follow the path as it winds up to the saddle of **Scarth Gap**, a good place for a breather before you tackle the rocky buttress of Haystacks itself.

02 The climb to the summit is steep but not too testing, although there are a few bits of clambering. After 20 minutes or so, you'll reach the top of **Haystacks**, with its twin cairns and cluster of little pools. The panorama from the top is grand, stretching northwest across Buttermere, west into Ennerdale and south towards Pillar and Great Gable. In *Fellwalking with Wainwright* the hillwalker likened the fell to a 'shaggy and undisciplined terrier'.

Alfred Wainwright

The inveterate fellwalker, cartographer and author Alfred Wainwright (AW to his fans) penned seven volumes of *The Pictorial Guides to the Lakeland Fells*. Well over half a century after their original publication, Wainwright's guides are still the preferred choice for many fellwalkers, thanks to their hand-illustrated maps, painstaking route descriptions and quirky writing – but most of all, perhaps, for Wainwright's enduring love of the Lakeland landscape, which is plainly apparent on every page. They're more than guidebooks; they're works of art.

MICHAEL CONRAD/SHUTTERSTOCK ©

03 From here, the path meanders eastwards past two high tarns: the reedy pool of **Blackbeck Tarn**, and **Innominate Tarn**, where Wainwright's ashes were scattered in 1991, as requested in his will. In his autobiographical book *Memoirs of a Fellwanderer*, he noted (with typically pithy humour): 'if you, dear reader, should get a bit of grit in your boot as you are crossing Haystacks in the years to come, please treat it with respect. It might be me.' As you descend east, you'll pass a left-hand path into Warnscale Bottom, an easy escape route that avoids Fleetwith Pike.

04 To reach Fleetwith Pike, descend towards the slate piles of Dubs Quarry and follow the quarry roads before cutting west under Honister Crag (Hopper Quarry is still in use). The path leads northwest along the ridge to the summit cairn of **Fleetwith Pike** (pictured), with a mind-blowing prospect along the length of Buttermere and Crummock Water beyond.

05 From the top, a clear but rocky path leads sharply down the spine of the pike; it's not too difficult, but it is steep and rubbly in places. A controversial plan to install the Lake District's longest zip-wire near here finally received the go-ahead in 2019, much to the chagrin of local conservation groups. At the bottom, the path levels out down to Gatesgarth.

☕ TAKE A BREAK

Buttermere has good options for a post-hike lunch: **Syke Farm** (www.sykefarmcampsite.com) serves sandwiches, cream teas and homemade ice cream and the **Fish Inn** (www.fishinnbuttermere.co.uk) serves reasonable pub grub. But it's worth heading over to nearby Loweswater for the **Kirkstile Inn** (www.kirkstileinn.com), which brews its own ales too.

06

CASTLE CRAG

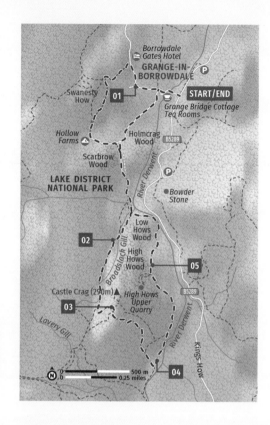

DURATION	DIFFICULTY	DISTANCE	START/END
2hr	Easy	4.5 miles/ 7.2km	Grange-in-Borrowdale

TERRAIN	Woodland and slate quarries

Borrowdale has many fells to conquer, but one of the most spectacular also happens to be one of the smallest. The former slate quarry of Castle Crag is less than a thousand feet in height, but offers a wraparound scene of the green farms and fields of Borrowdale.

GETTING HERE

Grange-in-Borrowdale is 5 miles south of Keswick. The easiest way to get here is on the 78 bus (at least hourly, half-hourly on weekends from July to August), which shuttles through Borrowdale as far as Seatoller, then heads back the same way to Keswick. Parking can be tricky: there is a small roadside car park a little north of Grange, and another larger one to the south near the Bowder Stone.

STARTING POINT

Grange-in-Borrowdale makes a lovely place to begin the walk, with its whitewashed cottages and pretty stone bridge.

01 Cross over the double-arched footbridge in Grange. This area was once the site of a monastic farm that belonged to the monks of Furness Abbey. Cross the bridge, walk through the village and follow the road towards the Borrowdale Gates Hotel. A gate leads left onto a path heading south past Swanesty How and Hollow Farms campsite. At the next junction, turn right along the edge of Holmcrag Wood.

02 At the next junction, follow the trail left past Dolts Quarry, with Low Hows Wood on your left. Near the southern edge of the wood, a path leads left (east). Take this, and then look out for another left-hand turn soon afterwards, which

Millican Dalton

Born in 1867, Millican Dalton pioneered a backwoods lifestyle long before Bear Grylls or Ray Mears. Having worked briefly in London as an insurance clerk, Dalton struck out for adventure in the 1920s, moving into an abandoned cave on the side of Castle Crag, where he spent most of the rest of his life, practising a self-sufficient lifestyle while leading people on hiking, climbing and camping adventures. A self-styled 'Professor of Adventure' and lifelong bachelor, he made most of his own clothes, and was never seen without his natty Tyrolean hat. He died in 1947, aged 79; his self-penned journal, *Philosophy of Life*, was sadly lost after his death.

OLIVER BERRY/LONELY PLANET ©

crosses a couple of stiles before the climb up **Castle Crag**. It's a fairly short walk up, but it is very steep – and there is one section near the summit that zigzags up and over a mass of shattered slate. Take extra care here, as the stone is unstable underfoot and can be very slippy in wet weather. Walking poles may come in handy.

03 At the top (pictured) you'll enter the **old quarry**, surrounded by upstanding stones and cairns arranged by previous hikers. For the best views, climb up a bit further to the grassy plateau just above: a dramatic vista opens up of a patchwork of green fields and farms, stretching away south and southwest to the summits of the Borrowdale and Buttermere Fells. A fantastic spot for a picnic.

04 Retrace your steps back down the crag, crossing the stiles until you reach the main path. Turn left (southeast) and follow the trail along the edge of the woods, before turning north along the banks of the River Derwent. You'll enter **High Hows Wood**; look out for a side trail on the left leading to an area of old quarry workings and caves. The legendary woodsman Millican Dalton lived here for nearly 30 years.

05 On the north side of Low Hows Wood, you'll rejoin the trail back to Grange. At the next junction, take the right-hand fork through **Holmcrag Wood**. Before long you'll be back in the village, enjoying a well-earned cuppa and slice of cake.

TAKE A BREAK

Many a walker stops off for tea and cake or a slice of leek-and-ham pie at the quaint **Grange Bridge Cottage Tea Rooms** (☏ 01768-777201), in an idyllic spot right next to the bridge in Grange. The prime tables are right by the river, but they fill up very fast on sunny days.

07

HELVELLYN & STRIDING EDGE

DURATION	DIFFICULTY	DISTANCE	START/END
6-7hr	Hard	8 miles/ 12.5km	Glenridding

TERRAIN	Exposed mountain ridge

Next to Scafell Pike, Helvellyn is the Lakeland fell that everyone has on their bucket list. The classic ridge route along Striding Edge and Swirral Edge is definitely not for the faint of heart, but few English hikes are quite as buttock-clenchingly thrilling.

GETTING HERE

Bus 508 travels from Penrith to Glenridding and Patterdale. Five buses continue over Kirkstone Pass to Windermere. The Ullswater Bus-and-Boat Combo ticket includes a day's travel on bus 508 with a return trip on an Ullswater Steamer; buy the ticket on the bus.

STARTING POINT

The trail begins at a very large public car park in Glenridding, next to the **Lake District National Park**

Ullswater Information Centre (☎017684-82414; ullswater-tic@lake-district.gov.uk; ☺9.30am-5.30pm Apr-Oct, to 3.30pm weekends Nov-Mar). There are several shops in the village where you can pick up supplies and gear for the trail.

01 Cumbria's third-highest mountain – at 950m – is a fairly formidable proposition even for experienced walkers, with dizzying drops and some all-fours scrambling. It's definitely best avoided if you're even slightly wary of heights, and don't even think about it in wintry conditions, when the arête is cloaked in treacherous ice and snow. Queues are also a problem in high summer, so this is another one to save for a clear, quiet day in late spring or early autumn. But don't let the challenges put you off: Helvellyn is well within the reach of most ordinary walkers. The key is not to rush, to watch your step on the trickier sections, and to try and take the easiest route wherever you can. You'll be on the top in no time. Well, alright – maybe not no time, but no more than 3½ hours for the averagely fit walker.

There are many possible routes to the top, but we've gone with the classic, starting in Glenridding. Follow the road up past the Travellers Rest pub, and take the bridleway signed to Glenridding Bridge. You'll pass Gillside Farm campsite, then take another steepening path along Mires Beck, climbing quite sharply up Birkhouse Moor. From here, the path continues to climb up to a drystone wall,

crossing over at a well-known point known as **Hole-in-the-Wall**, before emerging onto the ridgeline of **Bleaberry Crag**.

02 Follow the ridgeline along to High Spying How. This is where the real ascent begins. Dead ahead of you looms the formidable ridge of **Striding Edge**. It looks imposing, even impossible, but it's actually very achievable, as long as you take things slow and steady, and watch your footing. Several possible trails wind their way along the edge, offering various degrees of difficulty; the hardest involves scrambling directly up the ridge, but a path along the

right side avoids most of the hand-over-hand work. Whichever route you decide to take, the drops are pretty formidable, but you'll be fine if you take your time and watch your step.

03 At the end of the ridge, a final, semi-scrambly section heads up a rock buttress before levelling out onto Helvellyn's surprisingly flat summit plateau. After the airy ridge ascent, it seems rather strange that the mountain's top is so level. The views are truly fabulous: the glassy expanse of **Red Tarn** stretches out way beneath you, along with the needle-thin

Helvellyn's Hardiest Hikers

While you're tackling Helvellyn, spare a thought for the steel-legged Fell Top Assessors, who are employed by the national park to climb the mountain every day between December and Easter to assess the risk of possible avalanches, and measure weather conditions such as wind chill, snow depth and temperature.

The information is recorded on the **Lake District Weatherline** (☏ 0870 055 0575; www.lake-district.gov.uk/weatherline), a vital weather service relied upon by hundreds of thousands of hill walkers. You can follow them on Twitter @lakesweather.

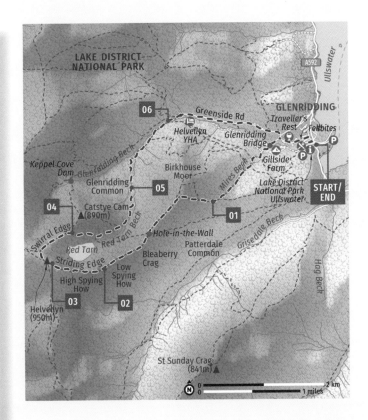

arêtes of Striding Edge and Swirral Edge, both cut out by the long-gone glacier that carved out the entire massif. Big views loom on all horizons: southeast to St Sunday Crag, northeast to the pointy peak of Catstye Cam, west to Thirlmere and east to Ullswater. Beyond, when the weather is really clear, you should be able to see all the way to the Solway Firth, Morecambe Bay and the Irish Sea.

Three **memorials** can be found around Helvellyn's summit. One commemorates the artist and climber Charles Gough who, in 1805, became the first recorded person to fall off the mountain. His body was found three months later; according to legend, his faithful dog Foxie was still waiting beside the skeleton (William Wordsworth wrote a poem about the dog's devotion called *Fidelity*, conveniently overlooking the rather inconvenient likelihood that Foxie more than likely survived by eating the remains of his owner). Another memorial concerns local man Robert Dixon, who slipped off the peak while following a foxhounds' trail in 1858. A third memorial champions two daring pilots, John Leeming and Bert Hinkler, who amazingly managed to land their planes on the top of Helvellyn in 1926.

The natural drama of Helvellyn made it a particular favourite of Wordsworth, who lived much of his life at nearby Grasmere. He is known to have ascended the mountain several times; one of the best-known portraits

of the poet, painted by Benjamin Robert Haydon in 1842, depicts him deep in thought with Helvellyn as an über-romantic backdrop. Samuel Taylor Coleridge is also known to have climbed Helvellyn a number of times: an entry in Dorothy Wordsworth's diary records an occasion in 1800 when the poet came to visit them at around 10 in the evening, having climbed the mountain the same day. The mountain's name is thought to derive from an ancient Celtic term for 'yellow moorland', although there is some debate about this, not least since the mountain isn't really very yellow at all.

04 The entire landscape around Helvellyn was carved out by massive glaciers that gouged out the surrounding rock during the last Ice Age (those boring geography lessons at school all about drumlins, moraines and cirques might finally come in handy). The descent from the summit is via **Swirral Edge**, another classic glacial arête that loops around the northern side of Red Tarn, a high lake formed by glacial meltwater. Water from the tarn was once used to power machinery at the nearby Greenside mines. The edge is steep and fairly exposed; in fact, some walkers find that they actually feel more exposed here than on Striding Edge – but it's the thrilling, tightrope-like walk that makes

 **On the Edge**

Striding Edge is a classic arête, a sharp mountain ridge formed by the action of glacial erosion. When snow and ice accumulates in hollows, known as corries, on opposite sides of the mountain, and slowly slips down the mountainsides, the underlying rock is gradually worn away. Over millennia, the rock is reshaped into a narrow, knife-edge ridge; the ice then melts away, leaving behind glacial pools like Red Tarn.

it the perfect companion piece. The ridge is overlooked by the pyramid-shaped peak of **Catstye Cam** (890m), another popular target for peak-baggers. Soon the trail heads down off the ridge and leads to a junction at the lake's eastern edge.

05 Bear left (north), following the course of Red Tarn Beck northwards through the old mine workings on the north side of Birkhouse Moor. As you cross Glenridding Common, you'll see **Keppel Cove** to the west; this was the site of a major disaster in 1927, when a dam failed following a severe storm, flooding the Glenridding valley below. Miraculously, no-one lost their lives – but the local topography means that the

area continues to be extremely flood-prone. The most recent floods were in 2015, when Storm Desmond swept through the village, causing Glenridding Beck to break its banks twice in a matter of days, resulting in major damage.

06 When you reach the old mine workings, the path crosses over Glenridding Beck and leads past **Helvellyn YHA** (✆ 0845 371 9742; www.yha.org. uk; Greenside; dm £13-30; ⊙ Easter-Oct), where many walkers choose to spend a night in order to beat the crowds by getting an early start on the mountain. From the hostel, it's a straightforward trek back down the old Greenside Road into Glenridding village.

 **TAKE A BREAK**

Fellbites (✆ 017684-82781; lunch mains £3.95-9.95, dinner mains £12.50-18; ⊙ 9am-8.30pm Thu-Tue, to 5.30pm Wed), beside the car park in Glenridding, has something to fill you up at any time of day: fry-ups for breakfast; soups, burgers and rarebits for lunch; lamb shanks and duck breast for dinner.

The luxurious **Another Place, The Lake** (✆ 017684-86442; www.anoth er.place; Watermillock; r £230-290, f £345-385; P 🛜 🐾 🐕) has a couple of in-house restaurants, and also offers lake activities including SUP, kayaking and wild swimming.

08

SCAFELL PIKE

DURATION	DIFFICULTY	DISTANCE	START/END
4-5hr	Hard	5.8 miles/ 9.4km	Wasdale Head
TERRAIN	Rocky, exposed mountain		

In terms of bragging rights alone, this is the biggest day out in England: the nation's highest hiking challenge at 978m. It might be relatively small compared to say, the Alps, but make no mistake, this is a proper, full-blown mountain: stark, wild and packed with drama.

GETTING HERE

Wasdale Head lies in a deep valley, 5 miles' drive from the Cumbrian coast. There are no bus services, so the only option is to drive, cycle or take a cab: try **Gosforth Taxis** (📞 01946-734800).

STARTING POINT

The car park at Wasdale Head fills up fast in summer. There is a second National Trust car park at the end of Wastwater.

01 Every year thousands of hikers set out to conquer England's highest mountain and, despite its elevation, it's achievable as long as you're fit and properly equipped – but it's a tough walk, no two ways about it. The exposed summit and altitude make this walk dangerous and difficult to navigate during bad weather. It's at its best on a clear day, or at the very least one without too much low cloud. It's important to stick to the path wherever possible, as trail erosion is becoming a big problem on Scafell Pike – the peak's popularity inevitably puts the mountain's delicate habitat under severe pressure, so you want to avoid adding to the problem if you can. A map and proper walking gear are essential for this walk; if you're attempting it in bad weather, which we don't advise, a compass is mandatory too.

As with most fells, there's a multitude of ways to conquer Scafell Pike, many starting from Wasdale Head. We've chosen one that also takes in the summit of nearby Lingmell, which offers a great view of the Scafell mountain massif, and is generally much quieter than the main motorway route through Hollow Stones. **Wasdale Head** is a dramatic place to begin a walk in its own right: hemmed in by brooding peaks on all sides, it's a view that's often voted one of the best in Britain, and that's before you've even got out of the car park. Take the trail leading southeast, crossing over **Lingmell Gill** via the footbridge. The path is faint to begin with, then becomes clearer as it ratchets up the west side of Lingmell. It's a taxing, tiring climb – on the plus side, it gets a good chunk of the ascent out of the way early, when your legs are still relatively fresh.

02 It's a steep push up the ridge, increasingly strewn with scree and rocks around **Goat Crags**. At around 550m, the path starts to level out and climb more gently eastwards towards the fell top. It veers around the Goat Crags, climbing up a gully towards the peak of **Lingmell**, which you'll reach at 807m. To the north, the moody summits of Kirkfell and Great Gable loom; to the east rises Great End; and to the south, the stark ridge line of Scafell Pike and the distinctive notched profile of Scafell occupy the sky. But the best part of the view from Lingmell is to the west – the long, glassy stretch of **Wastwater** (pictured), England's deepest lake, and the distant shimmer of the Irish Sea beyond. The summit cairn is a good place for a picnic and a rest before stage two: the push up to the Pike.

03 From Lingmell, the path drops south into the grassy dip of **Lingmell Col**, where you'll come to a junction with two alternative paths: the 'Corridor Route' from Seathwaite in Borrowdale, and the 'Hollow Stones' route from Wasdale Head. Make a mental note of

 Scafell or Scawfell?

Scafell Pike's name derives from the Old Norse *skalli fjall*, meaning 'the fell with the bald summit'; pike comes from *pic*, or peak. To early tourists, the mountain formed part of a circuit known as the Scawfell Pikes, along with nearby Ill Crag and Broad Crag (scawfell roughly reflects how it sounds when pronounced in a thick Cumbrian accent, and was used on maps for decades). Initially, early cartographers thought that Scafell was actually higher than Scafell Pike; in fact it's 14m lower.

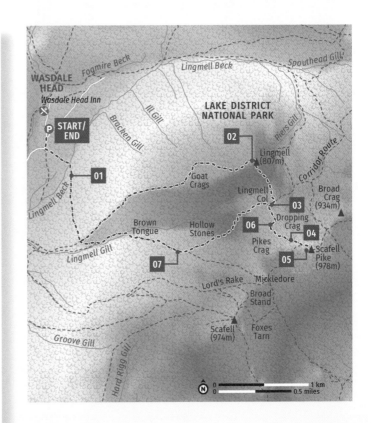

this junction, as you'll be coming back to it later. It can be incredibly windy up on the col, so keep a tight grip on anything that has the potential to fly off into the great blue yonder.

04 South of the Lingmell Col junction, you begin to share the path with the main 'tourist' route up Scafell Pike, so you are pretty much guaranteed to encounter more crowds after the glorious quiet of Lingmell. From the col, the path climbs between **Dropping Crag** and **Pikes Crag**, becoming ever more rocky as you ascend.

05 A great shattered expanse of broken rock and scree covers the summit plateau (pictured); it looks like something from an extraterrestrial planet, altogether harsher and more unforgiving than some Lakeland fells. There's no defined path as such, but when the weather's clear, it's fairly obvious where you need to go – cairns mark the way, and unless you're an extremely early bird, there are bound to be other walkers there before you. In bad weather, however, it's very easy to lose your way here, when the summit is likely to blanketed in cloud. Without a compass, it's easy to get lost in the mist.

At 978m, **Scafell Pike** is known to every schoolchild as England's highest mountain, but it wasn't always this way: until the peak was properly surveyed in the early 19th century, most people believed that either Skiddaw, near Keswick, or Helvellyn, near Ullswater, was Lakeland's loftiest

peak. Among those early walkers was Samuel Taylor Coleridge, who wrote a letter from the summit in 1802, and Dorothy Wordsworth, William's sister, who commemorated climbing the mountain in her journal (a rather extraordinary achievement at a time when hillwalking – let alone by a solo woman – was still in its infancy). In 1919 the peak was donated to the National Trust by its owner, Lord Leconfield, in memory of all the many Lakeland servicemen who laid down their lives during the Great War. The views across the valley are astounding, especially the interlocking panorama of peaks to the north, including Lingmell, from which you've just climbed – but if it's cloudy there won't be very much to see at all. Be prepared for fierce winds up

on the top: Scafell Pike's welcome can be a bit brutal.

Two paths lead away from the summit: one northeast over Broad Crag, the other southwest along the ridge of Mickledore. If you want to push on to the top of Scafell Pike's sister peak, Scafell, it's the Mickledore route you need to follow. When you reach the ridge, you'll find the way to the summit blocked by a massive, rather terrifying wall of rock. This is **Broad Stand**, a formidable challenge for the most seasoned rock-climbers (notoriously, this is the point at which Samuel Taylor Coleridge became 'cragfast' during his 1802 climb). Another equally treacherous route ascends westwards via the gully scramble known as **Lord's Rake**. Neither of these

SEBASTIAN WASEK/ALAMY STOCK PHOTO ©

～～～ Wastwater

In his 1810 *Guide to the Lakes*, William Wordsworth described Wastwater as 'long, narrow, stern and desolate', and it's a description that still seems apt. The lake itself is owned by the National Trust and is the deepest body of water in the national park (around 79m at its deepest point). It's also the coldest, and one of the clearest; very little life can survive in its inhospitable waters, apart from the hardy Arctic char.

is remotely suitable for walkers. The only sane route for hikers to the summit of Scafell drops south then west via Foxes Tarn, before ascending sharply up to the summit at 974m. It's doable for experienced walkers, but still a tricky, scrabbly climb that should be avoided in bad weather; a ridge walk then heads west back to Wasdale Head.

06 However, if you don't feel up to tackling Scafell, simply retrace your steps back from the summit of Scafell Pike to Lingmell Col and the junction you passed on the way down from Lingmell. In good weather, it shouldn't be too hard to follow the stone cairns – but there's no clearly defined path as you're walking through a fairly featureless plain com-

posed of rock and scree, so you need to pay close attention not to lose your way. This is where a compass really comes in handy if the weather has set in – you can just take bearings off the map to make sure you're on the right path. In practice, however, you're extremely unlikely to be alone on the summit – so if in doubt, there's no harm in asking another hiker if they're happy for you to follow them back down.

07 When you reach the junction at Lingmell Col, follow the path west down along the **river valley**. This is the well-trodden main path up and down from the Pike which most people follow, leading west through Hollow Stones, Brown

Tongue and Wasdale Head. Once you're back at the bottom, give yourself a pat on the back – you've just conquered England's rooftop. Now you've just got Ben Nevis and Snowdon to tick off…

TAKE A BREAK

A slice of hill-walking heritage awaits at the **Wasdale Head Inn** (☎ 019467-26229; www.wasdale.com; s £59, d £118-130, tr £177; P ☎). Hunkering beneath Scafell Pike, this 19th-century hostelry is gloriously old-fashioned and covered in vintage photos and climbing memorabilia. The wood-panelled dining room serves fine food, with pub grub and ales in Ritson's Bar, where many a Scafell Piker has congregated.

Also Try...

JEZ CAMPBELL/SHUTTERSTOCK ©

LOUGHRIGG FELL

Loughrigg Fell (335m) may be small, but its position right in the heart of the central fells means it offers unparalleled views (pictured), encompassing Windermere and the Langdale Pikes to the south, and the vale of Grasmere and Fairfield Range to the north.

There are numerous routes to the top, approaching from pretty much every point of the compass: the loop from Grasmere village is a good all-rounder, as it allows you to walk along the peaceful southern shores of Grasmere and Rydal Water, and also leads past the dramatic caves along Loughrigg Terrace, hollowed out by quarrying. If you feel up for a longer walk, you could also easily combine it with the Old Coffin Route from Rydal Mount to Grasmere.

DURATION 2hr
DIFFICULTY Moderate
DISTANCE 4.4 miles/7km

HELM CRAG

If you only do one fell walk around Grasmere, there's a pretty good argument that says you should make it Helm Crag.

It's sometimes referred to as 'the Lion and the Lamb', after the twin crags atop its summit, which (with a bit of judicious squinting) vaguely resemble the animals. Many people think it actually looks more like a hilltop cannon, and we're inclined to agree. It's a rewarding two-hour climb, but it's very steep in places, with around 335m of elevation gain. The there-and-back trail starts on Easedale Rd and is fairly well signposted. An optional and very worthwhile extension pushes eastwards to Easedale Tarn and the waterfall of Sourmilk Ghyll.

DURATION 2hr
DIFFICULTY Moderate
DISTANCE 3.6 miles/5.8km

STEVE HEAP/SHUTTERSTOCK ©

MELLBREAK

This is another of those Lakeland fells that looks relatively small, but takes a good deal more effort to conquer than you might think.

Standing in semi-isolation on the edge of Crummock Water, it involves a steep, tiring climb up slopes of scree to get to the top, but offers a prize panorama over Buttermere. On the fell's southern side, you can also visit the thunder of Scales Force – the highest waterfall in the Lake District at 170ft.

DURATION 3hr
DIFFICULTY Moderate
DISTANCE 6.5 miles/10.5km

OLD COFFIN ROUTE

An easy walk that follows the route used by pallbearers carrying coffins to St Oswald's Church (you'll pass stone platforms where the coffins were deposited while the bearers rested).

The trail begins at Rydal Mount, a former home of Wordsworth's, then leads along the north side of Rydal Water to Dove Cottage (another Wordsworthian residence), before circling round to Grasmere. Retrace your steps, or catch the 555 bus back.

DURATION 1½hr
DIFFICULTY Easy
DISTANCE 2.5 miles/4km

TARN HOWS

Two miles off the B5285 from Hawkshead, this famously photogenic lake (pictured) has a wealth of easy walks.

It's a particularly good place for red-squirrel-spotting, so a pair of binoculars would come in handy. It's hard to believe that it's not natural, but was in fact purpose-built by James Garth Marshall in 1865 according to the 'picturesque' principles of the day. The National Trust car park fills quickly; several buses, including the 505, stop nearby.

DURATION 1hr
DIFFICULTY Easy
DISTANCE 2 miles/3.2km

DEVON & CORNWALL

Explore
DEVON & CORNWALL

Sand, sea, surf – these are the three things that draw most people to Britain's most far westerly counties, and for clifftop scenery and coast walks, you really will be spoilt. If you like to walk with the scent of the sea in your nostrils, followed by a paddle in the ocean and a congratulatory pint at a seaside pub, this is very likely to be the corner of Britain for you. But there are other sides to Devon and Cornwall that feel quite different to the coast – two of Britain's great moorlands, Bodmin Moor and Dartmoor, straddle the granite spine that runs down the centre of the counties, while a web of pretty rivers and estuaries provides a wealth of tranquil waterside walks.

TRURO

Dominated by the three spires of its 19th-century cathedral, Truro is Cornwall's capital and its only city. It's the county's main centre for shopping and commerce: the streets here are packed with high-street chains and independent shops, and there are regular weekly markets held on the paved piazza at Lemon Quay (opposite the Hall for Cornwall).

Traces of Truro's wealthy past remain in the smart Georgian town houses and Victorian villas dotted around the city – especially along Strangways Tce, Walsingham Pl and Lemon St.

PENZANCE

Overlooking the majestic sweep of Mount's Bay, the old har-bour of Penzance has a salty, sea-blown charm that feels altogether more authentic than many of Cornwall's polished-up ports. Its streets and shopping arcades still feel real and a touch ramshackle, and there's nowhere better for a windy-day walk than the town's seafront Victorian promenade. It's a useful base for exploring the far west of Cornwall, including Land's End and the Penwith Peninsula. Buses serve most local villages.

EXETER

Well-heeled and comfortable, Exeter exudes evidence of its centuries-old role as the spiritual and administrative heart of Devon. The city's Gothic cathedral presides over pockets of cobbled streets; medieval and Georgian buildings and fragments of the Roman city stretch out all around. A snazzy contemporary shopping centre brings bursts of the modern; thousands of university students ensure a buzzing nightlife; and the vibrant quayside acts as a launch pad for cycling or kayaking trips. Throw in some stylish places to stay and eat, and you have a relaxed but lively base for explorations of central and southern Devon.

WHEN TO GO

Spring and autumn are usually the best time for walking in the far west. There are far fewer crowds once the school holidays are over, and the weather can often be a bit more settled, especially in May and September.

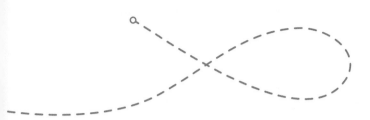

Resources

South West Coast Path (www.southwestcoastpath.org.uk) Excellent guide to walking the southwest's longest trail.

I Walk Cornwall (www.iwalkcornwall.co.uk) Good local guide to out-of-the-way Cornish walks.

Visit Dartmoor (www.visitdartmoor.co.uk) Walking advice, routes and guidance for Dartmoor National Park.

Prices at B&Bs and campsites often drop, and seasonal deals are available.

Summer is peak season in Devon and Cornwall. Prices are at their highest, beaches and attractions can be uncomfortably crowded, and most of the best hotels, B&Bs and campsites are usually full. On the plus side, warm weather and plenty of sunshine mean that this can be still a good time to walk – but expect plenty of foot traffic on the most popular trails.

Walking in winter means wrapping up: you'll often be battling fierce winds and sudden storms, but the winter storms bring real drama to the landscape. Snowfall is expected on the high moors of Dartmoor and Bodmin Moor, but is rare in other areas; if it comes, it's usually after Christmas.

TRANSPORT

Devon and Cornwall sit, gloriously, at the far end of England, and getting here sometimes feels like it. The main A30 runs down the centre of the counties, while the A38 travels along the southern edge via Plymouth and the Tamar Bridge. Expect traffic jams in summer.

GWR (☎0345 7000 125; www.gwr.com) runs hourly trains from Bristol and London, while **CrossCountry** (☎0844 811 0124; www.crosscountrytrains.co.uk) runs connecting services from the north. The most useful mainline stations are Exeter and Plymouth in Devon, and St Austell, Truro and Penzance in Cornwall. Several branch lines serve more out-of-the-way towns. National Rail Enquiries (www.nationalrail.co.uk) has timetables and fares: book ahead for the cheapest tickets. The journey time from London to Exeter is around three hours, to Truro 4½ to five hours, Penzance 5½ to six hours.

Travelling by bus to the southwest is cheap and reliable, but takes much longer than the train (around nine hours from London Victoria to Penzance). The main local operators are First (www.firstgroup.com) and Stagecoach (www.stagecoachbus.com).

WHERE TO STAY

Devon and Cornwall have a great range of accommodation, from cosy pubs to stylish B&Bs and hotels. Booking at least two months in advance for holiday periods (Easter, mid-July to early September, and Christmas) is strongly advised. A good selection of YHA hostels and rural campsites makes budget travel easy here, but again, you'll need to book ahead at the most popular in summer.

👍 WHAT'S ON

St Piran's Day (🕙5 Mar) Processions in honour of Cornwall's patron saint.

Padstow May Day (🕙1 May) Raucous 'osses cavort round Padstow.

Falmouth Sea Shanty Festival (www.falmouthseashanty.co.uk; 🕙Jun) Sea-songs fill the harbour air.

Eden Sessions (www.edensessions.com; 🕙Jul & Aug) Big bands play in front of the space-age biomes.

Dartmouth Royal Regatta (www.dartmouthregatta.co.uk; 🕙Aug) Yachties ply the waters round Dartmouth.

British Fireworks Championships (www.britishfireworks.co.uk; 🕙mid-Aug) Plymouth's skies are filled with bursts of colour.

09

TEIGN GORGE

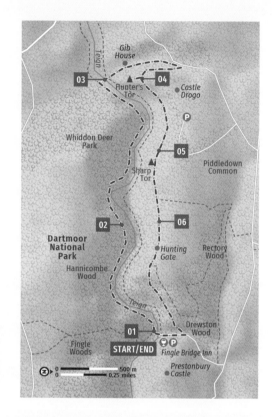

DURATION	DIFFICULTY	DISTANCE	START/END
2½-3hr	Moderate	4 miles/ 6.5km	Fingle Bridge car park

TERRAIN	Woodland and riverbank

Skirting the cliffs of a tree-cloaked, almost Alpine-esque valley, this woodland loop offers one of the most impressive vistas on Dartmoor, and visits one of the UK's largest forest restoration projects.

GETTING HERE

Castle Drogo is 3.3 miles northwest of the village of Chagford. Dartline Coaches (www.dartline-coaches.co.uk) bus 173 stops at Castle Drogo and Drewsteignton, from where it's about a mile's walk down to Fingle Woods.

STARTING POINT

From the Fingle Bridge car park (free) it's a short walk into Fingle Woods.

01 The walk begins in the middle of **Fingle Woods** (NT; ✆01647-433356; www.finglewoods.org.uk),

an 825-acre area of ancient woodland spanning the slopes of the River Teign. Damaged by the planting of non-native conifers, the forest was jointly acquired by the National Trust and Woodland Trust in 2013, with an aim to restore it by planting native species such as oak, ash and beech – a project that will take 200 years. It's a glorious spot for a stroll, especially on a sunny spring day, when the sunlight filters down through the trees and the woods ring with bird-song, or even better, in autumn, when the tree canopy lights up in reds, oranges and golds.

02 To begin with, a clear trail leads along the riverbanks all the way to **Whiddon Deer Park**. After around 1½ miles, you'll walk past a small hydroelectric turbine and begin to follow the course of an old drystone wall.

03 Near its end, a footbridge crosses the river, then leads up a quiet lane past Gib House.

🏰 Castle Drogo

This outlandish modern-day **castle** (NT; 📞 01647-433306; www.nationaltrust.org.uk/castle-drogo; near Drewsteignton; adult/child £11.60/5.80; ⏰11am-5pm mid-Mar–Oct; 🅿) – England's most recent, built between 1911 and 1931 – was an architectural flight of fancy designed by Sir Edwin Lutyens for self-made food millionaire Julius Drewe, who wanted to combine the drama of a medieval castle with the comforts of a country house. Unfortunately, the property was bone-chillingly draughty and leaked terribly, and is currently the focus of a huge six-year restoration project. Parts of the house remain open; mid-renovation displays include a scaffolding viewing tower.

Best for

A POST-HIKE PINT

OLIVER BERRY/LONELY PLANET ©

Look out for a sign on the right leading through a gate onto the **Castle Drogo** estate. The path climbs gently through the trees.

04 Before long you'll see another sign pointing to **Hunter's Tor**, an outcrop that juts out into the gorge like the prow of an ocean-liner. Pick your way along the gorse-lined path to the tip of the promontory for an east–west panorama along the gorge, and across Chagford to the high moors. The canopy of Fingle Woods stretches out handsomely below.

05 Backtrack to the main path, and continue east along the edge of the gorge, with ever-expanding views of the deep, tree-cloaked valley. The path leads across the open ground of Piddledown Common to another viewpoint, **Sharp Tor**, with a dizzying drop straight down: vertigo sufferers beware. Listen and you'll hear the clatter of the Teign below.

06 From Sharp Tor, the path continues east, dropping gently down into the trees. Walk through **Hunting Gate** and return to the car park, where a celebratory pint at the Fingle Bridge Inn awaits. High on the hillside above the inn are the remains of an Iron Age hillfort, **Prestonbury Castle**; you can clearly see the outline of the fort as you stand on Fingle Bridge.

 **TAKE A BREAK**

A more perfect place for a riverside pint you could not find than the **Fingle Bridge Inn** (📞01647-281287; www.finglebridgeinn.co.uk; Fingle Woods; ⏰11am-5pm Mon-Wed, to 10pm Thu-Sat, to 6pm Sun). Nestled in the middle of the woods, on the banks of the Teign, this delightful pub is popular with ramblers exploring the trails. Light pub lunches are served daily, dinners from Thursday to Saturday. Alternatively, there's a pleasant cafe at Castle Drogo.

10
WISTMAN'S WOOD

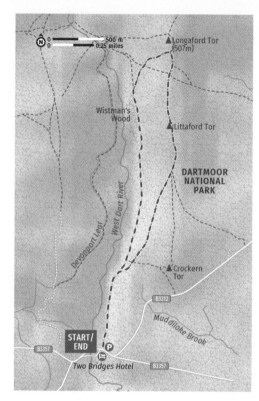

DURATION	DIFFICULTY	DISTANCE	START/END
2½hr	Moderate	4 miles/ 6.3km	Two Bridges car park

TERRAIN	Moorland and woods

This classic short walk visits one of the oldest surviving woodlands on Dartmoor, a last remnant of the mighty forest that once covered the entire moor, and much of southwest England.

Park opposite the Two Bridges Hotel, and follow the farm track north past a small white cottage. Head to the right of the cottage, climbing up onto the open moor.

After about a mile, you will come to the southern edge of the wood. The main path skirts its edge, but it's well worth taking a quick detour off the main trail just to experience the haunting, otherworldly atmosphere. There's no clear path through the trees, and it's very unstable underfoot – but the moment you enter the forest, it feels like entering a parallel world. It's a magical spot, with twisted, lichen-cloaked oaks sprouting from a chaotic jumble

of moss-covered boulders. Unsurprisingly, numerous local legends surround this place: it's said to have been a sacred grove for the druids, and many people claim to have spotted fairies here. It's also rumoured to be the home of demonic 'Wisht Hounds' who race through the woods by night in search of unwary travellers.

Assuming you haven't been bewitched by fairies or devoured by hell-hounds, once you've explored the wood, head back to the main path along the edge. After a while, it bears north away from the trees, then climbs up the grassy slopes to **Longaford Tor**, a jumble of granite stacks that looks as though it's been left behind by a giant. You can pick your way up to the top if you wish. From Longaford Tor, an indistinct and occasionally rather boggy trail leads south across **Littaford Tor**, then bears southwest down the hillside, before rejoining the farm track back to the Two Bridges car park.

11

RIVER DART WALK

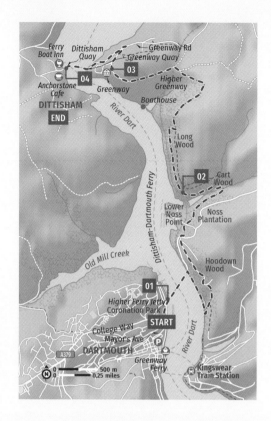

DURATION	DIFFICULTY	DISTANCE	START/END
2hr	Easy	4 miles/ 6.4km	Dartmouth/ Dittisham

TERRAIN	River path, woodland

The southwest's great estuaries were once the key to Britain's seagoing might, and few have as illustrious a history as the Dart. From the riverside town of Dartmouth, this route tracks the course of the river to Agatha Christie's summer home at Greenway.

GETTING HERE

Dartmouth is 13 miles south of Totnes. Stagecoach bus X64 runs every two hours Monday to Saturday, twice on Sunday. You can also catch the Dartmouth Steam Railway (www.dartmouthrailriver.co.uk) from Paignton to Kingswear.

STARTING POINT

Coronation Park in Dartmouth; the nearest car park is on Mayor's Ave.

01 From Coronation Park, walk to the jetty for the **Dartmouth–Kingswear Higher Ferry** (☎07866 531687; www.dartmouthhigherferry.com; car/pedestrian 1 way £5.60/60p; ⏰6.30am-10.50pm Mon-Sat, from 8am Sun), which crosses the river every six minutes. On the far side, walk up the road, and follow signs onto the permissive footpath on the right. The path leads along the river, then turns up into **Hoodown Wood**. Follow signs along the Dart Valley Trail towards Greenway Ferry and Maypool. The trail leads through the woods, turning into a lane above Lower Noss Point. Cross the road, and continue through the trees into Noss Plantation and Cart Wood.

02 The trail turns back sharply towards the river, then continues north through Long Wood, an important area of semi-ancient oak woodland. You're now walking on the long-distance **Dart Valley Trail**, roughly following the same course as the old Paignton and Dartmouth Steam Railway. The

 Coleton Fishacre

For a glimpse of jazz-age glamour, drop by the former home of the D'Oyly Carte family of theatre impresarios, **Coleton Fishacre** (NT; 📞 01803-842382; www.nationaltrust.org.uk/coleton-fishacre; Brownstone Rd, near Kingswear; adult/child £11.60/5.80; ⏱10.30am-5pm mid-Feb–Oct, 11am-4pm Sat & Sun Nov & Dec; 🅿). Built in the 1920s, its art deco embellishments include original Lalique tulip uplighters, comic bathroom tiles and a stunning saloon – complete with tinkling piano. The subtropical gardens afford sudden vistas of the sea. A 4-mile path leads along the cliffs from Kingswear.

TREVOR SMITH / ALAMY STOCK PHOTO ©

woodland is rich with birdlife, so bring binoculars: blue tits, jays, woodpeckers and even sparrowhawks can be seen.

03 Keep following the trail though the woods. At its north end, you'll see waymarkers pointing to Greenway; turn left past Higher Greenway, then left again downhill to Maypool. The lane leads down to **Greenway** (pictured; 📞 01803-842382; www.nationaltrust.org.uk/greenway; Greenway Rd, Galmpton; adult/child £11.60/5.80; ⏱10.30am-5pm mid-Feb–Oct, 11am-4pm Sat & Sun Nov & Dec), the captivating summer home of crime writer Agatha Christie. Christie owned the

house between 1938 and 1959, and it feels frozen in time – complete with piles of hats in the lobby, a book-stocked library and a wardrobe filled with clothes (you can even listen to her speak via a replica radio in the drawing room). In Christie's book *Dead Man's Folly*, Greenway doubles as Nasse House, with the boathouse making an appearance as a macabre murder scene.

04 Once you've explored the grounds of Greenway, hop across the river to the village of Dittisham on the foot ferry (it's summoned by ringing a ship's bell on Greenway's quay). From here, you can

catch the **Dittisham-Dartmouth Ferry** (📞 01803-882811; www.greenwayferry.co.uk; adult/child return £8.50/6.50; ⏱Easter–Oct) – a picturesque way to round out the day.

 TAKE A BREAK

For riverside dining, it's hard to beat Dittisham's **Anchorstone Cafe** (📞 01803-722365; www.anchorstonecafe.co.uk; Manor St, Dittisham; mains from £9; ⏱noon-4pm Wed-Sun mid-Mar–Oct) for crab, hand-dived scallops and local Sharpham wine. Less fancy is the waterfront **Ferry Boat Inn** (📞 01803-722368; www.ferryboatinndittisham.pub; Manor St, Dittisham; ⏱11am-11pm).

12

KYNANCE COVE & LIZARD POINT

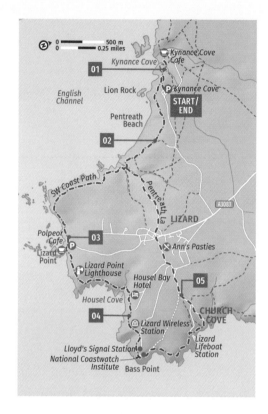

DURATION	DIFFICULTY	DISTANCE	START/END
3hr	Moderate	5.9 miles/ 9.5km	Kynance Cove

TERRAIN	Coast path, clifftops

This cliff walk takes in some of southern Cornwall's most postcard-worthy views, including an island-studded cove and a historic lighthouse.

GETTING HERE

Kynance Cove is 12 miles south of Helston. In summer, **First Kernow** (customer service 0845 600 1420, timetables 0871 200 2233; www.firstgroup.com/cornwall) runs hourly services between Helston and the Lizard.

STARTING POINT

Kynance Cove car park. NT members can park for free, but spaces go fast in summer.

01 Park at **Kynance Cove**. Studded with craggy offshore islands rising out of seas that seem almost tropical in colour, it's one of Cornwall's most ravishing beauty spots. The cliffs around the cove are rich in serpentine, a red-green rock popular with Victorian trinket-makers.

02 From Kynance, pick up the coast path and head south past **Lion Rock** and rocky **Pentreath Beach**. This is a good area to spot choughs: a member of the crow family, identifiable by its bright orange beak, the bird features on Cornwall's coat-of-arms, but was almost wiped out by pesticides and habitat loss. Since being reintroduced and protected, choughs are now breeding here in decent numbers.

03 One-and-a-half miles south, you'll reach the craggy outcrop of **Lizard Point**, the southernmost point of mainland Britain. Historically this is

🗼 Lizard Lighthouse

Rising above Lizard Point, the whitewashed **lighthouse** (📞 01326-290202; www.trinity house.co.uk/lighthouse-visitor-centres/lizard-lighthouse-visitor-centre; adult/child £3.50/2.50; 🕐 11am-5pm Sun-Thu Mar-Oct) **was built in 1751 and has protected ships from the treacherous rocks ever since. Although it's now automated, like all UK lighthouses, you can visit the heritage centre to learn more about its mechanics and the many ships that have come to grief nearby. It's also the only lighthouse in Cornwall you can actually climb; guided tours (adult/child £8/5) ascend into the tower to see the lamp room and foghorn.**

OLIVER BERRY/LONELY PLANET ©

Best for

🦌

WILDLIFE

one of Britain's deadliest headlands. Hundreds of ships have come to grief around the point, and are now a hub for scuba divers. A steep track winds down to the long-disused lifeboat station and shingly cove. Nearby, the white tower of Lizard Lighthouse hoves into view.

04 Continue around the coast to **Housel Cove**, home to a Victorian-era hotel, then trek onwards towards **Bass Point**. You'll pass a small building which, a century ago, housed a signal station; a plaque outside is dedicated to Guglielmo Marconi, often credited as the inventor of radio. There's a

small visitor centre inside. The main signal station is in a white building a little further east (you can't miss it – it's labelled in gigantic letters).

05 Trek north past the modern lifeboat station, which can be visited if you wish. A bit further north, you'll pass pretty **Church Cove**. From here, follow the main road from the cove back into the centre of **Lizard Village**. Once you've browsed around the village's souvenir shops, follow Pentreath Lane from the main car park, onto a lane which rejoins the coast path and leads back to Kynance Cove.

☕ TAKE A BREAK

Everyone has their favourite pasty shop, but **Ann's Pasties** (📞 01326-290889; Beacon Tce; pasties from £3.50; 🕐 9am-5pm) has the approval of many top chefs (including Rick Stein). They come in steak, cheese and vegan versions.

Alternatively, above Lizard Point, **Polpeor Cafe** (📞 01326-290939; mains £3-8; 🕐 10.30am-4.30pm or 5pm) serves lunches and cream teas, and claims to be Britain's most southerly cafe, and **Kynance Cove Cafe** (📞 01326-290436; www.kynancecovecafe.co.uk; mains £5-14; 🕐 9am-5.30pm) does cream teas, crab sandwiches and delicious cakes.

13

ST AGNES & CHAPEL PORTH

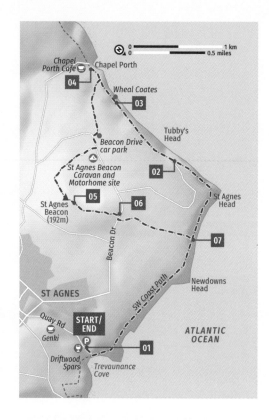

DURATION	DIFFICULTY	DISTANCE	START/END
3hr	Moderate	6.5 miles/ 10.4km	Trevaunance Cove

TERRAIN	Coast path, clifftops

This walk takes in the beautiful, windblown scenery around the old mining village of St Agnes, factoring in panoramic coastal views and a trip to the top of the area's highest point, the Beacon.

GETTING HERE

St Agnes is 9 miles from Truro. Bus 87 (45 minutes, hourly in summer) stops in St Agnes on its way from Newquay, via Crantock, Holywell, Perranporth and Trevellas, to Truro.

STARTING POINT

You can park in Trevaunance Cove opposite the pub.

01 Start at **Trevaunance Cove**. From the beach, the coast path climbs steeply around the clifftops to Newdowns Head. Offshore there are two rocks known locally as the **Bawden Rocks**, which

according to local legend were hurled there by the local giant, Bolster. The coast path then tracks round to St Agnes Head, travelling through thick heather and gorse.

02 The trail then swings south, opening out onto the exposed, heather-carpeted cliffs around **Tubby's Head**. This is among the most impressive stretches of the north Cornish coastline, with huge views stretching south all the way to Godrevy Lighthouse. Once an important mining area, the clifftops all around here are littered with the remains of disused shafts, engine houses and mine workings.

03 The most picturesque mine – and possibly the most photographed in all of Cornwall – is the engine house and chimney stack at **Wheal Coates** (pictured), dramatically framed against the blue Atlantic. There are various other workings nearby to explore, and you can peer down into a capped shaft.

Blue Hills Tin Streams

A mile east of St Agnes (signed to Wheal Kitty) is the rocky valley of Trevellas Porth, home to one of Cornwall's last remaining **tin manufacturers** (📞 01872-553341; www.cornishtin.com; adult/child £6.50/3; 🕐 10am-2pm Tue–Sat mid-Apr– mid-Oct). You can watch the whole tinning process, from mining and smelting through to casting and finishing. Handmade jewellery is sold in the shop. The valley's local name, Blue Hills, refers to the vivid blue heather that grows here in summer.

HELEN HOTSON/SHUTTERSTOCK ©

04 From here it's a steep walk downhill to the cove of **Chapel Porth**, where you can fuel up with a hot tea and hedgehog ice cream from the ever-busy little **Chapel Porth Cafe** (sandwiches & cakes £2-5; 🕐 10am-5pm).

05 Backtrack towards the Wheal Coates mine ruins, this time turning inland along the uphill path (roughly northeast). You'll reach the National Trust car park beside Beacon Dr. Turn left onto the road, then immediately right through St Agnes Beacon Caravan and Motorhome site. Walk up through the farm, picking up the path out onto the fields. A well-trodden trail climbs

sharply up the hilltop, giving majestic views of **St Agnes and the coastline**, and inland towards Carn Brea. In summer, it's covered in yellow gorse; by late summer, it's purple heather.

06 From the top, several trails lead back down onto Beacon Dr. It doesn't really matter which you take; when you get to the road, turn right. Walk along till you reach a bench with a rough lane opposite (if you reach a hamlet of houses, you missed the turning, so you need to backtrack).

07 Take the lane and follow it back to the coast path,

turning right (east) for the last section past the old **clifftop quarries** and a stone staircase down to Trevaunance Cove.

TAKE A BREAK

The whitewashed **Driftwood Spars** (www.driftwoodspars.com; Trevaunance Cove; mains £8-16; 🕐 11am-11pm; Ⓟ) has served generations of St Agnes drinkers, and brews its own ales. Downstairs is a hugger-mugger wooden bar, with upturned barrels and bench seats; there's a more refined restaurant upstairs. On the road up to the village, **Genki** (Quay Rd; mains £4-8; 🕐 9am-5pm) is a simple shack cafe that's ideal for paninis, smoothie bowls and salads.

14

BROWN WILLY & ROUGH TOR

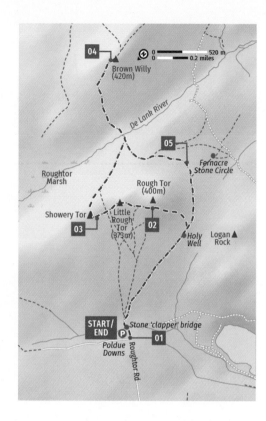

DURATION	DIFFICULTY	DISTANCE	START/END
2½-3hr	Moderate	5.2 miles/ 8.4km	Poldue Downs Car Park

TERRAIN	Moorland and rocky tors

Alright, alright, stop sniggering at the back. A perennial source of amusement for Cornish schoolkids, Cornwall's highest hill actually gets its name from the Cornish *bronn wennili*, or 'hill of swallows' – and if it's big, bleak views you're after, nowhere else in Cornwall compares.

GETTING HERE

The nearest town is Camelford, served by the 95 bus from Truro, Wadebridge and Bude, operated by First Kernow (p62). If you have wheels, follow the A39 north to Camelford, drive through the village and turn right onto Roughtor Rd.

STARTING POINT

There's a large, free car park at Poldue Downs at the end of Roughtor Rd. There's usually enough space for everyone. Look out for murmurations of starlings in autumn.

01 Head east from the car park and cross over the ford via the **stone 'clapper' bridge**. These rustic bridges, made of granite slabs, date back to medieval times: the one here is an unusual double span and is Grade II–listed. Follow the track south, passing through the remains of around 120 hut circles, relics of a **Bronze Age settlement** which once thrived in the shadow of the tor. Hidden among these ruins is a holy well, but you'll have to search a bit to find it.

02 From the holy well, ascend up the west side of **Rough Tor** (pronounced 'row' to rhyme with 'cow'). It's a steep hike to the summit at 400m, but the panoramic views from the top are stunning. The top of the tor (pictured) is marked by massive stacks of granite, carved out by aeons of wind and rain.

Bronze Age Bodmin Moor

Looking out over the empty wildness of Bodmin Moor, it might seem strange to find the remains of so many ancient settlements around Brown Willy. But several thousand years ago, the moor's landscape (like others in the southwest) was very different: it was covered by forest, which was cleared over the centuries for cultivation and agriculture, resulting in the barren landscape we see today. It's perhaps the earliest example in Britain of manmade climate change.

CHRIS JG WHITE/SHUTTERSTOCK ©

03 Brown Willy's bulk looms to the southeast, but for now, follow the ridgeline north towards **Showery Tor**, another granite stack at the far northern end of Rough Tor's ridge. At the end of the rocks, bear east down into the valley, following the De Lank River (it can be boggy round here). You'll reach a bridge; cross it and begin the slog up **Brown Willy**. You'll cross a couple of stiles en route to the summit; it's pretty obvious when you've reached the top, but a trig point marks the official spot.

04 Congratulations: you're standing on Cornwall's highest point, 420m above sea level. Take a breather and admire the views: on a clear day you can see all the way to the north coast. More **Bronze Age cairns** are littered around the summit, which may mark burial sites or even solstice calendars.

05 Double back down to the bridge, cross the ford, then follow the path along the fence-line, before turning west towards **Fernacre Stone Circle**. It's one of the largest in Cornwall, measuring 44m across and consisting of around 60 standing stones. Skirt round the southwest side of Rough Tor, and return north to the car park.

TAKE A BREAK

Run by well-known chef Emily Scott, the **St Tudy Inn** (☏ 01208-850656; www.sttudyinn.com; St Tudy; mains £14-25; ⊙ meals noon-2.30pm & 6.30-9pm Mon-Sat, noon-2.30pm Sun) is one of East Cornwall's top gastropubs, blending big British flavours with seasonal Cornish ingredients. It's in St Tudy, 6 miles southwest of Camelford.

Alternatively, for picnic supplies, the friendly **Hilltop Farm Shop** (☏ 01840-211518; www.hilltopfarm shop.co.uk; teas £3-6) in Slaughterbridge, 2 miles north of Camelford, is known for its Cornish fudge, pasties, cheeses and excellent cream teas.

15

PORTHCURNO TO LAND'S END

DURATION	DIFFICULTY	DISTANCE	START/END
3½– 4hr	Moderate	7.2 miles/ 11.5km	Treen/ Land's End

TERRAIN	Cliffs and coast

Is this the finest coast walk in all of Britain? Many a seasoned rambler might say so – and there are few who would sensibly argue. This walk really has it all: booming surf, massive cliffs, historic lighthouses and wild Atlantic vistas that will sear themselves onto your retinas.

GETTING HERE

Treen is about 7½ miles southwest of Penzance. The village is easily reached by bus: the A1 Coastal Cruiser operated by First Kernow (p62) runs three to five times daily. Some buses are open-top in summer.

STARTING POINT

There is a small car park near the Logan Rock Inn. Theoretically this could be done as a return walk,

but it'll make for a long day – an easier option is to take the A1 bus back from Land's End to Treen. A shorter option is just to follow the walk as far as St Levan, then circle back along the same route – it's about 3.8 miles return this way, but you'll be missing out on some serious coast views if you do.

01 This is a long walk, so starting out as early as possible is an extremely good idea – not least since the small private car park just past the Logan Rock Inn fills up fast. Once you've got your gear together, head out of the car park and turn left up the lane past the white building (a former chapel). Soon after, another narrow, easy-to-miss **lane** (signed for Logan Rock) turns left under the trees. If you miss it, don't worry, as you can just follow the main lane along to the coast path.

02 Either way, you'll eventually end up on the coast path, looking out towards a distinctive, fortress-like headland. This was the site of a large Iron Age hillfort, Treryn Dinas, but it's better known as the home of the **Logan Rock**. This massive boulder once famously rocked back and forth on its own natural pivot with only the slightest pressure; its name supposedly derives from the Cornish verb 'log', meaning 'to rock', used to denote the motion of a drunken man. Unfortunately, in 1871 a young naval lieutenant by the name of Hugh Goldsmith (the nephew of the Restoration playwright Oliver Goldsmith) commandeered his crew and knocked the rock off its perch. The locals were so incensed, Goldsmith was forced

to restore the rock to its original position under threat of his naval commission – a task that required the efforts of 60 men, winches borrowed from Devonport Dockyard and a total cost of £130 8s 6d (a copy of the bill can be seen in the Logan Rock Inn). The path out to it involves traversing narrow cliff paths and sheer drops, so take care if you want a closer look.

03 Turn west along the coast path. Before long, you'll pass the perfect little cove of **Treen Beach**, also known as Pedn Vounder, one of Cornwall's few nudist-friendly patches of sand. It can be accessed via a formida-

bly steep cliff path, but it's very easy to miss the turning - ideally you need someone to show you where it starts. It's followed soon after by the celebrated crescent of **Porthcurno**, as perfect a beach as you'll find in west Cornwall (and accordingly busy). It's a great place to swim, with a deep drop-off, although the waves can be rough. From the beach, look up: carved into the crags is Cornwall's celebrated clifftop theatre, the **Minack** (pictured; ☏ 01736-810181; www.minack.com; tickets from £10). Overlooking Porthcurno and the azure-blue Atlantic, it looks like a relic from ancient Greece, but it was actually built in the 20th

Porthcurno Telegraph Museum

This fascinating **museum** (☏ 01736-810966; www.telegraphmuseum.org; adult/child £9.50/5.50; ⏱10am-5pm) charts the unlikely tale of Porthcurno's role in transatlantic telecommunications. In 1870 an underwater cable was laid here, which enabled telegraph messages to be sent as far as Bombay in less than a minute. Over the next century, 14 cables ran into Porthcurno, carrying much of Britain's global telecommunications before being decommissioned in 1970. The museum features interactive morse-code kits, vintage equipment, archive footage and so on, plus a network of WWII-era tunnels.

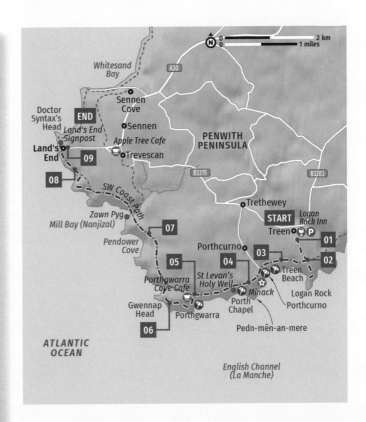

century; it was the lifelong passion of theatre-lover Rowena Cade, who dreamt up the idea in the 1930s. It's still a hugely popular place for al fresco theatre, with plays staged from mid-May to mid-September. A steep path leads up the cliff past the visitor centre.

04 Continue across the Minack car park, following the coast path around the headland of **Pedn-mên-an-mere** (Headland of the Great Stone). Just around the headland nestles another lovely beach, **Porth Chapel**, which usually stays a good deal quieter than its neighbour. Just off the path above the beach is **St Levan's Holy Well**, one of several such sacred springs in this part of West Penwith. The waters are said to have healing powers, but it would be a brave soul indeed who drinks the mucky water. Best stick to the water in your canteen.

05 A little further west hides the fishing cove of **Porthgwarra**, with a steep slipway leading down to the sheltered beach. It's another good spot for a dip, but take care not to swim out past the headland, where the sea currents can be strong. The little **Porthgwarra Cove Cafe** (☎01736 888515) serves sandwiches, snacks, pasties and ice creams, and has a pleasant little garden to sit out in.

06 Next looms **Gwennap Head**, the southernmost point of the Penwith Peninsula. A coastguard lookout station sits out on the point, and makes a

good place to take a break and enjoy the incredible Atlantic views. On a clear day, you might just about be able to spot the profile of Wolf Rock Lighthouse, 9 miles out to sea, a lonely beacon rising from a spur of rock jutting out of the Atlantic Ocean. Forty-one metres high, the granite lighthouse took eight years to build, from 1861 to 1869. Given its location, and the storms that regularly lash this stretch of coast, that it was ever built at all is something of an engineering marvel.

07 From Gwennap Head, the coast ducks and dips, passing Pendower Cove, before reaching the broad, boulder-strewn expanse of **Mill Bay** (pictured; known locally as

Nanjizal). There are plenty of sand and rock pools to investigate, and on one side of the beach is a natural arch called **Zawn Pyg** (from the Cornish for 'pointed chasm'), where the sea has worn a passage through the cliffs. Many locals know it as the Song of the Sea cave. There are many other zawns, or steep-sided inlets, pockmarking the surrounding coastline.

08 Beyond Nanjizal, you're within striking distance of the most westerly point of mainland Britain. The coast path opens up as you stride over wide cliffs all the way to **Land's End**. Famous as the last port of call for charity walkers on the 874-mile slog from John O'Groats in Scotland, this

Longships Lighthouse

Perched on a rocky reef, 1.25 miles out to sea from Land's End, this photogenic lighthouse is one of Cornwall's most upstanding feats of maritime engineering. Built to warn ships away from this infamously dangerous stretch of coastline, the first structure was built in 1795 but was swamped by waves, and subsequently replaced in 1873 at the considerable cost of £43,870. Since then it's somehow withstood even the worst of the Atlantic storms, and has been unmanned since 1988.

wild, craggy headland is where Cornwall (and, by extension, the rest of Britain) comes to a screeching halt, and the black granite cliffs fall away into thundering white surf and sea spray. The views are epic: the restless Atlantic seems to wrap itself around the horizon, shimmering and flashing in the late-afternoon light, and when the weather's clear you can often glimpse the faint outlines of the Isles of Scilly, 28 miles out to sea. It's a special spot – which makes the decision to build a tacky theme park here in the 1980s utterly inexplicable. Still, once you bypass the tat – and there's plenty of it here – the coast regains its wild splendour. The curiously named Doctor Syntax's Head was named after a fictitious schoolmaster who featured in a series of popular books in the early 1800s.

The signpost at Land's End marks the official end of the trail (unless you still have the legs to push on to Sennen, another 1½ miles further along the coast path). According to the signpost, it's 3147 miles to New York, 874 miles to John O' Groats, 1½ miles to the Longships Lighthouse and 28 miles to Scilly.

09 Heading back to Treen, it's a rather more manageable 4 miles; A1 buses run three to five times a day. The last bus of the day is usually between 5pm and 6pm, but double-check the First Kernow website to confirm timings.

TAKE A BREAK

A mile inland from Land's End, the **Apple Tree Cafe** (☎ 01736-872753; www.appletreecafe.co.uk; Trevescan; mains £6-12; ⏰ 10am-5pm Wed-Sun) is a real community hang-out – there are paintings and crafts by local artists, a menu of sandwiches, soups and wholefood salads, and a counter lined with sinful-looking cakes.

Alternatively, the 400 year-old **Logan Rock Inn** (☎ 01736-810495; www.theloganrock.co.uk; Treen; mains £6-14; ⏰ 10.30am-11pm, closes mid-afternoon winter) brims with old-time atmosphere – head-scraping ceilings, wooden seats, a crackling hearth and brassy trinkets.

Also Try...

WEWI-PHOTOGRAPHY/SHUTTERSTOCK ©

HARTLAND POINT

A rugged right-angle of land, the Hartland Penin-sula marks the edge of Devon.

In the late 19th century, this was among the most treacherous headlands anywhere in England – a macabre fact summed up by the local seaman's refrain 'From Pentire Point to Hartland Light, a watery grave by day or night'. The rusting fragments of the coaster *Johanna*, driven ashore on New Year's Eve 1982, can still be seen near Hartland Point Lighthouse (pictured). The cliffs reach their highest point at 350ft near Hartland Quay.

Nearby Hartland Abbey was founded in the 12th century, but is now a grand private house, known for the ornate Alhambra Passage and a Regency library designed in the Strawberry Hill Gothic style.

DURATION 3hr
DIFFICULTY Moderate
DISTANCE 6.4 miles/10.2km

HOUND TOR & HAYTOR

Probably the best-known tor walk on Dartmoor.

From the Haytor visitor centre, the route heads northwest past the prehistoric settlements around Smallacombe Rocks, then climbs the spookily named Hound Tor (414m), which some people claim inspired the title of Arthur Conan Doyle's classic Dartmoor-set Sherlock Holmes caper, *The Hound of the Baskervilles*. From here, the path loops back across Becka Brook over Haytor (454m), then visits an old flooded quarry, before following the line of a disused tramway that was built to transport granite to the port at Teignmouth. It now forms part of the 18-mile Templer Way.

DURATION 3hr
DIFFICULTY Moderate
DISTANCE 5.5 miles/9km

START POINT

Start Bay curves in an elongated crescent towards Devon's most southerly tip.

This loop walk begins at the abandoned village of Hallsands, which was literally swept out to sea by a great storm in 1917 (the ruins themselves are off limits). It then circles round the dramatic Start Point Lighthouse, built in 1836, before passing the beaches of Great Mattiscombe (pictured), Lannacombe and Woodcombe, returning via inland paths to Hollowcombe and Hallsands.

DURATION 3½-4hr
DIFFICULTY Moderate
DISTANCE 6.8 miles/11km

FOWEY & POLRUAN

This circular walk starts across the river from Fowey in Bodinnick, climbing cross-country to Lantic Bay, with an optional detour to nearby Pencarrow Head.

The path then follows the coastline to the harbour of Polruan, offering super views across the river to Fowey. From Polruan, circle back along the wooded banks of Pont Pill Creek before returning to Bodinnick, from where a ferry chugs back to Fowey.

DURATION 3½hr
DIFFICULTY Easy
DISTANCE 6.5 miles/10.5km

BOTALLACK & CAPE CORNWALL

The mineral seams around the Penwith coastline were once among the richest in Cornwall, a legacy that's still visible in the evocative mine workings around Botallack.

The Crowns engine house has featured in many a costume drama (including the BBC's recent adaptation of *Poldark*). To the south lies the ruined hillfort of Kenidjack Castle and rocky Cape Cornwall, topped by one of Cornwall's earliest Christian chapels.

DURATION 3hr
DIFFICULTY Easy
DISTANCE 4 miles/6.6km

SOUTHWEST ENGLAND

Explore
SOUTHWEST ENGLAND

Ancient Britons left an enduring mark on this corner of Britain, in the shape of a wealth of stone monuments, circles, menhirs and burial barrows. It's crossed by the Ridgeway, thought by many to be the oldest footpath in Britain, and offers varied terrain for the walker: coast walks, chalk plains, old woodlands and hilly heaths, as well as a network of canal paths and riverways. We've covered three neighbouring counties here (Somerset, Wiltshire and Dorset) as well as two major cities, Bath and Bristol, and the historic landscape of the New Forest.

BATH

Bath is one of Britain's most appealing cities. Famous for its Georgian architecture, it's also a lovely place to base yourself in for exploring Somerset and Wiltshire – although it has to be said, accommodation can be pricey and parking is difficult. There is a decent YHA hostel and a huge number of hotels and B&Bs to choose from, however, and the city is well connected by bus and train to most parts of Somerset.

BRISTOL

The southwest's biggest and buzziest city, Bristol is known for its alternative and slightly anti-establishment nature. It's a dynamic city with a creative edge. There are plenty of chain hotels to choose from, but only a couple of hostels, including a modern YHA by the harbour: short-term rentals or self-catering could be a good option here. It's well placed for Somerset and Wiltshire walks.

SALISBURY

Centred on a majestic cathedral that's topped by the tallest spire in England, Salisbury makes an appealing Wiltshire base. It's been an important provincial city for more than a thousand years, and its streets form an architectural timeline ranging from medieval walls and half-timbered Tudor town houses to Georgian mansions and Victorian villas. It's ideal for exploring Wiltshire, Hampshire, Dorset and the New Forest.

BOURNEMOUTH

A resort town since Victorian days, Bournemouth remains a popular beach retreat, but it's also a sensible launchpad for forays along the Dorset coast. The nearby town of Poole offers a slightly more chilled vibe. The town has good transport links and plenty of accommodation, especially a supply of budget-friendly B&Bs.

WHEN TO GO

The lack of significant elevation means that, theoretically, most of the southwest is open for

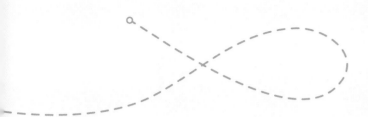

walkers nearly all year round. Indeed, hiking among the strange stones of Salisbury Plain on a crisp winter's day is an experience not to be forgotten. Spring brings colour and fragrance to the woods – Exmoor's displays of snowdrops, bluebells and daffodils are famous. Music-festival fever takes hold in June at Glastonbury – whatever you do, don't attempt to climb up Glastonbury Tor in the middle of June, as the roads for miles around will be blocked. As always, the summer holidays bring a swathe of visitors, particularly to hotspots such as Bath, Exmoor, Somerset and Stonehenge, with an according spike in accommodation prices and road traffic. The end of school summer holidays in September brings cheaper sleep spots, quieter beaches and warmer seas. Autumn is a pleasant time for walking, particularly on Exmoor, when the deer rut sees red stags clash antlers, and the winter storm-watching season begins.

TRANSPORT

The main motorway to the southwest is the M4, which runs west from London to Bristol, linking to the M5 which runs as far as Exeter. From here, the road connects to the A30 dual carriageway. An alternative route is along the A303 dual carriageway, which famously runs past Stonehenge. Traffic can be very heavy in summer, especially during school holidays.

The southwest is well served by trains. Frequent intercity services run from Birmingham and London to mainline stations including Bristol, Bath, Salisbury, Bournemouth and Southampton.

It is possible to travel the southwest using public transport, but services to remote areas are limited; using your own wheels gives you more flexibility. Traveline South West (www.travelinesw.com) provides region-wide bus and train timetable info. The main bus companies are First (www.first group.com), More (www.wdbus. co.uk) and Stagecoach (www. stagecoachbus.com).

WHERE TO STAY

Whatever style or budget you prefer, the West Country can accommodate you. From bare-bones clifftop campsites to clusters of hip eco-yurts; from seaside resorts thick with B&Bs to beam-heavy rural inns; from slick city crash pads to improbably plush country-house hotels – you can sleep in them all here. There's a wide choice in all the major towns and cities, with plenty more options in the countryside too.

👍 WHAT'S ON

Bath Festival (📞 01225-614180; www. bathfestivals.org.uk; 🗓️May) A multi-arts festival spanning music, literature, science and politics.

Glastonbury Festival (www.glaston buryfestivals.co.uk; tickets from £238; 🗓️Jun or Jul) The UK's biggest and best musical mudfest.

Upfest (www.upfest.co.uk; 🗓️Jul) Celebration of street art in Banksy's home city.

Bristol International Balloon Fiesta (www.bristolballoonfiesta.co.uk; 🗓️Aug) Hot-air balloons fill Bristol's skies.

Jane Austen Festival (www.jane austenfestivalbath.co.uk; 🗓️Sep) Bath's 10-day celebration of its beloved writer.

16

BATH SKYLINE

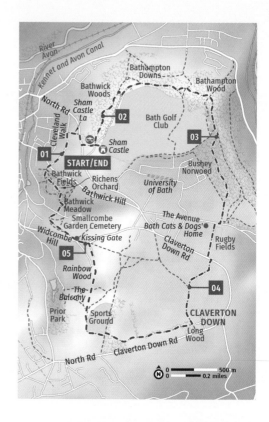

DURATION	DIFFICULTY	DISTANCE	START/END
3-3½hr	Moderate	5.9 miles/ 9.5km	Bathwick Hill

TERRAIN	Woodland, grassy fields

The belle of British cities, Bath is rightly famous for its Georgian architecture – but has some surprisingly green spaces nearby, too. This walk explores the hills and woods east of the city, ending with an eye-popping rooftop view.

GETTING HERE

Trains link Bath to London Paddington, Cardiff Central and Bristol. Several buses head up Bathwick Hill from the bus and train stations, including the U1 and U3, which run multiple times an hour. Parking along Bathwick Hill is permit-controlled, so leave the car in a city-centre public car park.

STARTING POINT

Start at Bathwick Hill, near the entrance to Bathwick Fields.

01 Take Cleveland Walk. Follow it along to a footpath on the right opposite Sham Castle Lane. The path climbs up through a small wooded area to North Rd. Turn right, then take the gate on the left which leads up through another area of woodland. At the top near a bench, there's a quick view of Bath's rooftops, and you can take a quick detour to see **Sham Castle**, a mock-medieval folly built by the entrepreneur Ralph Allen.

02 Backtrack to the bench, from where the trail enters **Bathwick Woods**, a surprisingly dense area of native woodland. There are several trails through the trees: take care to follow the waymarkers for Bath Skyline, indicated by a yellow arrow. Keep bearing right; eventually you'll turn uphill out of the trees, past some radio masts and onto the open fields of Bathampton Down. Walk along the slope, bearing slightly downhill towards the woods.

Prior Park

Prior Park (NT; ☎ 01225-833977; www.nationaltrust.org.uk; Ralph Allen Dr; adult/child £7.40/3.70; ⏰ 10am-5.30pm daily Feb-Oct, 10am-4pm Sat & Sun Nov-Jan) was established by Ralph Allen, who made his fortune founding Britain's first postal service, and owned many of the quarries from which the city's amber-coloured Bath stone was mined. The gardens were partly designed by the landscape architect Lancelot 'Capability' Brown, and include cascading lakes and a graceful Palladian bridge, one of only four such structures in the world. The house itself is now a private school.

OLIVER BERRY/LONELY PLANET ©

03 A gate leads down into **Bathampton Wood**. The trail is easy to follow; you'll pass several small abandoned quarries where stone was extracted, then enter another area of open fields, Bushey Norwood; the campus of Bath University is on your left. Follow waymarkers to The Avenue; turn left here, taking the path just before the Cats & Dogs' Home. Continue to Claverton Down Rd; cross over, turn left, and look out for the trail on the right past the rugby fields.

04 You'll cross Claverton Down, then enter **Long Wood**. Continue through the trees, turning north past playing fields.

You'll pass the edge of Prior Park, then walk along a lovely section of the woodland path called **the Balcony**, with rolling valley views away to your left. The trail leads through Rainbow Wood, emerging onto Widcombe Hill.

05 Walk down Widcombe Hill, then through a **kissing gate** on your right. Cross the field and walk down into the valley: Smallcombe Garden Cemetery is on your right. Climb steeply up the other side, passing the community-run Richens Orchard and coming out onto **Bathwick Fields**. This is where the views get really grand: as you cross the sloping hill,

the rooftops of Bath open up in front of you like a diorama from a Disney movie. Walk across the fields to where you began on Bathwick Hill.

TAKE A BREAK

Lodged above a vintage boating station, the **Bathwick Boatman** (www.bathwickboatman.com) serves lunches with lovely river views; afterwards, you can steer a wooden rowboat along the River Avon. On Walcot St, the olde-worlde **Star Inn** (☎ 01225-425072; www.abbeyales. co.uk) still has many of its 19th-century pub fittings. It's the brewery tap for Bath-based Abbey Ales; some are served in traditional jugs.

17

GLASTONBURY TOR

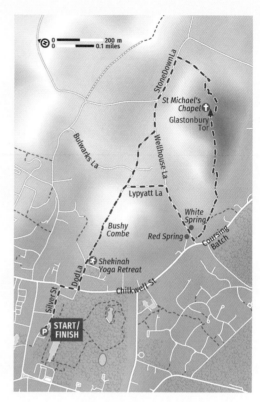

DURATION	DIFFICULTY	DISTANCE	START/END
1-1½hr	Easy	2.2 miles/ 3.6km	Silver St car park

TERRAIN	Country lanes, grassy hill

Myths and legends swirl around the strange hillock of Glastonbury Tor. Visible for miles around, it's one of Somerset's most unmistakable landmarks – and arguably its most unmissable view.

Depending on which legend you believe, the tor is either the home of the faerie king of the underworld, the last resting place of King Arthur or a mystical node where many ley lines converge. It's also a cracking short walk: steep but easygoing. Hike early or late in the day to avoid the crowds; at dawn or dusk, its mystical power is impossible to deny.

Walk up Glastonbury's main street, turning right onto Chilkwell St, then left up Dod Lane past the Shekinah Yoga Retreat. The path leads through a gate uphill across the fields of **Bushy Combe**. You'll cross Bulwarks Lane, then more fields to Wellhouse Lane. Continue uphill to the National Trust gate.

A steep, switchbacking path leads up the tor's northeast side.

The views across the Somerset Levels are breathtaking. In ancient times (when the Levels were often flooded), the tor would have appeared as an island, cut off by impassable marshes and bogs; this perhaps explains its legendary status as the Isle of Avalon. At the summit, the tower of **St Michael's Chapel** (pictured) spikes skywards; in 1539, the last abbot of Glastonbury Abbey, Richard Whiting, was hung, drawn and quartered here for refusing to denounce the pope.

Walk down the other side of the tor to Wellhouse Lane. Nearby, one of Glastonbury's sacred springs, the **White Spring,** bubbles up underground; the other, the **Red Spring,** emerges in Chalice Well & Gardens. Turn right (uphill) along Wellhouse Lane, left onto Lypyatt Lane, and back down Bushy Combe to the town centre.

18

AVEBURY & SILBURY HILL

Best for

ANCIENT HISTORY

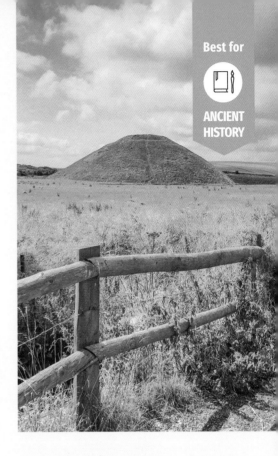

DURATION	DIFFICULTY	DISTANCE	START/END
2-2½hr	Easy	4 miles/ 6.4km	Avebury National Trust car park

TERRAIN	Grassy fields

Everyone's heard of Stonehenge, but far fewer people know much about Avebury – Britain's largest stone circle, so enormous they plonked a village right in the middle of it. It forms part of a vast ancient landscape whose exact purpose still remains shrouded in mystery.

GETTING HERE

Avebury is about 9 miles northeast of Devizes, 7 miles west of Marlborough. Bus 49 runs hourly to Swindon (30 minutes) and Devizes (15 minutes). There are six services on Sunday.

STARTING POINT

The National Trust has built a large car park just outside Avebury's village centre.

01 Around the same time the ancient Egyptians were building the pyramids, neolithic Britons were hard at work creating their very own wonders of the ancient world. Unlike the circle at Stonehenge, with its distinctive upright trilithons, the stone circle of Avebury takes imagination to decipher – not least because Avebury's stones are half-hidden among the buildings of its namesake village. But in terms of scale alone, Avebury dwarfs its better-known neighbour on Salisbury Plain – it's nearly 10 times the diameter of Stonehenge, and forms part of a sprawling complex of prehistoric monuments that must have taken decades, if not centuries, to construct. All of which suggests that, at least to its builders, Avebury may have been at least as sacred a site as Stonehenge – and perhaps, given its size, even more important.

Carrying a satellite map of the Avebury landscape is a good way to get your bearings, as it can be hard to make sense of the geography of the site from the ground alone. From the National Trust car park, cross the road and follow the signed track along the edge of the River Kennet. It's easy to follow, but can be gloopy in wet weather.

02 About half a mile south of the car park, you'll catch sight of your first ancient wonder of the day. To the southwest, a conical green hill (pictured) rises up in the middle of a nearby field. Unremarkable, you might think – until you realise it's too smooth, too uniform, too perfect to be a natural feature. And you'd be right. This is **Silbury Hill**, perhaps the strangest of all the monuments around Avebury. Forty metres high, this hill is the largest artificial earthwork in Europe,

comparable in height and volume to the Egyptian pyramids. It was built in stages from around 2500 BC. Incredibly, it's been estimated that it would have taken 500 men roughly 15 years to build, but despite countless theories, no-one really has any idea what its purpose was – a ceremonial platform, perhaps? A monument to the dead? Some kind of celestial marker? No one knows. Several tunnels have been bored into the middle over the decades, but so far, other than a few tools and bones, no significant archaeological artefacts have been found. Why did they feel building their own hill was so important? We'll probably never know – and since

the tunnels have now been filled with concrete to avoid the hill's collapse, the mystery of Silbury Hill is likely to remain one, perhaps forever.

03 It's not permitted to climb the hill – it looks solid, but is surprisingly delicate – but you'll get fine views as you walk south along the fields towards the A4. When you reach the busy main road, carefully cross over (look out for fast-moving traffic), and follow signs across the fields pointing to **West Kennet Long Barrow**. There is a clear path to follow; you'll head slightly uphill, reaching the barrow after about 10 minutes' walk.

The Restoration of Avebury

In the Middle Ages, when Britain's pagan past was an embarrassment to the Church, many of Avebury's stones were buried, removed or broken up. In 1934 wealthy businessman and archaeologist Alexander Keiller supervised the re-erection of the stones; he later bought the site for posterity using funds from his family's marmalade fortune. The small **Alexander Keiller Museum** on the High St documents his history and contains prehistoric finds.

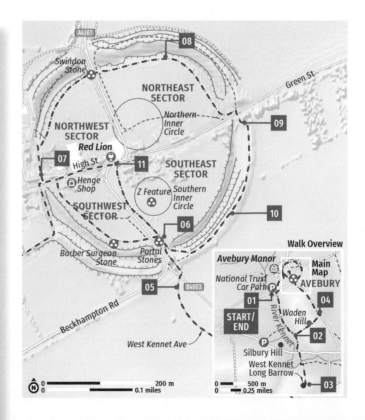

Like Silbury, it's an improbably massive structure: 100m long and 20m wide, far bigger than most other ancient barrows of its kind. Dating from around 3500 BC, its entrance is guarded by huge sarsen stones, and its roof is made out of gigantic overlapping capstones. Inside, several circular chambers have been excavated; about 50 skeletons were found interred here, but for some reason, at a later date, it appears the barrow was deliberately abandoned and infilled several centuries after its construction. Again, no-one really knows who was buried here, or why the monument is quite so enormous, or why it was abandoned. Another similar burial mound, **East Kennett Long Barrow**, sits on private land nearby, but is not as well preserved and is sadly off-limits to the public. The people who built Avebury are believed to have occupied a site at **Windmill Hill**, about 1 mile northwest of the circle.

04 Backtrack down the hill, cross the road and follow the Kennet River north until you reach a hedgerow fence leading away to your right. Here, a permissive path leads northeast over **Waden Hill**, offering superb views of both Silbury Hill and West Kennett Long Barrow. It's a fairly steep but short climb, which then drops down over the other side of the hill. As you approach the road, a double line of massive standing stones appears, leading away to the northwest: this is the **West Kennet Avenue**, a sacred processional route which ancient Britons used to approach the circle. It's hard not to get a haunting feeling as you walk through the massive stones, just as our ancestors of old would have done.

A second avenue is also once believed to have existed, leading to another site at Beckhampton.

05 The Avenue ends near Beckhampton Rd. Here, you'll get your first real glimpse of the great **stone circle** itself, although its scale is obscured by buildings and trees, so you'll have to use your imagination to picture how it must have originally appeared. With a diameter of approximately 330m at its widest point, Avebury is the largest stone circle in the world. It's also one of the oldest, dating from 2500 to 2200 BC. Originally, it's believed the henge consisted of an outer circle of around 100 standing stones of up to 6m in length, many weighing 20 tonnes. The stones were surrounded by another circle delineated by a 5m-high earth bank and a ditch up to 9m deep. Inside were smaller stone circles to the north (27 stones) and south (29 stones). Today, around 30 stones remain in place; the others were plundered or smashed up for stone long ago. Pillars now show where missing stones would have been.

06 Across Beckhampton Rd, you enter the circle through two huge **portal stones**. From the portal stones, walk in a clockwise direction around the circle. Modern roads into Avebury neatly dissect the circle into four sectors: the southwest sector between Beckhampton Rd and the High St contains 11 stones, including the **Barber Surgeon Stone**, named after the skeleton of a man found buried under it (the equipment interred with him suggests he was a barber-cum-surgeon).

The Sanctuary

A lost stone circle called **The Sanctuary** can be visited just south of the busy A4 road. Many human bones and food remains have been excavated here, suggesting the circle may have hosted sacred ceremonies and perhaps death rites. The stones have long since disappeared, but their location is marked by concrete slabs.

07 Cross High St and continue into the northwest sector, perhaps the most complete. Note how different the shapes are here: at Stonehenge, they were crafted into uniform pillars, but at Avebury, they're much more free-form. This sector contains the massive 65-tonne **Swindon Stone**, one of the few never to have been toppled: it's the one nearest the A4361.

08 Cross the main road into the northeast sector, where fewer stones have survived. Three sarsens remain of what would have been a rectangular cove.

09 Cross Green St, passing under a great oak tree into the southwest sector. This is the best place to appreciate the scale of the ditch around the circle: the amount of work required to excavate this channel from the bone-hard chalk underfoot is hard to comprehend even today, let alone with only stone tools. Aerial photos suggest that the ditch may originally have been filled with other structures, probably made of timber. One theory has suggested that the white chalk under Avebury and Stonehenge may have been important; originally, perhaps the monuments were completely cleared of grass and vegetation, so that they might have appeared as shining, white otherworldly platforms.

10 The path circles back to the portal stones. Once, a southern inner circle stood in this sector and within this ring was an obelisk, now marked by a stone plinth. Nearby, a curious line of stones, known as the Z Feature, may have served an important sacred purpose, as the row appears to be orientated to face the sunrise and sunset.

11 Follow High St to the **Henge Shop** (www.hengeshop. com; 9.30am-5pm) to pick up souvenirs, then head back to the National Trust car park.

It's worth stopping in at the **Red Lion** (www.oldenglishinns.co.uk; High St; 11am-11pm), if only to say you've had a pint in the world's only pub inside a stone circle. One seat covers a 26m-deep well dating from the 17th century. The cafe in the library of **Avebury Manor** (www. nationaltrust.org.uk; snacks from £4; noon-5pm Easter-Oct) serves soups, jacket potatoes and classic afternoon teas.

19
TARR STEPS

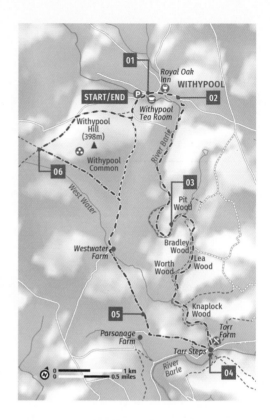

DURATION	DIFFICULTY	DISTANCE	START/END
3½-4hr	Moderate	8.3 miles/ 13.4km	Withypool

TERRAIN	Riverside trail, woodland, heath

Many walkers overlook Exmoor, but that's a mistake. This hike encapsulates all that's lovely about the UK's smallest national park: dappled woodland, peaceful fields, fast-running rivers and rural architecture – in this case, a famous stone clapper bridge.

GETTING HERE

Withypool is 9 miles northwest of Dulverton. There's no regular bus service so you'll need your own car; alternatively, Exmoor is good (albeit hilly) cycling country.

STARTING POINT

There is a small car park in Withypool, but spaces are limited.

01 Exmoor has a special, sleepy magic that's uniquely its own, and this hike along the banks of the River Barle explores some of the national park's loveliest countryside. The woodland cover makes this a particularly good autumn walk, but it's good in any season, even midwinter. The walk begins in the village of **Withypool**, where you can stock up on supplies from the village shop.

02 Walk east along the main road past the Royal Oak Inn. The road dips, then heads uphill; cross a stile on your right over a drystone wall and walk down towards the woods.

03 Follow the path south along the river, crossing the boggy meadows before rounding an oxbow bend and entering **Pit Wood**. Continue on through the trees, through Lea Wood, and across fords; waymarkers provide guidance at key points.

Exmoor's Red Deers

Exmoor supports one of England's largest wild red deer populations. In autumn during 'rutting' season, stags bellow and clash horns to impress prospective mates. The Exmoor National Park Authority runs regular free wildlife walks, which include evening deer-spotting hikes, or you can go on 4WD safaris: try **Red Stag Safari** (☎01643-841831; www.redstagsafari.co.uk; safaris £38) or **Barle Valley Safaris** (☎07977 571494; www.exmoorwildlifesafaris.co.uk; adult/child £35/25; ☾tours at 9.30am & 2pm).

Much of the riverside path is very rooty and rocky, so watch your step.

04 After climbing briefly, the path drops back down to the river, entering the gnarled trees of Knaplock Wood before reaching **Tarr Steps** (pictured). This is the largest and possibly oldest 'clapper' bridge on Exmoor, made of stone slabs propped on supporting columns embedded in the River Barle. Folklore claims the Devil used it for sunbathing; it first appears in the historical record in the 1600s, and recently had to be rebuilt after 21st-century floods.

05 Cross the bridge, then take the side trail uphill towards Parsonage Farm. You'll follow the hedgerows across the muddy fields, with views over the river valley. Continue across Parsonage Down to Westwater Farm, emerging onto a minor road. You can follow this road all the way back to Withypool, but it's worth detouring across Withypool Common; a waymarker points left after a cattlegrid.

06 The faint path peters out as you cross the down. Continue west till you pick up another faint footpath; turn right (northeast). You can sidetrack to the top of the hill, where the remains of a vanished **stone circle** and a **Stone Age tumulus** can be seen. If not, skirt the northern edge of the down before dropping back down to Withypool.

TAKE A BREAK

Beside the clapper bridge, **Tarr Farm** (☎01643-851507; www.tarrfarm. co.uk; ☾11am-5pm) is fab for cream teas and hearty lunches. Baked spuds, cakes and sandwiches are on offer at the little **Withypool Tea Room** (☎01643-831279; www. withypoolexmoor.co.uk/tea-rooms; ☾9.30am-5pm spring-autumn), while the **Royal Oak Inn** (☎01643-831506; www.royaloakwithypool. co.uk) pulls a decent pint.

JULIAN GAZZARD/SHUTTERSTOCK ©

20

THE NEW FOREST

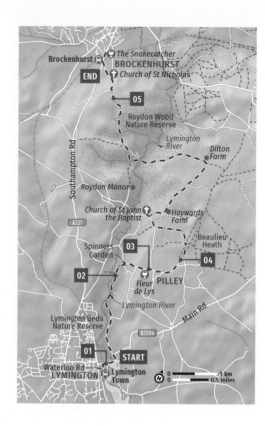

DURATION	DIFFICULTY	DISTANCE	START/END
3hr	Moderate	6 miles/ 11km	Lymington/ Brocken- hurst

TERRAIN	Boggy paths, woodland

The New Forest is a world apart, with a very distinct atmosphere, and even its own court and system of local law, drawn up in 1217 to counter oppression from William the Conqueror's descend- ants. Despite the name, its not all about trees here – there's a lot of open moorland, populated by small shaggy ponies that roam free. This plus a large deer population and otters in the Lymington River make it a special place for wildlife lovers.

GETTING HERE

This walk is ideal for those using public transport, as it starts at one train station and ends at another, a little way down the line. If you're driving you could park at Lymington and return by train from Brockenhurst.

STARTING POINT

The route starts at Lymington Town Station, which sits on the banks of the Lymington River on the eastern edge of the town. From here you're straight into a country walk, so detour if you want to buy any supplies.

01 From Lymington Station, turn right onto Waterloo Rd and then right again at the T-junction to cross the railway line and estuary. Over the bridge, turn left and, after 100m where there's a bend in the road, go straight ahead on the path signed for the **Lymington Beds Nature Reserve**. The path hugs the right-hand bank of the Lyming- ton River, across land that can be wet and boggy. From here, start looking out for ponies.

02 At the end of the Reserve go ahead on the paved path and then turn right towards

Watch Out for Wildlife

The adorable wee ponies are only the most visible of the New Forest's natural inhabitants. Varied habitats here – valley bogs, wet and dry heaths and deciduous woodland – support some rare and wonderful creatures. Among the wild gentian flowers and wild gladioli, you might spot southern damselflies and large marsh grasshoppers. Adders, grass snakes and rare smooth snakes slither around at ground level, while look up and you might spot woodlarks and wood warblers. Fallow, roe and red deer inhabit the woodland, while one of the most extraordinary sights is during autumn 'pannage' when scurrying pigs are set free to root around for acorns.

Best for

WILDLIFE

MIKE READ/ALAMY STOCK PHOTO ©

Pilley. Past Spinner's Garden (you pay a small fee to see the magnolias, azaleas and irises) you come into the village of **Pilley**, where the thatched **Fleur de Lys** pub – an amazing 1000 years old – has an upmarket restaurant as well as bar (a better bet for muddy boots).

03 Continuing through the village past the pub, you come to the wild expanses of **Beaulieu Heath**, which can be treacherously boggy and very hard to navigate without a detailed OS map.

04 Instead, follow footpaths which lead via clearings

and patches of woodland past the Church of St John the Baptist. Then head past Haywards Farm and round the back of Dilton Farm, eventually entering the **Roydon Wood Nature Reserve** (pictured). Some of the broad-leafed trees here are classified 'ancient'. Continue downhill to cross the Lymington River, and pass Roydon Manor to your right.

05 A sinuous network of bridleways lead out of the woods and onto a road. Turn right and you come to the **Church of St Nicholas**, where 'Brusher' Mills (see right) is buried. Carry on down the road to reach Brockenhurst station.

TAKE A BREAK

At the end of the walk and handily near the station you'll find **The Snakecatcher** (☎01590-622348; www.thesnakecatcher.co.uk; Lyndhurst Road, Brockenhurst; pub snacks £6.95, burgers £11.95, meals £11.95) pub. It serves five local real ales plus craft beers and ciders. There's a range of meals, but the big deal is the burgers, which include veggie and mushroom varieties. The pub is named for local character Harry 'Brusher' Mills, who drank in the pub when it was the Railway Inn; born in 1840, he spent a lifetime living in the woods here catching grass snakes and adders.

21

THE RIDGEWAY

DURATION	DIFFICULTY	DISTANCE	START/END
5hr	Hard	11 miles/ 18km	Foxhill/ Wantage

TERRAIN	Steep tracks and fields

The Ridgway is one of the most ancient walkways in the country. It runs for 87 miles, from Overton Hill in Wiltshire to Ivinghoe Beacon in Buckinghamshire. We've chosen a longish stretch – it's a little difficult to access, meaning you need an early start, and you'll probably want to stay at the hostel at the end. But it's well worth the effort to follow in the footsteps of some of England's first hikers, and the prehistoric sites you'll encounter – the tomb of Wayland's Smithy, the earthworks of Uffington Castle and the graceful White Horse – are some of the most mesmerising anywhere.

GETTING HERE

First take a train to the somewhat uninspiring town of Swindon, reached in an hour from London Paddington. From Swindon Station, head up Wellington St and turn left on Manchester Rd to reach the bus station. Take bus 46, 48 or 48a to Foxhill, which will take around 20 minutes.

STARTING POINT

Once at Foxhill, head up the minor road following signs to Hinton Parva. Soon after this, follow the Ridgeway sign which leads off to the right.

01 The route starts with a steepish climb up to the ridge of a hill, which gives views of **Lammy Down**, a tumulus (burial mound) which is the first of the ancient sites you'll spot along the way. Ahead you'll see the swelling mound of Uffington Castle. There's a signed detour here to the **Strip Lynchets**, medieval earth banks cut into the fields to create terraces for growing crops; the terraces may also have had a role in ceremonies. The route cuts across two narrow country lanes; down the second, en route to Idstone, is a fort known as **Alfred's Castle** where the heroic king is said to have defeated the Danes at the Battle of Ashdown at the age of just 22. Despite its possible epic place in English history, you may not want to make the 3-mile round-trip detour to the site with so many stunning attractions ahead. Alfred's Castle is a visually modest site, with low oval-shaped earthworks.

02 The Ridgeway runs on to a patch of woodland, emerging at one of its most thrilling sights: a Neolithic long barrow tomb fronted by tall stones, known as **Wayland's**

Smithy (pictured). The tomb's antiquity is astounding: the original chamber was constructed between 3590 and 3550 BC and held 14 bodies, then around 3400 another burial chamber was built on top. The name was given to the tomb in the early Middle Ages by the Saxons, who appropriated it for the mythical Wayland.

03 Continue on the route for around 30 minutes more, and you come to more exceptional sights: ascend a hill and then turn left at the gate where you'll see a National Trust sign. You emerge into the great sweeping earthwork known as

Uffington Castle – not, in fact, a castle at all, but a high hill fort dating back to the early Iron Age. Aside from the still-dramatic earth banks, no evidence of building was found here, but excavations have revealed pottery and loom weights. The Manger valley which falls below the fort has steep undulating banks, which were formed by retreating Ice Age permafrost. Nearby sits Dragon Hill, a natural conical hill with a flattened top which is poetically said to be the spot where St George slew the dragon. No grass grows on the top of the hill, something which is traditionally ascribed to the poisonous blood of the

Walkers on the Ridgeway

Set high on a long crest, the Ridgeway is often described as the oldest road in England; it has been tramped by drovers, itinerants and soldiers for at least 5000 years. Its elevation was a protection against attack – this was where the Saxons under Alfred the Great clashed with invading Vikings – as well as providing less boggy terrain for people and animals. Ancient hill forts along the way suggest that the Ridgeway was used as a secure trading corridor in ancient times. The route became formalised after the 18th-century enclosure act, but up until then it would have been a looser network of tracks and trails.

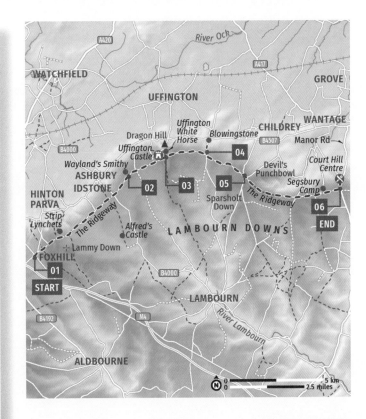

slaughtered dragon. Only slightly more prosaically, high levels of potash have been found here, suggestive of pagan ceremonies involving fire. Dragon Hill has clearly been a significant site for centuries: 46 Roman burials and eight Saxon ones were discovered here in the mid-19th century. Beyond the fort, on the slope of the glacial valley is the wonderfully artistic White Horse of Uffington, whose 3000-year-old, 110m-long form is stretched across the hillside.

04 Walk for another 2 miles or so, and you come to a minor road leading left down **Blowingstone Hill**. It's possible to make a detour here (2 miles in total, with a steep ascent back to the Ridgeway) to the Blowingstone itself, a weathered and rugged chunk of sarsen which, according to legend, is what King Alfred used to summon his army to battle. You can try yourself to emit a battle cry – a booming sound – by blowing into one of the holes in the stone.

05 Back on the route, you walk along fenced 'gallops' used for exercising race horses. The path climbs up to Sparsholt Down with a radio mast to the right. Turn right onto the paved road and then follow signs to where the Ridgeway resumes its course. Below you to the left is the steep green valley known as the Devil's Punchbowl. After around 20 minutes' walk, there's another detour by some farm buildings to Iron Age **Segsbury Camp**, an earthwork which was excavated

The White Horse

It is just one of the mysteries of the White Horse at Uffington (pictured) that it can only be clearly seen from the air. The horse is famously minimal and modern in appearance, a few bold lines cut deep into the chalk – the lines were dug up to a metre in depth around 2500 years ago. Indeed the jury is out on whether it does actually represent a horse – some claim the chalk lines may depict a sabre-toothed cat or a dog. Maintenance of the figure is now carried out by a group of National Trust volunteers, but until the late 19th century this work was done at hugely popular country fairs held on the hillside, with thousands in attendance.

in 1871 and was found to contain a Saxon burial, with human bones, a shield boss and urn fragments.

06 Another 15 minutes' walk brings you to Manor Rd, where you should turn left: here this stage of the Ridgeway walk ends at the **Court Hill Centre**. The centre is a great spot to get a simple meal and an equally simple bed for the night. Alternatively, call for a taxi, which can take you down the hill to Wantage.

 **TAKE A BREAK**

The independent **Court Hill Centre** (☎ 01235-760253; www.courthill.org. uk; Wantage; dorms £20, meals £12) was created out of five old barns, and enjoys a picturesque setting at the end of this route. It contains bunk beds and a few private rooms, and is a little spartan but very attractive. There's a lovely wood-beamed tea room, and simple but tasty meals are served for people staying overnight. It also provides breakfast and packed lunches for Ridgeway walkers.

Also Try...

NICOLA PULHAM/SHUTTERSTOCK ©

AVON GORGE & LEIGH WOODS

Slicing right through the centre of Bristol, and spanned by one of the great monuments of Victorian engineering, Isambard Kingdom Brunel's mighty Clifton Suspension Bridge (pictured; www.cliftonbridge.org.uk), the Avon Gorge makes for a super city walk.

Start in Leigh Woods, home to the Stokeleigh Camp hill fort, then cross the bridge to Clifton to visit the gorge-side lookout known as the Giant's Cave for one of the best vistas of the bridge. Return via the bridge, walking down through Nightingale Valley for a stroll along the edge of the River Avon, then a final climb back to the car park.

DURATION 3hr
DIFFICULTY Moderate
DISTANCE 4.6 miles/7.4km

STONEHENGE

Like Avebury, Stonehenge is much more than just a stone circle: it's part of a huge prehistoric landscape comprised of many different monuments.

North of Stonehenge and running roughly east–west is the Cursus, an elongated embanked oval; the smaller Lesser Cursus is nearby. Two clusters of burial mounds, the Old and New Kings Barrows, sit beside the ceremonial pathway known as the Avenue, which originally linked Stonehenge with the River Avon, 2 miles away. Trails connect all these monuments together – you can't even begin to understand Stonehenge without seeing how it sits within the context of this wider landscape. Few walks in Britain feel as moving, or as mysterious.

DURATION 2½-3hr
DIFFICULTY Easy
DISTANCE 6.4 miles/10.3km

OLD HARRY ROCKS

A classic Dorset walk along the World Heritage–listed Jurassic Coast, celebrated for its crimson cliffs and copious fossil deposits.

From the small village of Studland, the walk heads out around Handfast Point, affording views of the rock pillars known as Old Harry Rocks (pictured), sculpted into shape by the sea. It then heads west over Ballard Down, before looping round over Godlingston Heath and Agglestone Rock.

DURATION 3-3½hr
DIFFICULTY Moderate
DISTANCE 6.4 miles/10.2km

HAM HILL

Looming above the village of Stoke-sub-Hamdon, this is the highest point in Somerset at 125m.

It's served a variety of purposes – Iron Age hill fort, medieval village, stone quarry – and it's now a delightful park covering 390 acres. Recent archaeological excavations have revealed a huge Iron Age bone-pit. A great loop walk also crosses the parkland of nearby Montacute House.

DURATION 2-2½hr
DIFFICULTY Moderate
DISTANCE 5 miles/8km

THE QUANTOCKS

The 12-mile range of red sandstone hills known as the Quantocks are a mix of moors, valleys and ancient woods of coppiced oak.

They offer stirring views across the Bristol Channel: when the weather's fine, you can see across to the Gower coastline in South Wales. A super route travels west across Alfoxton Park from Holford to Bicknoller Post, then loops round to climb back up the wooded Holford Combe.

DURATION 2½-3hr
DIFFICULTY Moderate
DISTANCE 6.5 miles/10.4km

NORTHERN ENGLAND

Explore
NORTHERN ENGLAND

With rolling hills, wild moors, limestone outcrops and green valleys cut by scenic streams, the Yorkshire Dales and North York Moors national parks are among the most popular walking areas in England. Paths are a little gentler and conditions a little less serious than in the Lake District, with the happy addition of some delightful villages nestling in the dales. To the northeast, the rugged cliffs and vast empty beaches on the nearby Northumberland coast are less daunting but just as dramatic – perfect for wild seaside strolls.

PICKERING

Pickering is a lively market town with an imposing Norman castle that advertises itself as the 'gateway to the North York Moors'. That gateway is also the terminus of the wonderful North Yorkshire Moors Railway, a picturesque survivor from the great days of steam that offers a range of walks from its rural stations.

GRASSINGTON

A good base for hikes around the south Dales, Grassington's handsome Georgian centre teems with walkers and visitors throughout the summer months, soaking up an atmosphere that – despite the odd touch of faux rusticity – is as attractive and traditional as you'll find in these parts. Good riverside walks stretch out from the village, and the Dales Way passes right through the middle.

HAWES

Hawes is the beating heart of the Yorkshire Dales, a thriving and picturesque market town (market day is Tuesday) surrounded by rolling hills and hiking trails in the scenic setting of upper Wensleydale. It has several antique, art and craft shops, and the added attraction of a dozen or more walking routes radiating from the village centre.

ALNWICK

Northumberland's historic ducal town, Alnwick (pronounced 'annick') is an elegant maze of narrow cobbled streets around its colossal medieval castle. It's within easy striking distance of the Northumberland coast and has a youth hostel, a campground and a choice of hotels and B&Bs. Restaurants are mainly concentrated around Market Pl, and Alnwick's famous secondhand bookshop, Barter Books, has a cosy cafe.

WHEN TO GO

Although summer (June to August) means that the weather is usually warm and (hopefully!) dry, it's also the busiest time of year, especially during the school holidays (mid-July to end August). Hotspots like the Yorkshire Dales and Northumberland coast can get seriously overcrowded – it's not unusual for the road to Malham, for

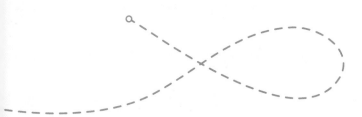

example, to be lined with parked cars for almost half a mile south of the village.

Late spring (May) and early autumn (September), on the other hand, are great months for walking, with fewer crowds and often mild and sunny weather. October and November can be good too, with the added advantage of autumn colours burnishing the woodlands.

 TRANSPORT

Trains on the East Coast Main Line run from London King's Cross to Edinburgh via York, Durham, Newcastle and Berwick; Northern Rail operates local and interurban services in the north.

Bus transport around Yorkshire is frequent and efficient, especially between major towns. Services are more sporadic in the national parks, but are still adequate for reaching most places. Bus transport around Northumberland can be irregular, particularly around the more remote western parts. Contact Traveline (www.traveline.info) for information on connections, timetables and prices. That said, a car is the most convenient way of reaching the starting point for most walks.

🧳 WHERE TO STAY

York, Leeds and Newcastle are the main centres for city-based accommodation, but most reasonably sized towns also have at least a couple of hotels and a dozen or more B&Bs. Many of the region's pubs also have rooms. Camping has always been a popular way to enjoy northern England's great outdoors, but there are now several glamping sites in the region with added luxuries, allowing visitors to enjoy the experience of sleeping in the near-wild without having to bring a tent.

Swaledale Yurts (www.swaledale yurts.com) Luxurious yurts with wood-burning stoves in Keld.

Lister Barn (www.listerarms.co.uk) Chic barn conversion B&B in Malham.

Ashcroft (www.ashcroftguesthouse. co.uk) Elegant Edwardian vicarage B&B near Hadrian's Wall.

Alnwick Lodge (www.alnwicklodge. com) Glamping in caravans, wagons and shepherds' huts.

Bramblewick (www.bramblewick. co.uk) Guesthouse set in old fishermen's cottages at Robin Hood's Bay.

Resources

www.daleswalks.co.uk Listings of walks in the Yorkshire Dales and North Yorkshire Moors.

www.nationaltrail.co.uk/ pennine-way/walk-the-way-in-a-day Day walks based on sections of the Pennine Way.

www.northyorkmoors.org.uk/ walking Walks in the North Yorkshire Moors National Park.

www.yorkshiredales.org.uk/ walking Walks in the Yorkshire Dales National Park.

www.lancashirewalks.com Walks in Lancashire.

 WHAT'S ON

Three Peaks Race (www.threepeaks race.org.uk; ⏱Apr) Challenging hill run held in Horton-in-Ribblesdale.

Grassington Festival (www.grassing ton-festival.org.uk; ⏱Jun) A two-week celebration of the arts.

Great Yorkshire Show (www.great yorkshireshow.co.uk; adult/child £25/12.50; ⏱mid-Jul) Farm animals compete for prizes, and entertainment ranges from showjumping and falconry to cookery demonstrations and hot-air-balloon rides.

Richmond Walking & Book Festival (www.booksandboots.org; ⏱Sep) Nine days of guided walks, talks, films and other events.

Harrogate Flower Show (www.flower show.org.uk; £17.50; ⏱late Sep) Has vegetable- and fruit-growing championships, a heaviest-onion competition, cookery demonstrations and children's events.

22

INGLEBOROUGH

DURATION	DIFFICULTY	DISTANCE	START/END
6-7hr	Hard	11 miles/ 18km	Clapham

TERRAIN	Rough, stony paths, often steep

Scenic Ribblesdale cuts through the southwestern corner of the Yorkshire Dales National Park, where the skyline is dominated by a trio of distinctive hills known as the Three Peaks: Whernside, Ingleborough and Pen-y-ghent. The ascent of Ingleborough (724m) from Clapham village is a classic Dales hike, full of interest and rewarded with fantastic and far-rainging views from the summit.

GETTING HERE

Clapham is 50 miles northwest of Leeds, and 57 miles north of Manchester. There is a regular bus service between Settle (served by trains from Leeds) and Clapham (20 minutes, every two hours, daily except Sunday). See www.dalesbus.org for timetables.

STARTING POINT

The National Park car park in the middle of Clapham village (£4.50 per car all day) has public toilets. About 120,000 people climb this hill every year, but don't let that lull you into a false sense of security. This is a proper hill walk, so pack waterproofs, food, water, a map and a compass.

01 Head north along Church Avenue, bear left past the church and cross the little bridge over Clapham Beck. The first half of the walk will be following the waters of this little stream almost to their source. Turn right on the far side of the bridge.

02 Where the street bends to the left, the gateway in front of you is the entrance to **Ingleborough Estate Nature Trail** (admission adult/child £1/50p), a scenic lakeside route to Ingleborough Cave. The estate was home to botanist Reginald Farrer (1880–1920), whose obsession with alpine plants led to the publication in 1907 of his book *My Rock-Garden,* which kicked off a British fashion for garden rockeries that persists to this day. Many of the features along the nature trail celebrate Farrer's contribution to botany and horticulture. An alternative route (which avoids paying the entrance fee) continues along the street for 80m and turns right on a gravel road (wooden signpost to Ingleborough Cave, Gaping Gill and Ingleborough). Another sign says Private Road, but walkers are welcome. Follow this road, keeping right at two forks, to reach Clapdale Farm.

03 Pass through the farmyard and turn right, heading downhill to join the gravel drive on the valley floor (the exit from Ingleborough Estate Nature Trail) where you turn left and follow the road alongside Clapham Beck to the entrance to Ingleborough Cave.

04 **Ingleborough Cave** is a show cave (adult/child £9/4.50) that has been open to the public since 1837. Easy concrete paths lead you for just over half a mile through floodlit passages and chambers filled with beautiful flowstone formations. This is where the waters that flow into Gaping Gill high on

the hillside above emerge into daylight once again as Clapham Beck. The walk continues past the cave entrance on a stony path, then turns sharp left and passes through a gate into the dramatic limestone canyon of Trow Gill.

05 Clamber up the boulder-strewn base of **Trow Gill** (pictured), which steepens and narrows before emerging into a narrow valley. The path hugs a stone wall on the left, and finally crosses the wall via a ladder stile to easier angled moorland with a view ahead to the summit of Ingleborough. A clump of bushes to the left of the path

The Three Peaks

Since 1968 more than 200,000 hikers have taken up the challenge of climbing Yorkshire's Three Peaks in less than 12 hours. The circular 24-mile route begins and ends at the Pen-y-Ghent Cafe in Horton-in-Ribblesdale (where you clock in and clock out to verify your time) and takes in the summits of Pen-y-ghent, Whernside and Ingleborough. Succeed and you become a member of the cafe's Three Peaks of Yorkshire Club.

Fancy a more gruelling test of your endurance? Then join the fell-runners in the annual Three Peaks Race (www.three peaksrace.org.uk) on the last Saturday in April, and run the route instead of walking it.

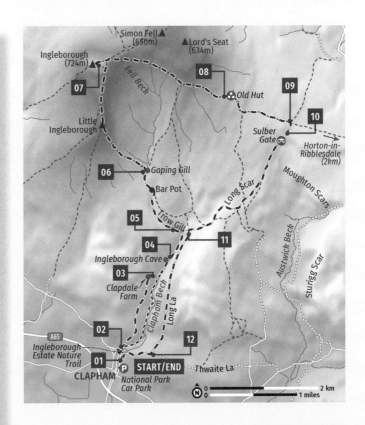

about 40m after the stile marks Bar Pot, one of the entrances to the Gaping Gill cave system. A short distance ahead fork right to view Gaping Gill itself, where the waters of Fell Beck plunge underground and flow through subterranean passages to Ingleborough Cave.

06 **Gaping Gill** (pictured) is one of the most famous caves in England. A huge vertical pothole 105m deep, it was the largest known cave shaft in Britain until the discovery of Titan in Derbyshire in 1999. Gaping Gill is normally off limits to non-cavers, but twice a year, on the late May and August bank holiday weekends, local caving clubs hold the Gaping Gill Winch Meet when a winch is set up so that members of the public can descend into the depths in a special chair (£15 per person). For details, see www.bpc-cave.org.uk and www.cravenpotholeclub.org, and click on the Gaping Gill link. Return to the main path, which begins to climb more steeply, via stone steps in places, onto the southern ridge of Ingleborough. It then traverses to the right before a final short, steep section leads onto the summit.

07 The summit of **Ingleborough** is a flat, featureless plateau about 300m across, marked at the highest point by a trig pillar, a huge pile of stones, and a cross-shaped drystone shelter. The view is stupendous, looking north across Ribblehead Viaduct to the Howgill Fells, northwest to the hills of the Lake District and south to Pendle Hill. In really clear

PAUL RICHARDSON/ALAMY STOCK PHOTO ©

weather you can make out the peaks of Snowdonia, 100 miles to the southwest. In pre-Roman times the summit of Ingleborough was occupied by a hill-fort settlement – you can still see the remains of a wall and some hut circles on the southern part of the plateau. Leave the summit in an east-northeasterly direction (towards Horton-in-Ribblesdale) past a prominent cairn on the edge of the plateau. Shortly after dropping down off the edge of the plateau bear right on a good footpath that leads steadily downhill, crossing a wall via a stile, to reach a small ruined building.

08 This old hut once served as a shelter for hunters shooting grouse on the nearby moor. Continue downhill with the wall on your left, cross another stile and bear left where the path forks. Soon you reach an area of **limestone pavement**, where the bare limestone bedrock is exposed at the surface. The path squeezes through a trench between wall and bedrock before crossing another stile and descending to a four-way junction of footpaths.

09 A prominent signpost marks **Sulber Crossroads**. This is where the footpath from Ingleborough to Horton-in-Ribblesdale intersects with the Pennine Bridleway. Turn right here on the bridleway, heading towards Clapham, and after 400m pass through a gap in yet another drystone wall.

Ingleton Waterfalls Trail

The village of Ingleton, perched precariously above a river gorge, is the caving capital of England. It sits at the foot of one of the country's most extensive areas of limestone, crowned by the dominating peak of Ingleborough and riddled with countless potholes and cave systems. The village is the starting point for a famous Dales hike, the circular, 4.5-mile Waterfalls Trail (www.ing letonwaterfallstrail.co.uk; £6), which passes through native oak woodland on its way past a series of spectacular waterfalls on the Rivers Twiss and Doe. Note that the walk involves a lot of uphill climbing, but in summer you can often find an ice-cream van at the highest point of the trail.

10 On your left is **Sulber Gate** – go through the gate for an impressive view of Moughton Scars, a sweeping curve of limestone escarpment with a large expanse of limestone pavement in the hollow below. Return through the gate and continue south with the stone wall on your left. The path forks three times in the next 0.75 miles – keep right at all three junctions. The last fork leads north on a grassy track around the outcrop of Long Scar, then curves back south and downhill to a ladder stile over a wall.

11 Turn left through a gate in the wall further downhill, where your path meets several other trails coming from the right. The wooded cleft on the far side of the valley is Trow Gill, where you clambered up during the first half of the walk. Follow this walled farm track (known as **Long Lane**) for 1.5 miles, with good views to the right across the valley. At its end is a T-junction.

12 Turn right and follow Thwaite Lane downhill, through woodlands and then tunnels beneath Ingleborough Estate (built in the 19th century to provide privacy for the estate gardens), to emerge in Clapham village beside the church. Turn left down Church Ave to return to the car park.

 TAKE A BREAK

There are several tearooms in Clapham, but for something a bit different head just 5km southeast on the A65 to the **Courtyard Dairy** (01729-823291; www.thecourt yarddairy.co.uk; Crows Nest Barn, Austwick, near Settle; 9.30am-5.30pm Mon-Sat, 10am-5pm Sun), a combined cheesemonger and cafe where you can try inventive grilled cheese sandwich wedges such as Wensleydale and caramelised carrot chutney. Don't miss the delicious rich fruit cake with a slab of local Dales cheese: a Yorkshire tradition.

23

PENDLE HILL

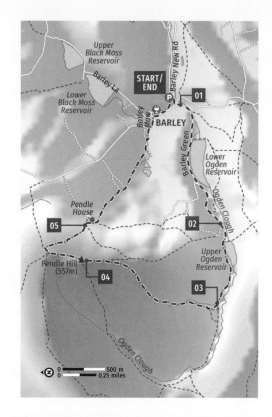

DURATION	DIFFICULTY	DISTANCE	START/END
3-4hr	Moderate	5 miles/ 8km	Barley

TERRAIN	Rough, stony paths, steep descent

Just east of Clitheroe in Lancashire lies one of England's most famous summits. Pendle Hill, forever associated with 17th-century witch trials, rises above the pretty village of Barley, commanding stupendous views that range from the Three Peaks of the Yorkshire Dales to the Isle of Man.

GETTING HERE

Barley is 32 miles (50 minutes' drive) north of Manchester, and 40 miles (1¼ hours' drive) west of Leeds. Bus 67 runs every two hours (Monday to Saturday) between Nelson and Clitheroe (both of which have train stations), stopping at Barley (20 minutes from Nelson, 40 minutes from Clitheroe).

STARTING POINT

The village of Barley has a large car park (£1 per car) with public toilets and a cafe. Nearby you will find a couple of pubs.

01 Turn right out of the car park entrance, cross the main road and head along the cul-de-sac opposite (signposted Barley Green). Follow the private road as it climbs to the right of the dam at **Lower Ogden Reservoir** and continues along its north bank. From its far end you are following part of the 45-mile Pendle Way, indicated by waymarks with a yellow arrow and a witch's silhouette.

02 The road leads along a narrow valley to a fork. Keep straight on, through a gate and up to the dam at **Upper Ogden Reservoir**. The way ahead now is on a rough and occasionally boggy footpath which leads to a wooden gate in a stone

Quakers & Witches

In 1652 George Fox had a vision atop the summit of Pendle Hill that would lead him to found the Religious Society of Friends, or Quakers. By then, the hill had become infamous as a centre of witchcraft: 40 years earlier, in 1612, 12 local women, some of whom were village healers in accordance with ancient traditions, were caught up in the religious tensions of the time and charged with witchcraft. On 18–19 August the women were put on trial in Lancaster and all but two were found guilty: the unlucky ones were executed on Lancaster Moor, where the Ashcroft Memorial in Lancaster's Williamson Park now stands.

RICHARD BRADFORD/SHUTTERSTOCK ©

wall with close-cropped grass on the near side and rough heather-and-bracken moorland beyond. Go through the gate and turn right immediately (not the carved stone Pendle Way marker at your feet), heading uphill and then leftwards across the slope.

03 After the path crosses a small stream, head uphill to the right (look out for two more stone markers). Follow the path as it climbs steadily past small cairns and crosses over the stream to merge with another, much more prominent, gravel path coming from the right.

04 The summit of **Pendle Hill** (557m) is marked by a trig pillar, and commands a fantastic view of the surrounding countryside – on a clear day you can pick out Blackpool Tower, 40 miles away on the western horizon. Walk north from the summit towards a stone wall, then turn right and head downhill on a stone-paved path that slants steeply down to meet and follow another wall.

05 Go through the gate just above Pendle House, and pass to the right of the house. Continue downhill, following the Pendle Way signposts back

to Barley village. At the road, turn right past the Barley Mow pub, and take the path inside the stone wall by the swings to return to the car park.

 **TAKE A BREAK**

The **Barley Mow** (☎01282-690868; www.barleymowpendle.co.uk; Barley Village; mains £7-15; ⏰7.30am-11pm Mon-Fri, 8.30am-midnight Sat, 8.30am-10pm Sun; 🛜👶🐾), a pub in the middle of the village, is a cosy rural retreat serving hearty breakfast, lunch and dinner menus aimed at refuelling weary walkers, from a full-on fry-up to fish and chips, Lancashire hotpot and Sunday roast with all the trimmings.

24

DUNSTANBURGH CASTLE

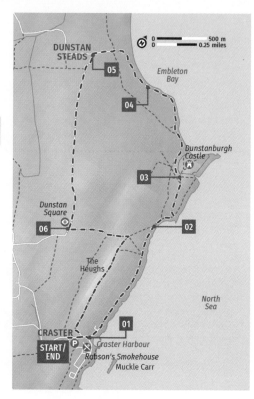

DURATION	DIFFICULTY	DISTANCE	START/END
2hr	Easy	4.5 miles/ 7km	Craster

TERRAIN	Firm paths, short grass, roads

Salty little Craster, famous for its kippers, is the starting point for one of northern England's finest coastal walks, following a sward of close-cropped turf northwards to the dramatic ruined towers of Dunstanburgh Castle and the golden sweep of Embleton Bay. It's an ideal hike to take young children on – easy going, no big hills, and a sandy beach to play on.

GETTING HERE

Craster is 40 miles (a one-hour drive) north of Newcastle-upon-Tyne, and 31 miles (45 minutes' drive) south of Berwick-upon-Tweed. Bus X18 runs to Craster from Berwick-upon-Tweed (1½ hours, three daily) and from Newcastle (2½ hours, three daily). From Monday to Saturday, bus 418 also links Craster to Alnwick (30 minutes, four daily).

STARTING POINT

Craster is a small fishing village on the Northumberland coast. The main car park is behind the tourist information office (£4 per car all day) – do not try to park in the village centre. There are toilets here (but none at Dunstanburgh Castle), and there's a pub, a tea room and a restaurant in the village.

01 From the tourist information office walk along the road to the harbour and turn left along Dunstanburgh Rd to its end. Pass through through two wooden gates and follow the grassy path along the coast.

02 After passing through another two gates, note the little bay on your right, which was once used as the harbour for Dunstanburgh Castle. At low tide you might be able to spot some rusting iron framework with scraps of timber still attached –

Craster Kippers

Craster, along with Seahouses further up the coast, is famous for its kippers (smoked herring) – in fact, the village is said to have invented the kipper. In the early 20th century, when the British herring fishery was at its height, around 25,000 herring were smoked here daily. Today only one traditional smokery remains in the village. Four generations of the same family have operated **Robson & Sons** (📞 01665-576223; www. kipper.co.uk; Haven Hill; kippers per kilo from £9; 🕐 9am-4.30pm Mon-Fri, 9am-3.30pm Sat, 11am-3.30pm Sun) for more than 120 years, smoking around 7000 fish a day over oak sawdust; loyal customers include the Royal Family.

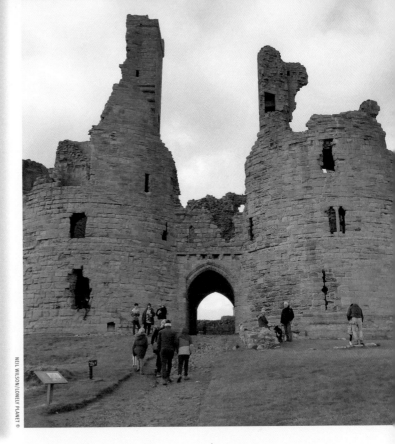

NEIL WILSON/LONELY PLANET ©

the wreckage of a Polish trawler that ran aground here in the 1960s. The path kinks to the left and rises up across a grassy field towards the castle.

03 **Dunstanburgh Castle** (pictured) was once one of the largest and most impressive fortresses in northern England, but fell into ruin by 1550. Follow the path along the inland side of the fortifications, and continue between the sea and a golf course.

04 At the southeastern end of **Embleton Bay** the coastal rocks give way to a magnificent sweep of golden sand.

Walk along the beach for 400m then turn left on a path through the dunes beside two concrete blocks, and continue along the road ahead.

05 At the first houses, turn left through a farmyard (signposted Public Bridleway), and continue for a mile to Dunstan Square farm, with views of the castle to your left.

06 At Dunstan Square turn left through a gate (signposted Craster), and follow the path through the gap in the ridge, then turn right before another gate and follow the grassy path back to Craster.

☕ TAKE A BREAK

The **Jolly Fisherman** (📞 016650-576461; www.thejollyfisherman craster.co.uk; Haven Hill; mains lunch £8-14, dinner £12-25; 🕐 kitchen 11am-3pm & 5-8.30pm Mon-Sat, noon-5pm Sun, bar 11am-11pm Mon-Sat, to 11pm Sun) is a gastropub with a beer garden at the back, which enjoys a view across the harbour to the distant towers of Dunstanburgh Castle. Crab (in soup, sandwiches, fish platters and more) is the speciality of the menu, but it also has a variety of fish dishes, as well as a house burger and steaks served with beef-dripping chips. A strong wine list complements its wonderful real ales.

25

HADRIAN'S WALL

DURATION	DIFFICULTY	DISTANCE	START/END
4hr	Moderate	7.5 miles/ 12km	Sill visitor centre

TERRAIN	Roads, stony paths, steep steps

Hadrian's Wall is the most dramatic and extensive legacy of the Roman occupation of Britain, stretching for more than 70 miles across northern England. This walk follows part of the famous Pennine Way along the most scenic stretch of the wall, as well as visiting the two best-preserved Roman forts in the country (the time given is for walking; allow at least two hours extra for exploring at Housesteads and Vindolanda).

GETTING HERE

The Sill visitor centre is 35 miles (a 50-minute drive) west of Newcastle-upon-Tyne, and 25 miles (a 40-minute drive) northeast of Carlisle. The AD122 Hadrian's Wall bus (hourly Easter to September) is a hail-and-ride service that runs between Hexham and Haltwhistle, calling at the Sill and other Hadrian's Wall sites.

STARTING POINT

The **Sill National Landscape Discovery Centre** (☎01434-341200; www.thesill.org.uk; Military Rd, Once Brewed; ⏰9.30am-6pm Apr-early Nov) was built in 2017 as a state-of-the-art visitor centre, with grasses and wildflowers growing on the roof to help it blend in with the landscape. It has a permanent exhibition on the landscape, culture and history of Northumberland alongside various temporary exhibitions. The car park charges £5 for all-day parking.

01 Head across the main B6318 road (be careful of traffic) and go north along the roadside path leading towards Steel Rigg viewpoint, steadily gaining height as you climb towards the rocky ridge of the Great Whin Sill.

02 Turn right through a wooden kissing gate at the far side of Peel Cottage (signposted Public Footpath to Hadrian's Wall). Bear left across the field to another gate in a stone wall and join a larger footpath on the other side. You are now on part of the **Pennine Way** national trail (note the acorn symbol waymarks). The path descends into a dip with rocky outcrops to the left, and then climbs steeply up stone steps to the crest of the ridge.

03 Looking back to the west, the pointed hill is **Winshield Crags** (345m), the highest point of the Great Whin Sill. The sill is one of northern England's most significant geological features, a layer of black dolerite (hard, erosion-resistant igneous rock) that stretches from Holy Island and Dunstanburgh Castle on the Northumberland coast to the western flank of the Pennines and the northern fringes of the Yorkshire Dales. Wherever it outcrops it creates prominent crags and ridges, including those at High Cup Nick, and much of Hadrian's Wall was built along its top. The path continues to the east along a well-preserved section of Roman wall, with broad views south across the valley of the River South Tyne to the high moors of the northern Pennines.

04 After another dip with a kissing gate, the wall on your left now little more than a low, turf-covered mound, you reach **Castle Nick**, a hollow in the ridge housing the stone outline of Milecastle 39. Every Roman mile (0.95 modern miles) along Hadrian's Wall there was a gateway guarded by a small fort (called a milecastle), and between each milecastle were two observation turrets (these are less well preserved and not usually visible).

05 A steep descent leads into **Sycamore Gap**, another hollow in the ridge with a dramatically sited sycamore

The Roman Wall

Named in honour of the emperor who ordered it to be built, Hadrian's Wall was one of Rome's greatest engineering projects. The 73-mile-long wall was built between AD 122 and 128 to protect against attacks from the Pictish tribes to the north. Today, the awe-inspiring sections that remain are testament to Roman ambition and tenacity. When completed, the mammoth structure ran across northern Britain's narrow neck from the Solway Firth in the west almost to the mouth of the Tyne in the east. A series of forts was built some distance south (and may predate the wall), and 16 lie astride it, including the impressive sites of Housesteads and Vindolanda.

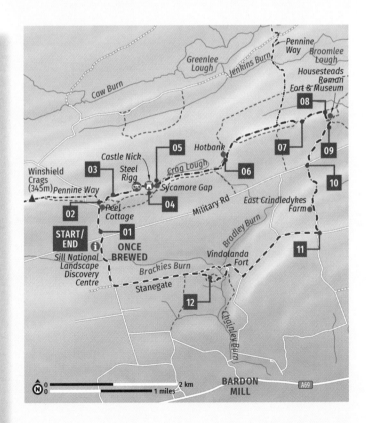

tree, one of the most photographed trees in the country (in 2016 it won the Woodland Trust's Tree of the Year award). The path now crosses the line of the wall and climbs gradually onto the crest of Highshields Crags, crossing a drystone dyke via a ladder stile (keep dogs and children close by here, as there is a vertical drop to the left); you may see rock climbers here. The little lake of Crag Lough lies at the foot of the cliffs as the path enters a picturesque stretch where it is lined with Scots pine trees. Another ladder stile over a wall marks the end of the woodland.

06 After crossing a farm road, easy going on a grassy path leads to a section of trail paved with stone slabs curving away from Hotbank farmhouse and back again, marking the site of **Milecastle 38**. Pass through a kissing gate and climb up past woods on the left. A section of rebuilt drystone wall runs along the crest of the ridge, with Greenlee and Broomlee loughs off to the left. At the next dip, the Pennine Way diverges to the north across a ladder stile on the left. Your route keeps straight on, through the small gate just ahead.

07 Another rise leads lead to **Milecastle 37** (pictured), which contains some well-preserved structures. You can see the remains of an arched gateway in the main wall, and the remains of barracks or storerooms in the eastern part (each milecastle was garrisoned by 20 to 30 Roman soldiers). Beyond

NEIL WILSON/LONELY PLANET ©

the milecastle a gate leads into an area of woodland. At the far end of the woods go through a gate in the wall on your right into a grassy field. The stone structure ahead is Housesteads Roman Fort.

08 The most dramatic site on Hadrian's Wall – and the best-preserved Roman fort in the whole country – is at **Housesteads** (EH; ☎ 01434-344363; www.english-heritage.org.uk; Haydon Bridge; adult/child £7.80/4.70; ⏰10am-6pm Apr-Sep, to 5pm Oct, to 4pm Nov-Mar). Set high on a ridge and covering 2 hectares – up to 800 troops were based at Housesteads at any one time – the fort commands the moors of Northumberland National Park to the north. Its remains include

an impressive hospital, granaries with a carefully worked out ventilation system, and barrack blocks. There's a scale model of the entire fort in the small museum at the far side of the field.

09 Descend past the museum and turn right along the tarred access road that leads southwest from the old farmhouse next to the museum (don't take the gravel path that leads to the museum car park, where most visitors will be heading).

10 When you reach the main B6138 road, turn right for only 20m and cross the ladder stile beside the gate (signposted Public Bridleway). Follow the grassy path across the field then slant left up the hillside to a

Hadrian's Wall Path

The Hadrian's Wall Path (www.nationaltrail.co.uk/hadrians-wall-path) is an 84-mile national trail that runs the length of the wall from Wallsend in the east to Bowness-on-Solway in the west. The entire route should take about seven days on foot, giving plenty of time to explore the rich archaeological heritage along the way. Preserved remains of forts and garrisons and intriguing museums punctuate the route, along with sections of the wall you can freely access. Another coast-to-coast option is Hadrian's Cycleway (www.hadrian-guide.co.uk), a 174-mile route between South Shields or Tynemouth and Ravenglass in Cumbria along the general line of Hadrian's Wall.

marker post. Bear right across a muddy dip and rise past two more marker posts, and pass to the left of East Crindledykes Farm via a pair of gates. Continue along the farm access road to reach a minor road.

11 Turn right and follow this road for a mile past two junctions, one to the left, and then one to the right. Turn right at the next junction (signposted Roman Vindolanda), and follow the road downhill past the car park to reach the site of Vindolanda Roman Fort. Turn left at the museum if you plan to visit the site; otherwise keep straight on along the minor road, passing an original Roman milestone (on the right, just after crossing the stream).

12 The extensive site of **Vindolanda** (☎01434-344277; www.vindolanda.com; Bardon Mill; adult/child £7.90/4.75, with Roman Army Museum £11.60/6.80; ☉10am-6pm Apr-Sep, to 5pm early Feb-Mar & Oct, to 4pm Nov-early Feb) offers a fascinating glimpse into the daily life of a Roman garrison town. The time-capsule museum is just one part of this large, extensively excavated site, which includes impressive parts of the fort and town (excavations continue) and reconstructed turrets and temple. Exit the site via the turnstile at the western end (or reach this point via the minor road) and continue west on the country lane for 0.75 miles. At a T-junction, turn right – another 0.5 miles leads back to your starting point.

 **TAKE A BREAK**

Just west of The Sill is the **Twice Brewed Inn** (☎01434-344534; www.twicebrewedinn.co.uk; Military Rd, Once Brewed; ☉10am-11pm; 📶), the ideal spot for a post-walk pint. Beer was first made on this site over half a millennium ago. Today, the pub's own brews include Ceres (wheat beer), Sycamore Gap (pale ale) and the brilliantly named Ale Caesar (American amber ale). There's a large beer garden with live music in summer, a roaring open fire in winter, and hearty food made with local Northumberland produce.

26

MALHAM LANDSCAPE TRAIL

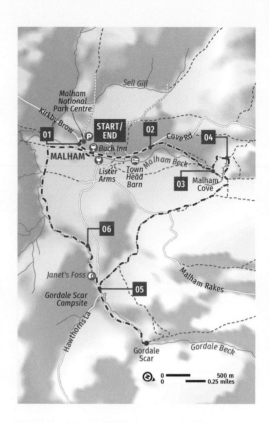

DURATION	DIFFICULTY	DISTANCE	START/END
2-3hr	Moderate	4.5miles/ 7 km	Malham

TERRAIN	Roads, rough paths, steep steps

Even in the Yorkshire Dales, where competition is fierce, Malham stands out as a strikingly attractive village. It sits within the largest area of limestone country in Britain, stretching west from Grassington to Ingleton – a distinctive landscape pockmarked with potholes, dry valleys, limestone pavements and gorges. This walk takes in two of the most spectacular features – Malham Cove and Gordale Scar.

GETTING HERE

Malham is 38 miles northwest of Leeds, and 52 miles north of Manchester. There are at least two buses a day Monday to Saturday year-round from Skipton to Malham (35 minutes). The scenic Malham Tarn Shuttle bus route links Settle with Malham (30 minutes), Malham Tarn and Ingleton

six times daily on Sundays and bank holidays only, Easter to October. Check the DalesBus website (www.dalesbus.org).

STARTING POINT

The car park at Malham National Park Centre (£4.50 per car all day) has an information centre and public toilets. Note that Malham is reached via narrow roads that can get very congested in summer, especially at weekends.

01 Turn left out of the car park and follow the road through Malham village, keeping left at the fork in front of the Buck Inn.

02 About 150m after passing Town Head Barn, go through the double gate on the right (signposted Pennine Way) and continue on the well-made hardpacked path through rolling pastures (there may be sheep and cattle grazing here). Pass

⛰ Malham Cove

Malham Cove (pictured) is a huge rock amphitheatre lined with 80m-high vertical cliffs, a playground for local rock climbers. A large glacial waterfall once tumbled over this cliff, but it dried up thousands of years ago. You can hike up the steep steps on the left-hand side of the cove (follow Pennine Way signs) to see the limestone pavement above the cliffs – a filming location in *Harry Potter and the Deathly Hallows*.

Peregrine falcons nest on the cliffs in spring, when the Royal Society for the Protection of Birds (RSPB) sets up a birdwatching lookout with telescopes near the base of the cliff – consult the national park centre for the schedule as it changes every year.

Best for

A POST-HIKE PINT

NICK BRUNDLE/SHUTTERSTOCK ©

through two more gates to reach a fork in the path.

03 Take the right fork to visit the base of **Malham Cove**, where the waters of Malham Beck reappear after their underground journey from Malham Tarn up above (the trail as far as the bottom of Malham Cove is accessible for all-terrain wheelchairs). Retrace your steps and bear right to reach the foot of a long flight of stone stairs that lead to the top of the Cove.

04 At the top of the stairs go through the gate and turn right to wander across the rugged limestone pavement and soak up the view. At the far side of the pavement, go through the gate in the stone wall and bear right uphill. Follow this path for just over a mile, crossing a road halfway, to emerge onto another road at a layby (there may be a snack bar here in summer).

05 At the road turn left, then left again along a level path that leads into the spectacular gorge of **Gordale Scar**. Return to the road and turn right, past the layby. Just as the road begins to climb uphill, go left through a gate (National Trust signpost) and along a wooded path to the pretty waterfall of **Janet's Foss**.

06 From Janet's Foss, follow the waymarked path along the river, across two stiles and through fields back to Malham village.

☕ TAKE A BREAK

The **Lister Arms** (☎ 01729-830444; www.thwaites.co.uk; Cove Rd; mains £10-18; ⏰ 8am-11pm Mon-Sat, to 10.30pm Sun; P 📶 🚼 🐾) is the best spot in Malham to kick back after a walk, with open fires for chilly days, a beer garden out back and classic pub meals plus chalkboard specials. In the busy summer months drinkers lounge out on the grass in front of the pub.

27

ROBIN HOOD'S BAY

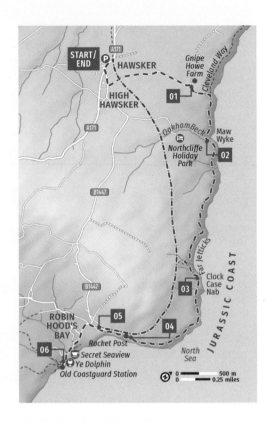

DURATION	DIFFICULTY	DISTANCE	START/END
4-5hr	Moderate	9 miles/ 14.5km	Hawsker

TERRAIN	Grass, gravel paths, can be muddy

The North Yorkshire coast is famous for its dramatic scenery and picturesque fishing harbours, and this walk makes the most of both, following part of the Cleveland Way national trail along the fossil-rich seacliffs south of Whitby to visit the storybook village of Robin Hood's Bay.

GETTING HERE

Hawsker is a small village on the A171 road, 3 miles southeast of Whitby. It's 75 miles southeast of Newcastle-upon-Tyne, and 51 miles northeast of York. Bus 93 runs hourly between Whitby and Scarborough via Hawsker and Robin Hood's Bay.

STARTING POINT

There is a car park (free) beside the village hall at the north end of Hawsker village. There are no facilities here, but there are toilets and cafes at

Robin Hood's Bay. From Hawsker village hall, head along the B1447, turn left at the bus stop (signpost for Swan Farm), and follow the track across the old railway line towards the coast.

01 At the entrance to Gnipe Howe farm, go through a gate on the right and aim for the corner of an old stone wall. Head downhill with the wall on your left and cross a stile to reach the **Cleveland Way** coastal path. Turn right.

02 Beneath the caravans of Northcliffe holiday park, the seacliffs of **Maw Wyke** are home to nesting seabirds in late spring and summer, notably a colony of kittiwakes – delicate-looking seagulls with black wingtips and a distinctive call that echoes their name.

03 As the path rounds Clock Case Nab there is a grand view back along the cliffs of **Far**

Robin Hood's Bay

Picturesque Robin Hood's Bay has nothing to do with the hero of Sherwood Forest – the origin of its name is a mystery, and the locals call it Bay Town. But there's no denying that this fishing village is one of the prettiest spots on the Yorkshire coast. Its maze of narrow lanes and passages is dotted with tearooms, pubs, craft shops and artists' studios (there's even a tiny cinema), and at low tide you can go down onto the beach and fossick around in the rock pools. The **National Trust visitor centre** (www.nationaltrust.org.uk; The Dock; ⏰10am-5pm Apr-Oct, to 4pm Sat & Sun Nov-Mar; ♿) houses an exhibition about local geology and natural history, with pamphlets on local walks.

Best for

COASTAL SCENERY

Jetticks. These layered rocks are part of Yorkshire's famous Jurassic Coast, which has yielded many of Britain's most important dinosaur fossils.

04 A tall wooden post to the right of the path marks the National Trust's '**Rocket Post Field**'. This is a replica of the original post used to practise rescuing shipwrecked sailors from the sea below the cliffs – a line was fired by rocket to the stranded ship, and the survivors winched ashore (an information board provides details). There is a fantastic view across the bay from the bench opposite the Rocket Post.

05 As you pass through a gate into the village of **Robin Hood's Bay** (pictured), note the signpost marked 'Cinder Track' – this indicates the start of your return route. Meanwhile, go straight ahead and turn left at the main street, then steeply downhill to explore the village.

06 The old coastguard station above the shoreline marks the end point of the famous Coast to Coast Walk. Retrace your steps uphill to the Cinder Track sign, and follow this track (an old railway line) for 4 miles back to Hawsker.

☕ TAKE A BREAK

It's debatable who wins the contest for most atmospheric pub; the Laurel Inn is a snug spot, Bay Hotel is the only pub with sea views, and **Ye Dolphin** (☎01947-880337; King St; ⏰11.30am-11pm Mon-Sat, noon-11pm Sun; 📶🐾) is good for real ale. Housed inside Robin Hood's 18th-century former chapel, **Secret Seaview** (www.swell.org.uk; Chapel St; mains £5-9; ⏰9.30am-3.30pm Mon-Fri, to 4pm Sat & Sun; 📶♿) unfolds into an impressive casual dining space with a lofty ceiling and petite terrace overlooking the beach. Great coffee, cakes, simple breakfasts, sandwiches and jacket potatoes are on the menu.

28

RIEVAULX

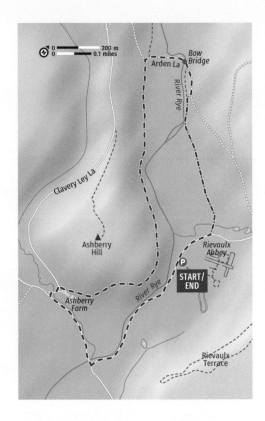

DURATION	DIFFICULTY	DISTANCE	START/END
1-2hr	Easy	2.5 miles/ 4km	Rievaulx Abbey

TERRAIN	Grassy paths, some uphill, muddy

In the secluded valley of the River Rye stand the magnificent ruins of Rievaulx Abbey. This idyllic spot was chosen by Cistercian monks in 1132 as a base for their missionary activity in northern Britain. St Aelred, the third abbot, famously described the abbey's setting as 'everywhere peace, everywhere serenity, and a marvellous freedom from the tumult of the world' – an atmosphere well captured by this woodland and riverside walk.

Head north from the abbey entrance (car parking £5) and turn left through a wooden gate beside a stable (signposted Bow Bridge). Cross a small stream, pass through another gate and follow the path alongside the hedge. The ditch to the right was originally a channel cut by the monks to supply water to the abbey. Follow the path for 800m along the banks of the River Rye.

Go through a gate at a marker post and turn left along a country lane. Cross the 18th-century stone arch of Bow Bridge and follow the lane ahead for 120m before turning left through a wooden gate (signposted Ashberry). Bear right through another gate, and as the path climbs steadily through the woods there are glimpses through the trees of the abbey and the mock temples of Rievaulx Terrace on the hillside above.

The path emerges from the woods at Ashberry Farm. Turn left, cross the red brick bridge and go left along the road. After 300m you cross a bridge over the River Rye – turn left to return to your starting point. The romantic ruins of the **abbey** (EH; www. english-heritage.org.uk; adult/child £8.90/5.30; ⏱10am-6pm Apr-Sep, to 5pm Oct, to 4pm Sat & Sun Nov–mid-Feb, daily Mar; P) are well worth a visit before or after your walk.

Also Try...

WONDERLUSTPICSTRAVEL/SHUTTERSTOCK ©

HOLY ISLAND

Remote, windswept Holy Island (also known as Lindisfarne) is one of the cradles of Christianity in Britain (St Aidan founded a monastery here in 635).

You can walk a clockwise circuit of the island from the main car park, taking in the bird-haunted sand dunes of the north coast (look out for seals on the offshore rocks), the restored 16th-century castle (pictured) perched picturesquely atop a prominent crag, and the red and grey ruins of the priory where the illuminated manuscripts known as the Lindisfarne Gospels were created in the 8th century. The island is only accessible at low tide – pay close attention to crossing-time information, posted at tourist offices and on notice boards throughout the area, and at www.holy-island.info.

DURATION 2hr
DIFFICULTY Easy
DISTANCE 4 miles/6.4km

THREE PUBS WALK

Pubs and walking go together, and this lovely hike in the heart of the Yorkshire Dales combines the two perfectly.

The route heads north from Buckden to Cray, where the White Lion makes a great lunch stop, then traverses high above the valley floor, with grand views down the length of Wharfedale, to Scar House (George Fox, founder of the Quakers, preached here in 1652). It then descends to the village of Hubberholme and the George Inn. The ashes of the writer JB Priestley, who loved the Yorkshire Dales – and Hubberholme in particular – are buried in the churchyard. Then it's back along the riverside to your starting point, where a pint awaits at the Buck Inn.

DURATION 3hr
DIFFICULTY Moderate
DISTANCE 5 miles/8km

BRIMHAM ROCKS

Set on a hilltop 14.5km north-west of Harrogate is the other-wordly landscape of Brimham Rocks (pictured).

Here wind and weather have carved the sandstone outcrops into weird and wonderful shapes, offering a fun-filled family outing (free admission, parking £6 for four hours). Easy paths meander through the rock formations – pick up a 'Spot The Rocks' leaflet at the information office and see if you can find the imaginatively named rock formations.

DURATION 1hr
DIFFICULTY Easy
DISTANCE 1.5 miles/2.5km

TOP WITHENS

Starting from Haworth, the home of the Brontë sisters, this walk visits the ruined farm-house of Top Withens.

The ruin is said to be the inspi-ration for the Earnshaw home in Emily Brontë's novel *Wuthering Heights*. Follow signs to the Brontë Waterfalls, a local beauty spot, cross the stream and continue uphill onto the moors, along a stony path (signpost-ed Top Withens) to the ruins. Return via the Pennine Way and minor roads through the village of Stanbury.

DURATION 4hr
DIFFICULTY Moderate
DISTANCE 7 miles/11.3km

TAN HILL INN FROM KELD

Tan Hill Inn, set at an elevation of 328m, is Britain's highest pub.

From Keld village near the head of Swaledale, follow the Pennine Way north for 4 miles on an old packhorse track to reach the inn. Return via the public footpath over Robert's Seat to Ravenseat Farm, then along the east side of Whitsundale Beck and down across a bridge over the River Swale to the B6270 road. Follow this back to Keld, past a superb wild swimming spot at Wain Wath Force.

DURATION 6hr
DIFFICULTY Challenging
DISTANCE 11 miles/17.5km

CENTRAL ENGLAND

Explore
CENTRAL ENGLAND

The best known and most ruggedly beautiful landscape in central England is the Peak District National Park, with its epic moorland, crashing waterfalls, rushing rivers and caverns. The area, whose literal and scenic high point is the moorland plateau of Kinder Scout, makes challenging hiking country. Indeed, it's a something of a pilgrimage spot for walkers, as the place where the right to access the countryside was established. Further southwest towards the Welsh border, the abundant Shropshire Hills are less dramatic but no less lovely, as the designation of Area of Outstanding Natural Beauty suggests. South again, the hills around the spa town of Malvern rise up in a green wave, and the Cotswolds are picture-perfect England.

MATLOCK

Matlock was developed as a spa town in the 19th century, and as a result has some gorgeous and fantastical Victorian architecture, in addition to a steep scenic location. It has long been a magnet for pleasure-seeking day-trippers, with a hydro, show caverns, pleasure gardens and cable railways. There's a plethora of great B&Bs in the handsome Victorian villas, and Thai, Italian and Indian restaurants as well as fine old pubs. The town sits just outside the national park, with easy access to it by bus, bike or car.

MALVERN

As with Matlock, mineral springs were the making of Great Mal-vern, the beautiful 19th-century centrepiece of the wider town of Malvern. Victorian villas climb uphill to a magnificent 11th-century priory church which sits at the top of Church St. You can taste Malvern's fabled spring water at wells dotted around the town, and you'll find decent places to eat and drink close by, plus some cracking pubs. If you'd like a musical soundtrack to your walking, bear in mind that the area's favourite son was Edward Elgar, who lived in and around the Malvern Hills, and found musical inspiration in their beauty.

BURFORD

The Cotswolds area is not short of beautiful settlements, whose golden-stone buildings light up the rolling hills, known locally as the wolds. One of the loveliest and most historic spots is Burford, whose history goes back at least a thousand years. The steep high street of the town with its tall houses and ancient cottages looks across at the High Wold, and down to the willows that fringe the River Windrush. In addition to the 15th-century parish church, there's a Tudor museum, plus some great old pubs, tearooms and excellent hotels and guesthouses.

 WHEN TO GO

The high elevations in the Peak District mean that thick snow

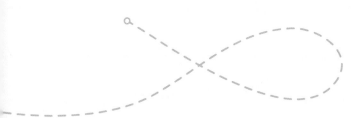

can be a possibility in winter, when driving is best avoided and you'll have to wrap up with lots of layers for hiking. Otherwise, the weather in central England is generally moderate, and there's no particular time to avoid, other than high summer in the Cotswolds, when this tourist honeypot can be swamped with visitors. Spring is a beautiful time across the region, perhaps especially in densely green Shropshire which is famed for its dense hedgerows. Autumn, in harvest time when the leaves change colour, is also gorgeous.

TRANSPORT

You'll be able to take trains to most of the major places mentioned in this chapter – in fact Great Malvern station is a sight in its own right, dating back to 1862 and featuring the award-winning Lady Foley's Tearoom. For Burford, the nearest stations are Oxford or Charlbury and then you'll have to switch to a bus or coach.

WHERE TO STAY

In the Peak District there's a campsite at Stanage with pitches and camping pods; you'll find sites at Malvern and Little Stretton in Shropshire, plus there are campsites and glampsites scattered across the Costwolds. B&Bs and Airbnbs abound for all budgets, with some particularly attractive options in honey-stone Cotswold homes. Hartington Hall in the Peak District is one of the YHA's best hostels, housed in a spectacular 17th-century manor house; it also has bell tents and cute land pods. YHA Costwolds in Cirencester occupies a beautifully restored brewery warehouse, and has good facilities and an adjoining arts centre.

WHAT'S ON

Y Not (www.ynotfestival.com; ☺Jul) This indie music festival held in Pikehall has a glorious Peak District setting, plus elements of carnival, comedy and cinema.

Walking festival (www.churchstret tonwalkingfestival.co.uk; ☺Jul) Church Stretton has themed rambles such as the Map and Compass Course, the evening Stars in Your Skies Walk, and a Landscape Photography Walk.

The Big Feastival (www.thebigfeast ival.com; ☺Aug) Hosted by Alex James of Blur fame on his farm, this Costwolds festival is all about good food and great music.

Ludlow Food Festival (www. ludlowfoodfestival.co.uk; ☺Sep) Take time off from your hiking for this three-day celebration of good food, held in the fine medieval market town of Ludlow.

Matlock Illuminations (www.visit peakdistrict.com/whats-on/mat lock-bath-illuminations; ☺Sep/Oct) Held in Derbyshire, the Matlock Bath Venetian Boat Builders' Association (yes really) place lighted models onto boats and float them up and down the River Derwent.

Resources

Cotswolds AONB (www. cotswoldsaonb.org.uk) The lowdown on the Cotswold Way National Trail and other routes in the area.

Miles without Stiles (www. peakdistrict.gov.uk/visiting/ miles-without-stiles) Includes a handy index of accessible walks in the Peak District.

Peak District National Park (www.peakdistrict.gov.uk) All you need to know about staying, eating, drinking and hiking in the national park.

Shropshire's Great Outdoors (www.shropshiresgreatout doors.co.uk) Explores the practicalities of the Shropshire Way, Offa's Dyke and other shorter routes.

Visit the Malverns (www. visitthemalverns.org) The website has a whole section on Malvern Hill walks, plus listings of places to stay and eat in the town and around.

29

KINDER SCOUT

Best for

WILD VIEWS

DURATION	DIFFICULTY	DISTANCE	START/END
4-5hr	Hard	8 miles/ 13km	Edale

TERRAIN	Rocky ascent, some boggy ground

The highest peak in the Peak District, Kinder Scout is a brooding moorland plateau that offers some of the area's most challenging walks. The place is famous not least because of the role it played in securing the right to roam: it was the site of the 1932 Kinder Mass Trespass, often cited as one of the most successful examples of direct action in British history. This route from Edale is popular for its scramble up Grindsbrook Clough and the peculiar rock formations along the southern edge, before it loops back down Jacob's Ladder – the first section of the Pennine Way.

GETTING HERE

Edale railway station is served by Manchester and Sheffield. There's pay-and-display parking at Edale Village Hall Car Park.

STARTING POINT

Whether you park or take the train, the walk starts at the bottom of the road heading through Edale village, a popular destination for ramblers.

01 Walk north up the road through Edale from the car park or station, passing the Moorland visitor centre to your right, to the Old Nags Head – the official start/end of the Pennine Way. Carry on along the road behind the pub to where it becomes a gravel track. Follow this track until you see the footpath to your right, marked 'Grindsbrook'. Follow this path down into the woods to cross Grinds Brook and bear left, sticking to the paved path which leads through the valley into **Grindsbrook Clough**, the original route of the Pennine Way.

02 As the valley narrows, the paved path begins to deteriorate and the route now becomes more interesting as you clamber over rocks and boulders to follow the stream uphill. As you climb higher, some hand work may be necessary, but this is classed as an easy Grade 1 scramble that can be managed by most with a decent level of stamina. As you near the top of the clough (gorge), the route forks. Stick to the left path for the steeper but more direct

route, or if you choose to take the slightly easier option up the stream to your right, head left at the top to follow the rim and rejoin our route.

03 At the top of **Grindsbrook Clough** you're greeted by a cairn. From here you can savour the views back down the valley, and for the first time appreciate the isolated wilderness of Kinder's vast and featureless plateau. In poor visibility Kinder can be confusing, so knowledge of how to use a map and compass is strongly recommended. Head west leaving Grindsbrook Clough – the path here can be a little difficult to locate but after

the first section you'll essentially keep to the path along the southerly rim, enjoying the weird and wonderful rock formations (pictured) along the way until you reach Crowden Clough. Cross the clough and head left to ascend to the rocky outcrop of Crowden Tower.

04 Carry on to reach **the Woolpacks**, a scattering of large, weather-sculpted rocks, so-called because of their likeness to old-fashioned wool bales. The path winds through this remarkable site and continues along to two other notable rock formations: **Pym Chair** and the anvil-shaped **Noe Stool**.

Mass Trespass

On 24 April 1932, more than 400 men and women marched upon the moorland – then used exclusively by gentry for grouse shooting – to demand access for all. At the fore was 20-year-old Benny Rothman, who argued that all peaks and uncultivated moorland should be accessible to everyone, especially workers in polluted industrial towns and cities. The protest resulted in Rothman and four others being jailed, but paved the way for the establishment of Britain's national parks (the first of which, fittingly, was the Peak District), and ultimately led to today's Countryside and Rights of Way (CRoW) Act.

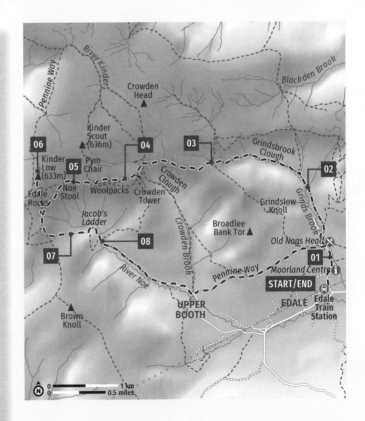

05 From Noe Stool continue along the path until you meet the Pennine Way. Although you'll eventually head left here to return to Edale, on a clear day it's worth making the 400m detour right to reach **Kinder Low** – as close to a summit as you'll find on Kinder Scout. Although 3m lower than the actual highest point (which lies unmarked to the northeast of Kinder Low, and is rather underwhelming), it's somewhat easier to find, being marked by a trig point, and has become a pilgrimage destination for ardent hikers. It was along here that hundreds of brave trespassers took on the gamekeepers to fight for access to the countryside: be sure to say a silent thank you to the protesters to whom we owe the sense of freedom that can be felt up in places like Kinder Scout. You'll find the trig just to the east of the Pennine Way, but it can be disorientating in poor visibility. It gazes down towards Hayfield where the mass trespass began, another popular starting point for a Kinder Scout hike.

06 Retrace your steps heading south from the trig point, passing Edale Rocks to the cairn marking the top of the Pennine Way. Bear right slightly and continue down to where the path forks. Take the left along the broad, eroded path and then left again to pick up the more established path of the Pennine Way and former packhorse route leading from east to west.

07 Descend along this track until you reach the top of

Kinder Scout Wrecks

This area of the Dark Peak – notably Kinder Scout and neighbouring Bleaklow, the region's second highest peak – is littered with aircraft wreckages. More than 150 aircraft are believed to have crashed in the Peak District in the last century and there are as many as 11 crash sites on Kinder alone. The weather here can be very changeable, and in low rain or thick fog (known by local hillwalkers as 'clag') it's easy to imagine how a pilot could become disorientated and the endless moorland slopes could pose a danger to low-flying aircraft. Due to the vast and featureless nature of the high moorland, it's recommended that you enlist a local guide to visit these wreckages unless you are an experienced navigator. Alternatively, Peak District rangers often run organised walks to these remarkable and eerie sites.

JOHN MORRISON/ALAMY STOCK PHOTO ©

Jacob's Ladder (pictured). Turn left for a steep but more direct route along Jacob's Ladder – named after Jacob Marshall who occupied Edale Head Farm and kept a small enclosure for packhorses, the ruins of which are close to the packhorse bridge at the bottom. He is credited with constructing the steep path to give the packhorsemen respite while their horses took the zigzagging route to the right (a longer but gentler option). Both routes emerge at the packhorse bridge across the River Noe.

08 From here follow the Pennine Way through Upper Booth and up the lower slopes of **Broadlee-Bank Tor** – the last slog before a well-earned beverage. After this you'll head through several gates and stiles before emerging back at the Old Nags Head.

TAKE A BREAK

The obvious choice for walkers descending from Kinder Scout is the **Old Nags Head** (☎01433 670291; www.the-old-nags-head. co.uk; Grindsbrook Booth, Edale; soup £4.95; steak & ale pie £11.95; ⏱noon-9pm Mon-Sat, to 8pm Sun), a packhorse inn (and former smithy) with tankards hanging from the beams and rugged flagstone floors. This is a proper walkers' pub with good food and log fires; it even serves its own ale, the 'Nags Head 1577'.

30

MAM TOR

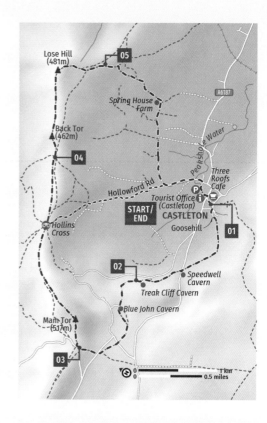

DURATION	DIFFICULTY	DISTANCE	START/END
4hr	Hard	6.5 miles/ 10.4km	Castleton visitor centre
TERRAIN	Steep inclines, rocky trails, steps		

Mam Tor, meaning 'Mother Hill' – also known as the 'Shivering Mountain' for its frequent shale landslides – is consistently voted one of Britain's best walks for its vast panoramic views. This route takes you from the enticing town of Castleton up to Mam Tor and along the Great Ridge.

GETTING HERE

Buses run here from Sheffield; alternatively, there's a pay-and-display car park at Castleton Visitor Centre.

STARTING POINT

The walk starts and ends at the visitor centre in Castleton town centre.

01 Cross the main road in front of the visitor centre and walk behind the jewellers to follow the footpath running beside Peakshole Water. Cross the bridge and walk up Goosehill, until it turns into a stony path with the wall on your right. Follow this path until it meets the road, with Speedwell Cavern to your left, and cross over to take the path to **Treak Cliff Cavern**.

02 Take the steps up to the cavern and follow the path right behind the building and up the hillside to **Blue John Cavern**. Cross the car park in front of the cafe-shop and go through a gate to take the path uphill. Veer right to head through a gate in the corner of the field. Continue straight along this path all the way up to the foot of Mam Tor, crossing two roads along the way.

03 Take the stepped path up to the summit of **Mam Tor** and hold on to your hat as you do – the winds can be strong up on top. On a fine day, you're likely to spot gliders taking off from the edge.

Mam Tor in history

As well as being a great place for a hike, Mam Tor is an important archaeological site; evidence of prehistoric use (two round barrows near the hilltop) dates from the Bronze Age, and even earlier finds include flint tools and a Neolithic polished stone axe. During the late Bronze and early Iron Ages it was occupied as a hill fort, one of the largest and highest in Britain. Look out for the iron plaques set into the steps up to Mam Tor, whose designs conjure these early settlers and are a good motivator for children to make it to the top. Among the images are a round house, a dagger, a neck torc (an item of jewellery), a plough, an urn and the face of the sun god Lugh.

LOOP IMAGES/GETTY IMAGES ©

Continue along the ridge to **Hollins Cross** – if you look to your right you can see the old Mam Tor road beneath you, closed in 1979 due to repeated landslips. At Hollins Cross you have the option to cut the route short by heading down to the right, back into Castleton.

04 Otherwise continue along the ridge, taking the stile left to climb the steep section up to the rocky outcrop of Back Tor and along to the final summit at **Lose Hill Pike** (if you don't fancy the steep ascent, take the lower path which misses out these two summits). On a clear day you can see right along the ridge, back towards Mam Tor. From Lose Hill, bear right down the stone path and cross two stiles before following the path down to your left, alongside the field boundary.

05 Continue on this path down the hill, passing a line of trees on your right. Shortly after, as the path veers left towards Hope, fork off right and continue down the hill (which is quite steep in places) until you emerge on a farm track. Turn right and head down the hill to Spring House Farm, after which you'll turn right into Castleton. Then keep going straight ahead, through a series of gates while ignoring any turnoffs, until you reach the training and conference centre. Turn left on to Hollowford Rd leading back into Castleton – a shortcut right before the Ramblers Rest takes you straight back to the car park.

 TAKE A BREAK

The **Three Roofs Cafe** (www.threeroofscafe.com; The Island; dishes £5-11; ⊙9.30am-4pm Mon-Fri, to 5pm Sat & Sun; 🛜), opposite the Visitor Centre, is Castleton's most popular purveyor of cream teas, and dishes up filling sandwiches, pies, fish and chips, burgers and jacket potatoes plus teas, coffees and a selection of alcoholic drinks.

31

STANAGE EDGE

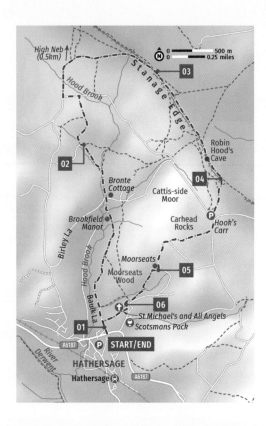

DURATION	DIFFICULTY	DISTANCE	START/END
3-4hr	Moderate	5.6 miles/ 9.1km	Hathersage

TERRAIN	Footpaths, tracks, some rocky terrain

Loved by walkers and climbers alike, Stanage is one of the Peak District's best-known gritstone edges. This varied, circular route from the village of Hathersage offers some of the best views over Hope Valley as well as of the edge itself.

GETTING HERE

Hathersage station is served by Manchester and Sheffield. There's a pay-and-display car park on Oddfellows Rd.

STARTING POINT

Baulk Lane, just off the main road (A6187) in Hathersage. You'll spot the public footpath sign immediately to the right of outdoor shop Alpkit.

01 Follow Baulk Lane for almost a mile to where it passes **Brookfield Manor** and reaches

Birley Lane. Cross the road, with **Bronte cottage** to your right, and take the footpath through the field opposite and into woodland. Where the path forks, take the footbridge left and head uphill into open fields, the second of which has a small boardwalk over boggy ground. Cross a stile in the wall, then go up the narrow path.

02 Where the path reaches a T-junction, turn left (signposted Stanage). Just after the wide gate, follow the footpath sign right up the hill. As this path tapers right, go through the gap in the wall so it's now on your left. Stick to this path until you reach the lane, where you turn left to a car park. Then turn right along the track leading up to **Stanage Edge** (pictured).

03 At the top, turn right to follow the edge. If you want to summit the highest point, first head left to the trig at **High Neb** (458m) before

Stanage Edge in Literature

You may recognise Stanage Edge from the 2005 film version of *Pride & Prejudice*. In an iconic shot, Elizabeth Bennet – played by Keira Knightley – stands on a rocky outcrop with her coat blowing behind her, feeling the full force of her freedom. It's become a local sport to emulate Knightly's pose, one to be undertaken with a bit of care given the dramatic drop. And, as mentioned in the route description, Moorseats is where Jane Eyre flees to 'the grey small antique structure, with its low roof, its latticed casements, its mouldering walls, its avenue of aged firs all grown aslant under the stress of mountain wind.'

Best for

WILD VIEWS

TOM_SANDERSON/SHUTTERSTOCK ©

retracing your steps. You'll pass above a cave where Robin Hood is rumoured to have sheltered.

04 Take the path diagonally down to Hook's Carr car park. Turn left out of the car park and immediately right along the road (The Dale). Shortly after, take the gate in the wall on your right leading uphill towards Carhead Rocks. At the top, you're treated to great views of Stanage Edge. Follow the path down the other side to a farm track. Turn right and continue down into the grounds of **Moorseats**, which inspired Moor House in Charlotte Brontë's *Jane Eyre*.

05 Walk through the grounds and immediately upon exiting go right through a wooden gate between two pillars. Follow this path down through **Moorseats Wood**, where you'll pass through a freestanding stone gateway. Upon emerging from the woods, continue straight where the path forks, ignoring the left turn to the metal kissing gate, until you reach a gate and stile with the church ahead.

06 Turn left onto Church Bank. Either follow the road down to the Scotsman's Pack Inn and the village, or pass through the second gate on your right into St Michael's and All Angels churchyard, where Robin Hood's right-hand man Little John is reputedly buried. Exit through the gate opposite where you entered and walk down to rejoin Baulk Lane into the village.

TAKE A BREAK

The **Scotsman's Pack** (☏ 01433 650253; www.scotsmanspackcountry inn.co.uk; School Lane, Hathersage; mains from £12; ⏰ 11am-midnight Mon-Sat, from noon Sun) is a traditional inn that's ideal for a post-walk pint: it serves hearty food and real ale. The place is named for the Scottish packmen who stopped here to sell tweeds.

32

THE MALVERN HILLS

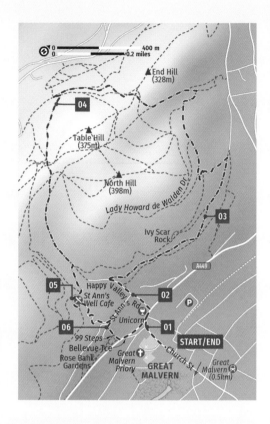

DURATION	DIFFICULTY	DISTANCE	START/END
1½hr	Moderate	2.5 miles/ 4km	Great Malvern

TERRAIN	Steep grassed paths

The green spine of the Malvern Hills rises to unexpected heights out of the gentle contours of three counties: Worcestershire, Herefordshire and Gloucestershire. The rocks from which the hills are formed are the most ancient in the country, something which perhaps adds to the mystical feel of the area, with its mineral springs, prehistoric earthworks and caverns. All this beauty has provided plenty of inspiration, from the 14th-century *Visions of Piers Plowman* by William Langland, to the works of JRR Tolkien and CS Lewis and the music of Elgar.

GETTING HERE

Great Malvern is best reached by train; a 2½-hour journey northwest of London's Paddington Station.

STARTING POINT

The walk starts in the heart of picturesque Great Malvern (pictured from the hills), close to the ancient Great Malvern Priory, which is a 10-minute walk west of the town's beautifully preserved Victorian train station.

01 Starting at the top of Church Street just north of Great Malvern Priory, turn right onto the main road and then, at the **Unicorn** pub, almost immediately left onto St Ann's Rd.

02 Where St Ann's Road bears left, go straight ahead away from the houses and onto Happy Valley Rd. Continue along the path, which eventually joins a gravel track, looking down to the clustered houses of Great Malvern.

03 Continuing past the outcrop of Ivy Scar Rock, take the left-hand path rather than

HARRY GREEN/SHUTTERSTOCK ©

Spring Water

Sixty litres of collected rainwater per minute shoot out of the tough limestone and granite rock of the Malvern Hills, in the past providing hoped-for relief for those suffering everything from poor eyesight to gout. The water-cure fad reached its height in the Victorian period: Charles Darwin brought his daughter Anne here for the cure, though sadly she died at the age of 10 and is buried in the priory graveyard. Spring water spurts from 70 locations around the town and the hills, famously at St Ann's Well. Malvern water has been commercially bottled since the 1920s, though a more eco-friendly way to sample it is from one of the town's wonderfully artistic water fountains.

following the North Hill sign. From here the path rises steeply for a stretch. Continue straight ahead, then follow the sharp left turn, then zig zag to the right on Lady Howard de Walden Dr and continue to ascend the curve of North Hill.

04 The track begins to descend and then splits – turn left and head uphill past the little quarry. Head up and over the hill, from where you can detour up **Sugarloaf Hill**. Otherwise, start to head downwards. You cross a path and walk down an avenue of sycamores, turning right at the paved driveway.

05 Continue on the path as it bears left to St Ann's Well Cafe, a worthy refreshment stop, then take the zig-zagging path back to St Ann's Rd.

06 Turn right on St Ann's Road, and then left down the staircase known as **99 Steps**, with the spacious Rose Bank Gardens to your right. The steps deposit you back in Great Malvern; at their foot there's a plaque which credits the local gas lamps with inspiring *The Lion, the Witch and the Wardrobe*. Turn left on wide Bellevue Tce to arrive back at the top of Church St where the walk started.

☕ TAKE A BREAK

Quaint **St Ann's Well Cafe** (✆ 01684-560285; www.stannswell.co.uk; St Ann's Rd; mains £5.50, cakes £2.90; ⏰ 11.30am-3.30pm Tue-Fri, 10am-4pm Sat & Sun; 🖊) is set in an early 19th-century villa, with mountain-fresh spring water bubbling into a Sicilian marble basin by the door. All-vegetarian food (including vegan options) spans warming soups to cheese-topped homity pies and veg chilli, filled baguettes, cakes, pastries and puddings. Drinks include homemade elderflower cordial and dandelion latte. The well here is said to have been used by the monks who built the priory back in 1085.

33

CAER CARADOC

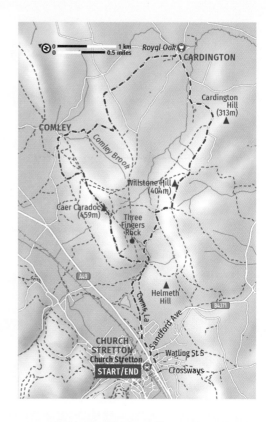

DURATION	DIFFICULTY	DISTANCE	START/END
4hr	Moderate	8 miles/ 13km	Church Stretton station

TERRAIN	Grassed paths

Caer Caradoc is ancient Britain at its most ruggedly appealing: this prehistoric hill fort was the last stand of the Celtic Catuvellauni against the Romans, and swirls with Arthurian legends. The walk starts in the attractive market town of Church Stretton, leading via the fort to a fine village pub.

Go straight ahead out of the station, crossing Crossways, then turning left onto Watling St. Carry on, crossing over Sandford Ave, then branch right onto Cwyms Lane. Ascend the lane, with a lake to your left, and turn right at the T-junction, clipping the woodland of Helmeth Hill.

From here it's a stiff climb of 459m (1500ft) to the volcanic summit of **Caer Caradoc**, passing outcrops known as Three Fingers Rock. At the top you'll see the circular outlines of prehistoric defensive ditch-

es; there are also superb views of Long Mynd and the Breacon Beacons.

Cross Caer Caradoc and descend it, passing the small amphitheatre-like **quarry** at Comley: since the 1880s it has been revealing fossils of trilobites, which went extinct before the dinosaurs appeared.

At Comley the path veers right, and continues in an easterly direction, bringing you to the village of Cardington, where the 15th-century **Royal Oak** pub serves locally renowned Fidget Pie.

Take the lane south out of the village, then follow the paths which run west up Cardington Hill, then along the ridge of Willstone Hill.

Here you rejoin the path in the woodland at Helmeth Hill. Take the route you took earlier in the day, back to Church Stretton station.

34

THE COTSWOLD WAY

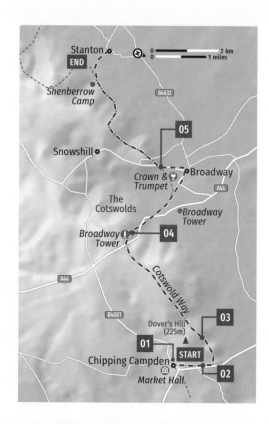

DURATION	DIFFICULTY	DISTANCE	START/END
4hr	Moderate	9 miles/ 16km	Chipping Campden/ Stanton

TERRAIN	Paths, steep ascents

This long-distance walk runs in all its glorious entirety for 164km (102 miles), along the Cotswolds escarpment from the lovely little wool town of Chipping Campden to the Georgian splendour of Bath. We've focused on the first day of the walk, which breaks in Broadway, a wonderfully attractive village with strong Arts and Crafts connections, and ends at idyllic Stanton. It's well worth factoring in time to explore the start, middle and end points of this lovely route.

GETTING HERE

The nearest train station to Chipping Campden is Moreton-in-Marsh, 9km to the south. Buses run here from all the major nearby towns.

STARTING POINT

The walk starts in the heart of town at a limestone disc marker, poetically inscribed with a quotation from TS Eliot and place names from along the Cotswold Way. It sits near the arcaded market hall on the High St.

01 From the Cotswold Way marker, turn right on Lower High St and then take a right on Hoo Lane. Heading up the lane, a **cottage** on the left has a blue plaque recording that Graham Greene lived here in the early 1930s.

02 At the T-junction cross Kingcombe Lane, turn left briefly and then go straight ahead to ascend steep **Dover's Hill**, an exhilarating high point with views of the Worcestershire Plains. This is the site of the archaic spring Olimpick Games, which started in 1612 and continue to this day with

Broadway & the Arts

Part of the beauty of Broadway stems from the Art and Crafts influence on its architecture; the movement found its spiritual home in the village, with William Morris setting up his studio in Broadway Tower. Writers and artists flocked here, including John Singer Sargent, who painted the luminous *Carnation, Lily, Lily Rose* here in 1886. Turner sketched the village, Alma Tadema and Evelyn Waugh drank in Tudor coaching inn the Lygon Arms (pictured), and JM Barrie, creator of *Peter Pan*, played cricket on the green. The June Broadway Arts Festival (http://broadwayartsfestival.com) pays homage to the village's creative past, as well as nurturing current talent with workshops, talks and concerts.

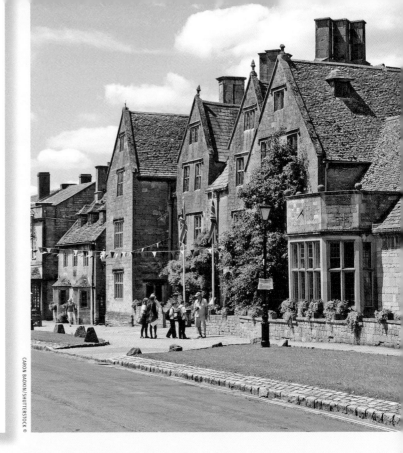

CARON BADKIN/SHUTTERSTOCK ©

tugs of war, shin kicking and other capers.

03 The Cotswold Way runs west for a short stretch to a National Park car park, where you turn left down the lane. At the crossroads turn right, continuing on the Cotswold Way. After 500m take the track which leads off to the left. Having climbed the escarpment, the route eventually crosses Fish Hill road and reaches **Broadway Tower**, a 1794 folly conceived in the style of a Saxon turret by Capability Brown.

04 The path takes a sharp right turn at Broadway Tower, running to the beautiful village of **Broadway** (pictured). Go through the village and turn left on Church St, where you'll see the Crown & Trumpet pub on the left. Just beyond is **St Michael and All Angels church**, built in 1839 but incorporating elements such as an ornate 17th-century pulpit from an earlier chapel.

05 Beyond the church, turn right to pick up the Cotswold Way once more. From here the path meanders for 4km to **Shenberrow Camp** with its Iron Age hill fort, before taking a sharp right to lead to lovely Stanton where the walk ends.

 **TAKE A BREAK**

Much the nicest of Broadway's pubs, its cosy bar and front garden filled at the weekend with lively locals, the 17th-century **Crown & Trumpet** (☎01386-853202; www.crownandtrumpet.co.uk; 14 Church St; soup £5.45, sandwiches £5.95, mains £9.95; ⏱11am-11pm; 📶) has been honoured by CAMRA (the Campaign for Real Ale) for its carefully kept, seasonally varying array of fine beers. It also offers a tempting bunch of ciders. There's good pub grub on offer, including classics such as ploughman's lunches, steak and kidney pie and breaded scampi, and frequent live music.

Also Try...

STEVE HORSLEY/SHUTTERSTOCK ©

PADLEY GORGE

Padley Gorge (pictured) is a favourite among Peak District photographers. This stunning, woodland-shrouded chasm has an entirely mystical feel to it at any time of year, but especially in autumn when orange leaves burn bright against green mossy boulders and dappled sunlight.

From Grindleford Station, walk up through Yarncliff Wood, initially with Burbage Brook to your left but crossing over midway to follow it up on your right, enjoying the small waterfalls and cascades. The top of the gorge, where grassy banks border shallow pools, is a popular spot for picnics and paddling. From here head west to the road, passing Surprise View car park, before taking the path down through Bolehill Quarry – a former industrial site now covered by silver birch trees – and back to Grindleford.

DURATION 1½hr
DIFFICULTY Easy
DISTANCE 2.3 miles / 3.7km

MALVERNS END TO END

Earlier in the chapter we describe a short Malvern Hill hike. But hardy hikers might want to tramp the full rollercoaster ridge. It includes North Hill, traversed in the route we describe previously, as well as Perseverance and Raggedstone Hills, to name a couple of the ridge's wonderfully titled features. It's not an especially long walk, but ascents are steep, making it a challenging option.

The first ascent is of North Hill, then you attack Sugarloaf Hill and, beyond it, the imposing Worcestershire Beacon. Summer Hill is next, followed swiftly by Perseverance, Jubilee, Pinnacle and Black Hills. Next up are the ancient fortifications of the Herefordshire Beacon. The next crest is Swinyard Hill, then Midsummer. Those who are flagging need to brace themselves for steep Raggedstone Hill; smaller Chase End Hill comes last. And then a well-earned rest!

DURATION 4½hr
DIFFICULTY Hard
DISTANCE 10 miles / 16km

ILAM TO DOVEDALE

This walk is a great choice for families. Starting in picturesque Ilam (pictured) with its Alpine-style houses, head east out of the village.

After the last house, cross the road and go through a gate which descends to the footpath. Turn right and walk along the bottom of Bunster Hill, continuing along through fields and stiles until you reach Dovedale car park, from where a track leads to the popular stepping stones. Add to the adventure by ascending Thorpe Cloud from the stepping stones, or you can continue further into the limestone valley.

DURATION 1hr
DIFFICULTY Easy
DISTANCE 1.5 miles/2.4km

LANDSOWN TO BATH

Earlier in this chapter we describe the starting stages of this long-distance path, which has you dipping in and out of heavenly Cotswolds villages.

The route is usually divided into at least six discrete day walks, taking you past manor houses and long barrows and across limestone grassland dotted with wild flowers. The final stage of the Cotswold Way starts at Landsown, looping via a prehistoric barrow known as the Kelston Round Hill and taking you to the imposing abbey that sits at the heart of the city of Bath.

DURATION 1½hr
DIFFICULTY Easy
DISTANCE 10 miles/6km

STOKESAY CASTLE

The starting point of this circular route is Stokesay Castle, a fortified manor house dating back to the 13th century.

Head south from Stokesay, passing a pond and then taking the footpath which crosses the railway and leads to Stoke Wood. From here head to View Wood. A network of paths and a sunken lane run to Brandhill; then follow the streamside path to Stonehouse Pools, and head to Onibury and on to Aldon. Take the Shropshire Way, head along some meadows, then follow the railway and cross it to return to the start.

DURATION 4hr
DIFFICULTY Moderate
DISTANCE 8 miles/13km

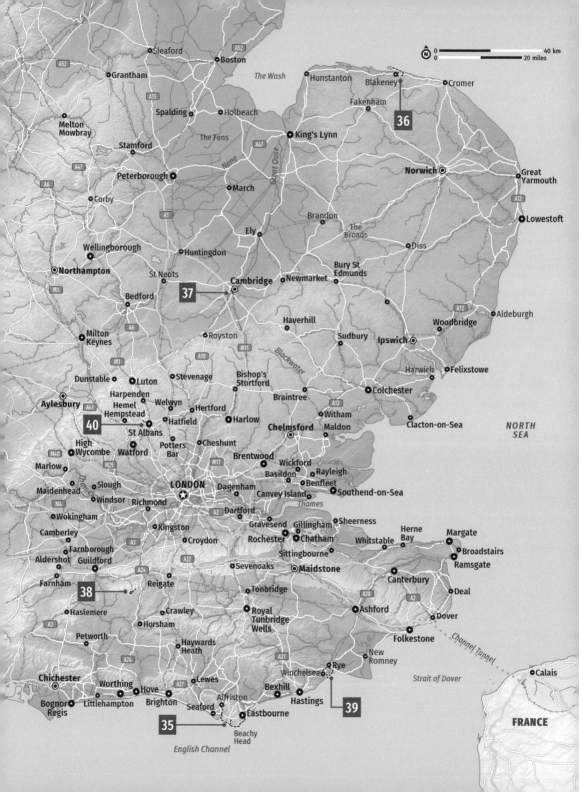

SOUTHEAST & EAST ENGLAND

Explore
SOUTHEAST &
EAST ENGLAND

The southeast corner of the country, dominated by London, is in some people's minds little more than commuter belt territory. But this idea can be quickly disproved: take a train trip for an hour or so and you'll find an amazing richness and diversity of landscapes, from the open spaces of the South Downs with their white cliffs to the densely forested ridges of the home counties. This chapter takes you on a trip to downland, woodland, sandy strands and lush meadows, as well as to the mysterious sea marshes of East Anglia and the back streets and river banks of lovely Cambridge. In this area you're never far from an ancient country church, or a rustic old pub where you can break your walk.

ALFRISTON

If you're planning to walk the Seven Sisters and the South Downs, or explore the curlicues of the Cuckmere River, the village of Alfriston is a lovely place to site yourself. The seaside towns of Brighton and Eastbourne are bigger and buzzier, but Alfriston offers country seclusion as well as some excellent eating and pub options, including superb afternoon teas. The village church is known as the Cathedral of the South Downs for its grandeur, and there are a couple of ancient half-timbered hotels to stay in, as well as cottage and farmhouse B&Bs.

CAMBRIDGE

The university city of Cambridge is a lovely spot if you're exploring The Backs walk in this chapter, and is a couple of hours' drive south of the north Norfolk coast. Founded back in 1209, the University of Cambridge comprises marvellous Gothic and medieval architecture. The place is well used to accommodating and feeding students, university staff and tourists, and there are plenty of great places to stay, eat and drink, perhaps the best of them being the riverside pubs. Cutting through town, the Cam river provides sylvan walking routes which guide you away from the tourist crowds, and is also fabled for its punts: shallow gondola-like vessels pushed through the water with a long pole.

ST ALBANS

Sitting comfortably in the county of Hertfordshire northwest of London, St Albans is a small and handsome city with a very long history: it was known in Roman times as Verulamium, and has substantial Roman walls and the remains of an amphitheatre as well as a magnificent cathedral. You'll find excellent places to eat and drink, including some medieval inns, and boutique hotels and B&Bs provide cosy accommodation. The sedate farmland surrounding the city is undramatic but quietly attractive.

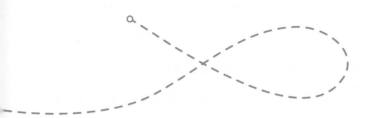

WHEN TO GO

The south of England has a mild climate and, while the weather can be wet and grey, it's not often you have conditions so severe that walking is impossible. The main obstacle to a decent hike is the shortness of the days in winter. Otherwise, spring is a lovely time to walk, and summer days can be gloriously warm and long. Autumn brings seasonal bounty in the form of apples, pears and wild blackberries in the hedgerows, as well as the sight of the leaves changing colour.

TRANSPORT

This is a well-connected region: nearly all towns have a railway station, and some villages too. Train prices are annoyingly unpredictable, and peak times should be avoided as you pay more at commuting time. Country buses are an option, though services tend to be infrequent. It's generally not a great region for cycling, with hills, sometimes narrow roads and fast cars, though in flat Norfolk and Cambridgeshire you at least have topography on your side. A couple of walks in this chapter are not well served by public transport; you may want to consider driving, though we have made suggestions for trains and buses.

WHERE TO STAY

You'll find some great youth hostels in this region – the South Downs for example has a new state-of-the-art hostel, and there are also smaller quirky properties with lots of character. These provide communal and affordable accommodation and can be great for families. Camping in summer is a good option, as well as glamping in pre-erected tents. Otherwise, it's the land of the B&B, with many comfortable and welcoming places where a large breakfast will fuel you up for a day's walking.

WHAT'S ON

The Great Escape (www.greatescape festival.com; ☺May) Held on Brighton Beach, Great Escape is a festival of new music, with gigs, debates and speeches.

Latitude Festival (www.latitudefest ival.co.uk; ☺Jul) Music and performing arts festival held near Southwold, where you can dance and party among the trees.

Into the Wild Festival (www.into thewildgathering.com; ☺Aug) Nature lovers can experience this festival in West Sussex, which features woodland crafts and bushcraft classes as well as world music.

Lost Village Festival (www.lost villagefestival.com; ☺Aug) Held in Lincolnshire, Lost Village has a sublime woodland setting, with music, food, workshops, talks and comedy events.

Kent Green Hop Beer Fortnight (www. kentgreenhopbeer.com; ☺late Sep) This boozy event held across Kent gives you the chance to sample 30 newly released brews, made with fresh rather than dried hops.

35

THE SEVEN SISTERS

DURATION	DIFFICULTY	DISTANCE	START/END
5hr	Hard	12.5 miles/ 20km	Eastbourne/ Alfriston

TERRAIN	Grassed paths and woodlands

Brace yourselves for a big bold walk, which leads from Eastbourne, with its long stone beaches and grand Edwardian seafront, up onto the high chalk cliffs whose most famous landmark is the red-and-white-striped Beachy Head lighthouse. You're then on the ups and downs of the famous Seven Sisters, which will give your legs a great workout and your eyes some gorgeous English Channel vistas. The route drops down to the Friston Forest, winds past lovely Westdean village, then follows the bends of the Cuckmere River to the beautiful downland settlement of Alfriston.

GETTING HERE

Eastbourne, which sits southeast of London on the Sussex coast, is easily reached from London's Victoria Station – trains take around 1½ hours.

STARTING POINT

The route starts at Eastbourne station, from where it's a 1.5km walk through the streets and along the fabled seafront to the base of the cliffs.

01 From the station, head south down Gildredge Rd, which leads into College Rd. At the T-junction where College Rd meets Carlisle Rd you'll see the **Towner Art Gallery** (free entry). It's well worth making a stop here: the purpose-built structure has temporary shows of contemporary work on the ground and 2nd floors, while the 1st floor is given over to rotating themed shows created from the gallery's 5000-piece collection. From the Towner, go left briefly onto Carlisle Rd, then take a right onto Wilmington Gardens and then head straight down to the **Wish Tower**, a blunt structure built in the early 1800s as a defence against feared Napoleonic attack.

02 Beyond the Wishtower Slopes garden and before you reach the sea, the South Downs route commences. Turn right onto the route, heading towards the high cliffs. This is a lovely stretch before the walk proper begins – to the right are Eastbourne's grand hotels, and to the left are shingle pleasure beaches, divided by distinctive

wooden sea defences known as **groynes**.

03 A narrow wooded path takes you for a vertiginous walk up the hillside, skirting Beachy Head Rd and landing you at the famous beauty spot of **Beachy Head**, the candy-striped lighthouse (pictured) sitting below. This has a much sadder reputation too, as there have been a high number of suicides here. On a sunny day though it's a wonderfully uplifting place: it's the highest sea cliff in Britain, rising 162m above the crashing English Channel below. You'll notice the lack of a beach here – it's said that the name Beachy

Head instead derives from the French for 'beautiful headland': *beau chef*. From here you begin the roller-coaster ride part of the walk, plunging up and down the undulations of the cliff top. The open landscape is a perfect habitat for skylarks, radiant songbirds who nest on the ground and feed their chicks on spiders and other insects. Look to the skies when you hear their trickling song, and you may see a skylark high above.

04 After 3km you reach **Birling Gap**; it's a tiny settlement that comprises little more than a collection of windswept 19th-century coastguard

👓 Adonis Blue

Striding across the Seven Sisters with just a few sheep for company, you may feel you're in an almost empty landscape. But the Downs, cleared of forest by our Neolithic forebears thousands of years ago, shelter some 30 or 40 species per square metre. The most famous is the Adonis blue butterfly, which feeds on the nectar of the horseshoe vetch; males are a brilliant cobalt blue, while the females are chocolate brown. Their pupae produce a honey-like goo which feeds ants, and the ants in turn protect the pupae, sometimes even burying them in the ground for safekeeping. This delicate symbiotic relationship is just one of the wildlife marvels of the Downs.

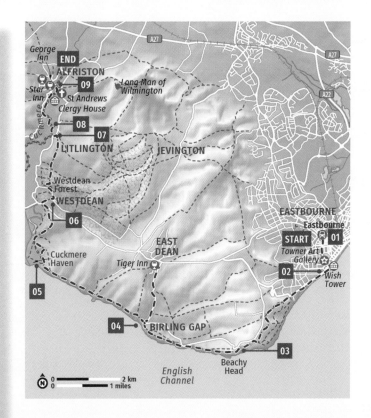

cottages. A detour may not be the first thing on your mind on this long walk, but if you leave the cliffs here on Birling Gap Rd and head inland, in around 15 minutes you'll arrive at **East Dean** village, where the Tiger Inn is renowned for its pub food and bucolic village green setting. If you make the detour, return the same way to continue the route or, to save your legs, you have the option of walking the high ridge road leading west to Westdean village.

05 Back on the sea cliffs, more undulations lead along to the point where the Cuckmere River joins the sea. It's a steep descent to **Cuckmere Haven**, as the scenic estuary with its oxbow lakes is known. Once infamous for smuggling, the estuary is an important site for overwintering wildfowl, and you might also see aquatic birds such as oystercatchers.

06 The route runs downhill, crossing the East Dean Rd, and entering the woodland of the **Westdean Forest**, which shelters the medieval village of Westdean. You might see 13th-century Charleston Manor through the trees (not to be confused with Charleston Farmhouse, the spiritual home of the Bloomsbury Group).

07 Exiting the woodland, the path leads on through farmland to Litlington, where a bridge takes you over the Cuckmere.

Alternative Route

There's another way to tackle the South Downs Way, which takes sea views out of the equation, but gives you instead the Long Man of Wilmington, an ancient chalk figure cut into the hillside depicting a man carrying two staffs. This route (10km) cuts inland from Eastbourne along a high downland ridge, and goes via the historic smugglers' village of Jevington and the 300-year-old Eight Bells pub. The Long Man sits between Jevington and Alfriston. A great way to get the best of both worlds would be to start at Eastbourne, take this route to lovely Alfriston for an overnight stay, and return the next day via the cliff walk to Eastbourne.

DAVID C TOMLINSON/GETTY IMAGES ©

08 The next stretch of the walk is particularly lovely, as you follow the gentle meanders of the Cuckmere, lined by rushes and surrounded by lush meadows. In around 30 minutes, the river walk deposits you in beautiful Alfriston.

09 The village of **Alfriston** is well worth a few hours of anyone's time, and if you haven't factored in an overnight stay here you may wish you had. The Tudor Star and George Inns are equally historic spots for a pub meal and a bed for the night. Fourteenth-century **St Andrews** is surprisingly grand for a village church, and is known as the cathedral of the Downs. Another compelling sight is the thatched **Clergy House**, now a National Trust property. You'll find other enticements in the form of tearooms and an excellent independent bookshop, Much Ado Books. Leaving Alfriston, the nearest station is at Berwick; take a bus or taxi from the village to reach it.

☕ TAKE A BREAK

Located inland from Birling Gap in the village of East Dean, the 15th-century **Tiger Inn** (The Green; mains £6-14; ⏱noon-10pm; 📶) is one of Sussex' best taverns, serving a gastropub menu to walkers and day trippers alike. In summer the action spills out onto the village green.

36

BLAKENEY POINT

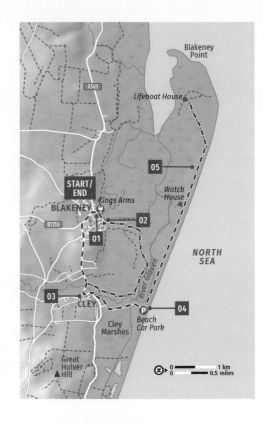

DURATION	DIFFICULTY	DISTANCE	START/END
4hr	Easy	12 miles/ 20km	Blakeney

TERRAIN	Paths, soft shingle

This is a walk of two halves, through extraordinary north Norfolk terrain. The first part describes a loop round the Blakeney Freshes, a freshwater grazing marsh that's a fantastic spot for birders. The route then takes you to Cley next the Sea, from where you can head out to the elongated shingle strand of Blakeney Point, which is famous for its seal colony. From the end of October until the middle of January seal pups are born, adding extra magic to this unearthly landscape.

GETTING HERE

Blakeney is frustratingly hard to reach by public transport. Take the Coastliner bus to Wells Next the Sea, then the CH1 Coasthopper bus to Blakeney. As Blakeney has a fairly remote location, we've suggested a pub stop that's an overnight stay as well as a great place for a post-walk pint. Otherwise, there are several car parks in Blakeney.

STARTING POINT

The route starts in the heart of Blakeney village, on the main coastal road.

01 From the main junction with the coastal road through Blakeney, head north on Westgate St, passing the **Kings Arms** which will either set you off with a pub lunch or provide a good incentive at the end. The road curves round to become The Quay as it follows the east bank of the River Glaven. Where Mariners Hill leads off to the right, turn left to follow the North Norfolk Coast Path.

02 Follow the path along the bank, with the Freshes down to your right, and continue as the path curves round the often waterlogged marshes, passing **Stiffkey Freshes** to the left. Keep to

Seals & Sea Kale

The ground beneath your feet on this route is vegetated shingle, a precious habitat that nurtures some rare plants. Crinkly sea kale and shrubby sea blight grow in thick clusters, sea lavender turns patches of shingle purple in summer, scurvygrass produces delicate white flowers and scarlet pimpernel may be spotted in the grasses. These and other low-growing beauties help to create the unique ambience of this ragged coastline. And the spit is home to Britain's largest seal colony, with 3000 pups being born in winter. Adorable to look at, the seals can be aggressive, especially when pups are around. Stick to the fenced paths, and keep a wide berth round the creatures.

ANDY333/SHUTTERSTOCK ©

the footpath on the bank until you reach New Rd, between Blakeney and Cley next the Sea.

03 Turn left onto New Road, then left again, following the High St as it heads into **Cley** (pronounced Cly). Unbelievably, this small place was a thriving medieval port, till it was hit by plague and a silted-up harbour. Just after the point where the road curves right, turn left on The Quay, which leads to the village's 19th-century windmill. From here you join the Norfolk Coast Path, which runs north, crossing the River Glaven and heading north to the Beach Car Park.

04 From the car park, walk north to the sea and turn left, to begin the long walk up the shingle spit. Pass the Watch House building, and continue along the water. Eventually you ascend a ridge and turn left, towards the blue wooden **Lifeboat House**; from here a boardwalk leads through the dunes to the beach, and gives a wonderful view of the seals.

05 This is the end point of the route; retrace your steps along the spit, and from the car park head south, returning to Cley. Once back at the coastal road on the edge of Cley, it'll take around 20 minutes to walk back to Blakeney, where the Kings Arms awaits.

TAKE A BREAK

Situated at the north end of the village en route to the shingle spit, the **Kings Arms** (☎ 01263-740341; www. blakeneykingsarms.co.uk; Westgate St; s/d £65/85; P 🐾) offers sweet, simple, old-style rooms (expect bright colours and pine) in a pub that's so welcoming you might not want to leave. Order some substantial pub grub (its fish and chips are famous; mains from £9 to £18; meals served noon to 9pm), then, for great theatre gossip, ask landlady Marjorie about her career on the stage.

37

THE BACKS

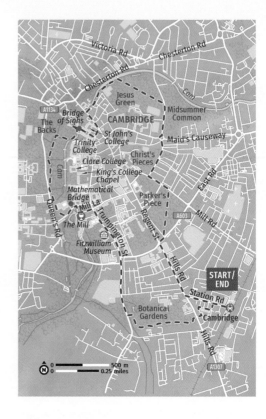

DURATION	DIFFICULTY	DISTANCE	START/END
2hr	Easy	4 miles/ 7.5km	Cambridge station

TERRAIN	Streets and paved paths

Cambridge University was founded way back in 1209, and the town is dotted with ancient colleges, whose Gothic vaults and pinnacles create a townscape like no other. All this is best viewed from the lush Backs, the spacious lawns along the River Cam which are the green lungs of the city. Watch the punters drift by, and round off your walk with a riverside pint.

Leaving the station, head up Station Rd, then turn right on Hills Rd. Cut across the open parkland of Parker's and Christ's Pieces. Head along Midsummer Common, cross Jesus Green and turn left to walk along the River Cam.

Follow the river heading south, crossing it by entering ancient St John's College (fee applies),

and heading over the the famous covered **Bridge of Sighs**, built in 1831 and named for its counterpart in Venice. Here the path leads through The Backs, providing sublime views of King's College Chapel and Trinity and Clare Colleges.

Cross the river again: look out for the wooden **Mathematical Bridge**, ingeniously built from straight pieces of timber which appear to curve. The 19th-century **Mill** is an excellent pub stop on the river. For a longer rural walk, head south down the Cam for 3km to **Granchester**, associated with the war poet Rupert Brooke, where you can take a break in the orchard tearoom.

To get back to the station, walk up Mill Lane and then turn right onto Trumpington St, passing the treasure-house Fitzwilliam Museum. Head south, then cut through the beautiful **Botanical Gardens** (pictured) back to the station.

38

LEITH HILL

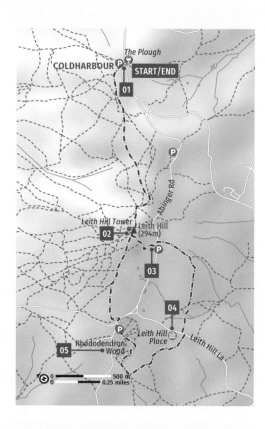

DURATION	DIFFICULTY	DISTANCE	START/END
2hr	Moderate	4 miles/ 7km	Coldharbour

TERRAIN	Paths and tracks, some steep

Leith Hill, like Box Hill, is a fabled Surrey beauty spot, with elevations that seem almost exotic in the south of England. This route takes you from the scenic village of Coldharbour, and then leads in a loop through wooded hills. It takes in the Gothic folly of Leith Hill Tower, and Leith Hill Place, the former home of Ralph Vaughan Williams, who composed the ecstatic tribute to the 'Lark Ascending'. You're likely to see plenty of birds on this bracing and sometimes steep route, including red kites and hovering goshawks.

GETTING HERE

Coldharbour is a little tricky to reach by public transport. There's an intermittent bus service between here and Dorking, but a more realistic option is to take the train to Holmwood (45 minutes from

Clapham Junction), and then take a taxi for the 10-minute journey to the village. Otherwise, you can drive to Coldharbour and park up there.

STARTING POINT

The walk starts at the Surrey Hills village of Coldharbour, in an area of almost Alpine beauty. There's an excellent pub-shop where you can buy a picnic for the walk.

01 Cross the road from the Plough pub in Coldharbour, and take the paved path that leads gently uphill, keeping the red post box to your right. The path climbs the ridge into woodland, then crosses the ground of the Coldharbour Cricket Club. From there it's back into the woodland, until you emerge at Leith Hill Tower.

02 Lofty **Leith Hill Tower** (pictured) is a decidedly quirky construction, built in the 1760s by

The Battle for Leith Hill

Bizarre as it seems, until 2018 leafy Leith Hill was the centre of a battle over oil. Despite its status as an Area of Outstanding Natural Beauty, Europa Oil & Gas wanted to sink a borehole for oil and gas explorations under Leith Hill, with a horizontal rig passing under Coldharbour village. The locals were horrified, and launched a campaign vigorously opposing the drilling work, fundraising a legal defence. The debate went on for almost 10 years, and the oil company's lease on the land expired before the work could begin. The lease was not renewed, and to the relief of locals this unspoiled spot looks to stay that way.

GELL/GETTY IMAGES ©

Richard Hill, the then owner of Leith Hill Place, in order that it should be the highest point in southeast England. The tower was restored by the National Trust in the 1980s; you can stand at the top and see as far as the London Eye through the telescope.

03 From the tower the track leads downhill through dense and lovely woodland, crossing Abinger Rd. Further on you come to a junction, which you cross over to pass Leith Hill Place.

04 **Leith Hill Place** dates from 1600, but was entirely refaced by the energetic Richard Hill in 1760. The composer Ralph Vaughan Williams was brought up here; inside, a soundscape pays homage to the composer, and you can see his piano. With the house on your right, go through the kissing gate and cross the field, going through the gate below a pond to head uphill through some woodland.

05 You emerge at a **rhododendron wood**, where you pass through a car park. Just beyond this point, cross the road, and follow the path along a wall to head up through more woodland and get back to Leith Hill Tower. This last section of path follows the Greensand Way (see p160).

TAKE A BREAK

The Plough (01306-711793; www.ploughinn.com; soup £5.95, mains from £13.95; 11.30am-11pm Mon-Sat, noon-9pm Sun) is a warmhearted community-owned pub in the high Surrey Hills village of Coldharbour. Pick up a packed lunch for the walk in the form of a fresh pasty or a bacon butty at the wonderfully old-fashioned Shop at The Plough. And after the hike, return to sample one of their own ales, made using traditional methods and all natural ingredients.

39

RYE TO WINCHELSEA

DURATION	DIFFICULTY	DISTANCE	START/END
4hr	Moderate	9 miles/ 15km	Rye

TERRAIN	Path, track, shingle

This walk takes in two of the Cinq Ports, seaside towns which formed a defensive cluster in Anglo-Saxon times; the beautiful little settlements of Rye and Winchelsea were latecomers to the federation in the 12th century. Along the way you'll explore the unique watery marshland and reedbeds of the Rye Harbour Nature Reserve. There's even a shingle beach en route, so bring a swimming costume in good weather. And there's a pub stop at the ancient Mermaid Inn in Rye, where you might want to stop over for a night.

GETTING HERE

Trains to Rye from London's St Pancras station take 70 minutes, with a change at Ashford International.

STARTING POINT

The route starts and ends at Rye station, leaving town to the west initially, but circling back to Rye's enchanting town centre at the end of the walk.

01 Exit the arcaded red-brick train station and turn right, with the railway line to your right. Where the road splits, turn left, crossing the railway line. Head down Ferry Rd (the B2089), passing whitewashed cottages and brick terraces. Follow the curve of the road left; it turns into Udimore Rd. Where you see the Udimore Rd street sign on the red-brick house on the left and the blue cycling sign on the lamppost, turn left up the lane named West Undercliff. The houses soon peter out and the lane turns into a rough track. Where the track veers left, go straight ahead up the path.

02 You're now cutting across the farmland of Rye Marsh on a short stretch of the **1066 Country Walk**, which, in its entirety, follows the route the Norman conquerors took from Pevensey to Battle. Follow this path for 1.5km till it joins the weirdly named Dumb Woman's Lane. There are two stories behind this: one says that a woman witnessed contraband goods being smuggled here, and had her tongue cut out so she couldn't tell the tale, another that a mute woman dispensed herbal remedies here. Follow the lane for a few metres, then turn left down hedgerow-lined Winchelsea Lane. You pass Winchelsea Station off to the right, then walk down the lane (now Station Rd) which follows the undulations of the River Brede as it leads south, crossing a bridge towards the beautiful little town itself.

03 Station Road emerges at a tight curve in the A259. Cross over onto the pavement, then follow the right-hand part of the road, which climbs gently up Ferry Hill. The entrance to Winchelsea is unmissable: a **medieval stone gate** on the left. Go through the gate, and head down North St. There are all sorts of ways of exploring the town's little grid, but we suggest taking a right onto School Hill.

04 The hill follows a gentle rise, lined by tile-hung and timbered houses with lush gardens. Where the lane emerges you'll see the 18th-century New Inn ahead of you. Turn left here onto the High St, passing an ancient lattice windowed building on your left – to the right is the grand **Church of St Thomas** (pictured), much damaged but containing some lovely 14th-century effigies. Walk down a couple of blocks, then follow the road (now Strand Hill) straight ahead; it curves left, departing Winchelsea via another ancient stone gate and running gently uphill to a T-junction.

Cinq Ports

Before Britain ever had a navy, its southern towns allied to provide a fleet for the monarchy, initially for Edward the Confessor and then for the Norman kings. The original five ports in the alliance were Dover, Hastings, Hythe, New Romney and Sandwich, with Rye and Winchelsea joining in the 12th century. The power of the Cinq Ports – still pronounced, in Norman French, as *sink* rather than *sank* – was at its greatest in the 13th and 14th centuries. Ultimately the greatest enemy of the proud ports was silting, which reduced Winchelsea, for example, to a shade of its former self. Only Dover now remains as a major port.

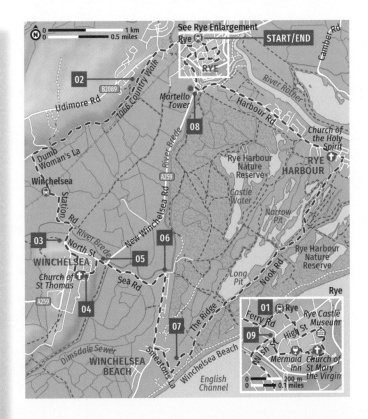

05 Turn right at the T-junction, crossing over to follow the pavement for a short stretch on the A259. Where the road curves left at an unlikely log cabin store, turn right onto Sea Rd. This is a pleasant and leafy suburban stretch, with verdant grazing opening up to your right. On your left you'll see Sutton's Fish Shop.

06 Follow the road, and take the sharp right as it runs south; to your right you'll see Dimsdale Sewer (which is actually a water channel) and some flower-dotted meadows. Eventually, opposite the Co-op store turn left, then immediately go left again down Smeatons Lane. Follow this lane for 600m, then take the first left, onto The Ridge. Or, if you fancy a swim, go straight ahead onto the shingle strand of Winchelsea Beach.

07 The Ridge, which turns into Nook Road, takes you on a ramble through the **Rye Harbour Nature Reserve**, with its atmospheric mix of salt-marsh, lagoons, reedbeds, gravel pits and grazing marshes. Nook Rd emerges at some semi-industrial sprawl, where you should turn left, up Harbour Rd. After a short stretch you'll see the Church of the Holy Spirit to your left. Continue up the road past more sprawl, and then back into open country-side. Eventually the road makes a sharp right, joining New Winchelsea Rd at a T-junction.

Immediately across the road is a circular **Martello Tower**, one of many low defensive structures build to resist a feared Napoleonic attack.

08 Turn right onto New Winchelsea Road (the A259), which after 500m curves right and crosses a roundabout to join Wish St. Take the first right onto Wish Ward at the Pipemakers Arms to enter the lovely heart of Rye.

09 Walk down Wish Ward, passing Rye Pottery, established in the 1700s, on your right. Take the first left up **Mermaid St**, which soon narrows to become cobbled. It's one of the prettiest streets in this enchanting town, bristling with 15th-century timber-framed houses with quirky names such as 'The House with Two Front Doors' and 'The House Opposite'. Towards the end of the street on the left is the ramblingly characterful Mermaid Inn, a great stop for a pint. At the end of the street take a right, and follow the lane as it curves round Church Sq, stopping to look at medieval **Church of St Mary the Virgin**, which has a Burne-Jones window. At the top northeast edge of the square turn right onto Market St, and then left onto East St, passing the Rye Castle Museum on the left. At the T-junction turn left onto the High St and then right onto Market Rd. Go straight ahead to reach the station.

Rye Harbour Birds

The waterlogged harbour is a haven for birds, including many winter visitors; the Sussex Wildlife Trust estimates you can spot more than 40 species at any given time of year. Year-round, look out for grey heron feeding at the water's edge, or egret (pictured) using their yellow feet to disturb fish and shrimp from their hiding places. Oystercatchers plunge their orange bills into the ground to root out worms, and lapwing nest in the wet grassland. Come the colder months, Brent geese winter on the saltmarshes after breeding in the Arctic, and linnets form large undulating flocks, while stonechats sit in pairs on posts. There are five hides dotted around the harbour, where birders train their binoculars on the open skies.

TAKE A BREAK

Few inns can claim to be as atmospheric as the ancient **Mermaid Inn** (☏ 01797-223065; www.mermaidinn. com; Mermaid St; s/d from £90/140; P 🛜), dating from 1420. Each of the 31 rooms is different, but all are thick with dark beams and lit by leaded windows, and some are graced by secret passageways that now act as fire escapes. The inn also has one of Rye's best restaurants, where you can dine on Rye Bay cod and Romney Marsh lamb.

40

ST ALBANS

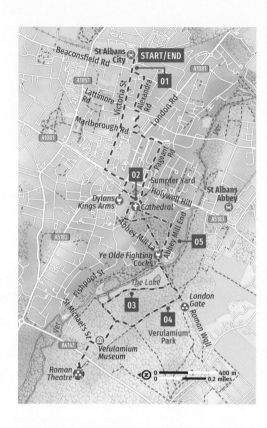

DURATION	DIFFICULTY	DISTANCE	START/END
2hr	Easy	5 miles/ 8km	St Albans City station

TERRAIN	Streets, paved paths

The medieval market town of St Albans is one of the most attractive places within easy striking distance of London. For a small place it has a mighty impressive cathedral, as well as dramatic Roman remains and some exceptional pubs. This walk explores all three aspects of the town, leading you round the spacious ruins of the former Roman settlement of Verulamium, which was sacked by Boudica way back in AD 61.

GETTING HERE

Despite its cosy county town feel, St Albans is just a 25-minute train journey north of London's St Pancras station.

STARTING POINT

The route starts at St Albans City station, which sits just east of the cathedral and historic centre.

01 From the station, turn right up Victoria St, heading into the historic heart of St Albans. At the T-junction, turn left on Chequer St and right on the High St. If you'd like lunch before you set off, go straight ahead for 350m to Dylans Kings Arms on the left. Otherwise, an alley on the left by the Raindrops on Roses charity gift shop leads into the cathedral precinct.

02 It's well worth pausing to explore the mighty Norman brick and flint **cathedral** (pictured), with its tomb to St Alban, the first Christian martyr in Britain. The onward path leads round the north side of the cathedral, then cuts horizontally across the lawns to the extraordinary **Ye Olde Fighting Cocks**, which makes a strong claim to be the oldest

Verulamium

The impressive walls and amphitheatre you see in St Albans still convey the power of Verulamium, as the town was called in Roman times: this was once the third largest city in Roman Britain. It had a forum, a basilica and a theatre, and was powerful enough to be raided by Boudica, the warrior queen of the Celtic Iceni, back in 61 AD: a layer of black ash has been excavated at the site dating back to her attack. Later, stone from the settlement was plundered to help built the cathedral. It's a tantalising thought that much of the ancient town remains unexcavated, lying under the green parkland that you traverse on the walk.

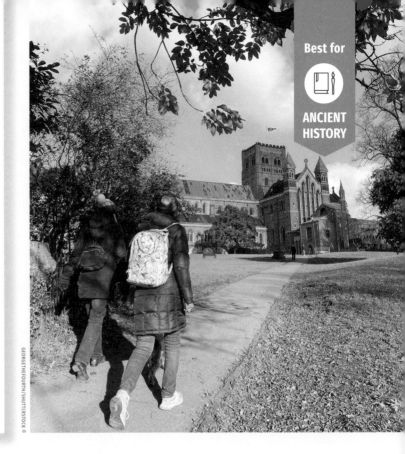

GEORGETHEFOURTH/SHUTTERSTOCK ©

Best for

ANCIENT HISTORY

pub in England. The octagonal pub is thought to be 11th century, but built on 8th-century remains with – allegedly – secret tunnels running to the cathedral.

03 From the Fighting Cocks, continue past the lake and then turn right and walk up along it. The path leads to the absorbing **Verulamium Museum**, which displays five floor mosaics from around 200 AD. From the museum, continue up St Michael's St, cross the road and carry on up to the Roman Theatre, with tiers of seating still visible. Retrace your steps via the museum.

04 Turn right to cross Verulamium Park, then left to follow the course of the impressive **Roman city walls**. You pass the remnants of the London Gate, then pass the southern end of the lake and Ye Olde Fighting Cocks.

05 Turn right onto Abbey Mill End, then left to skirt the edge of the parkland. At the cathedral turn right onto Sumpter Yard, then carry on down Pageant Rd, turning left at Keyfield Tce. Carry on – the terrace turns into Marlborough Rd, and then turn right on Victoria St to return to the station.

TAKE A BREAK

Dylans Kings Arms (☎ 01727-530332; www.dylanskingsarms.com; 7 George Street; bar snacks £8, 2/3 courses £26/30; ⏱ noon-11pm Tue-Sun; 🚇) took a long-closed Tudor pub and turned it into an eating and drinking destination. Mains – dished up in the back room of the pub – might include potato Dauphinoise with mushroom Wellington or ox cheek slow-cooked in port, while classy bar snacks such as sole goujons in beer batter are way out of the ordinary. Craft beers, ales and good wines are served. The timbered exterior is spectacular, the modernised interior stylish but unostentatious.

Also Try...

FLYSBT/SHUTTERSTOCK ©

PILGRIMS' WAY

Stretching all the way from Winchester, and joined by pilgrim routes from London, the Pilgrims' Way has been taking the faithful to Canterbury for centuries. This final stretch runs from the Kentish village of Chilham, via apple orchards and woodlands to Canterbury and its fabled cathedral.

It's well worth having a wander round the timbered houses and flint church of Chilham before you set off. The route runs via the oddly named village of Old Wives Lees, through a lime tree avenue and across hop fields to Chartham Hatch. From here you enter No Man's Orchard and head uphill to Harbledown, before entering the medieval West Gate at Canterbury, and walking through town to the cathedral.

DURATION 3hr
DIFFICULTY Moderate
DISTANCE 7.5 miles/12km

GREENSAND WAY

This long-distance walk takes you on a bucolic route through Surrey and Kent, leading from Haslemere to Hamstreet via a high sandstone ridge. The entire route runs for 175km, but we've selected the section that links Sevenoaks with Shipbourne, via some extraordinary country houses.

You leave the town of Sevenoaks via farmland and parkland, heading to vast 15th-century Knole (pictured), built by an Archbishop of Canterbury, enlarged by Henry VIII and once the home of Vita Sackville-West. From here you walk through the ancient woodland of One Tree Hill, and then enter the Ightham Mote estate. With its moat and 13th-century great hall, this is old England at its most magnetic. The route then runs across country to Shipbourne.

DURATION 2½hr
DIFFICULTY Moderate
DISTANCE 6 miles/10km

HELEN OGBOURN/GETTY IMAGES ©

BOX HILL

Anyone who thinks there's no drama in the landscapes of southeast England should try Box Hill (pictured). This fabled beauty spot, immortalised by Jane Austen, rises to nearly 200m, its chalky folds dotted with evergreen box trees.

Box Hill and Westhumble Station is the starting point for the route, which first runs to the downland village of Mickleham. From here ascend Mickleham Downs, before tackling the steep slopes of the Box Hill itself to reach the remnants of a 19th-century fort, where there's a handy National Trust tearoom.

DURATION 3hr
DIFFICULTY Moderate
DISTANCE 5.5 miles/9km

LEA VALLEY

This route explores a stretch of a long-distance walk, which in its entirety leads from the source of the Lea near Luton to the Thames in London.

Leaving Harpenden for the medieval mill town of Wheathamstead, the route explores the prehistoric earthworks known as Devil's Dyke before circling back to Harpenden. For the first half of the walk you'll be following the leafy banks of the Lea, leaving it for the Devil's Dyke and some steep fields before descending back to the water.

DURATION 4hr
DIFFICULTY Moderate
DISTANCE 10 miles/16km

SOUTH DOWNS WAY

The Seven Sisters walk described in full earlier in this chapter is the last stage of this 160km trail, which starts in Winchester and ends at Eastbourne. Most people take around 10 days to traverse the entire route.

Here we've chosen the gorgeous stretch between Pyecombe and Lewes, via two windmills, ancient dew ponds and the chalky summit of Ditchling Beacon. It's well worth factoring in time at the end to explore handsome Lewes.

DURATION 4hr
DIFFICULTY Moderate
DISTANCE 7 miles/11km

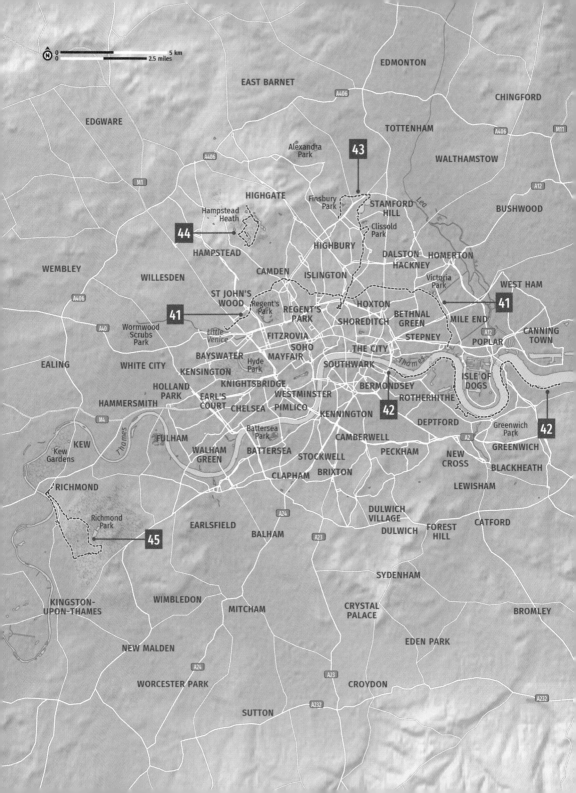

LONDON

Explore
LONDON

While it may not be your first impression, London is a remarkably and refreshingly green city – estimates are that 47% of the capital is made up of parkland and gardens. Some 2% of the city is comprised of 'blue' space, referring to canals, reservoirs and rivers whose banks and towpaths make for some lovely walking. The Royal Parks in the centre of the city are manicured idylls with artful planning, while Hampstead Heath and Richmond Park in particular offer a real wilderness feel and some stands of ancient trees. The New River route takes you on a trip from the northeast into the heart of town, via an ingenious 17th-century canal.

LONDON

London is a huge metropolis, which becomes manageable if you treat it as the locals do – as a series of villages, each of which harbours diverse and largely harmonious communities.

The proper name for London's administrative areas is boroughs, but in reality most people place their loyalty in smaller and more distinct areas. In terms of green spaces, north London has some wonderfully wild places: Hampstead Heath, Queen's Wood and Highgate Woods with their remnants of old English forest, and more open and spacious Finsbury Park.

Way out west, genteel Richmond boasts both the largest

park in the city (which has a huge deer population), and some inspiring river walking: you can follow the gentle curves of the wide Thames from here down to Hampton Court Palace and beyond.

Stay central to explore the three connected royal parks at the geographical heart of the city, or take a hike down the endlessly diverting Thames Path as it runs east to Greenwich.

East London, parts of which are gritty and built-up, also has a surprising amount of greenery, and a network of canals whose towpaths make for refreshing strolls.

Wherever you go in London you're never too far from a great

pub or cafe, and while accommodation can be expensive it is possible to find bargains, as well as affordable ethnic eats from all round the world.

 ## WHEN TO GO

There's no bad time to see London, though the winter months can feel rather drab, with low temperatures, grey skies and short days which may curtail your walking, but only rarely the compensating sight of thick snow. The city sees lots of tourists year-round, particularly in the summer months of July and August, but the routes we've suggested have space enough for everyone, and are unlikely to feel overcrowded.

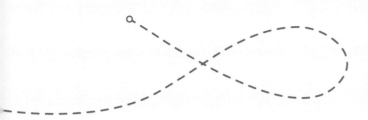

Resources

London Walks (www.walks.com) Guided rambles through the city, one of which explores the watery history of Rotherhithe.

Time Out (www.timeout.com) A weekly listings map sold citywide, giving the most comprehensive lowdown on what's new in the capital.

Transport for London (www.tfl. gov.uk) The website helps you navigate London, and also has good suggestions for green city walks such as the Green Chain walk and the Capital Ring.

Visit London (www.visitlondon. com) The official tourist board site features a comprehensive section on the city's parks. There's also plenty of information on outdoor London more widely, including outdoor events and markets, peaceful green spots, picnic places, riverside pubs and open-air swimming pools.

Spring in London, with cherry blossoms in bloom on many streets and daffodils brightening up the parks, can be lovely.

TRANSPORT

The city's transport is relatively pricey, but also in the main quick and efficient. The Underground system – the world's first – connects the major spots. It doesn't reach all the corners of east London you might want to explore, but a network of red double-decker buses and nippy overground trains fills the gaps.

Buses are by far the cheapest form of transport in the city. London has become a pretty decent city to cycle, with few hills and a growing network of cycle superhighways. You'll find an affordable bike-hire scheme and docking stations in the centre of the city, and a growing number of scattered bikes which you can access via apps. Driving in London tends to be stressful, bad-tempered and congested, and is not recommended.

WHERE TO STAY

Centrally sited accommodation in London doesn't come cheap,

though there are a few decent hostels, and some comfy but bland chain hotels have fabulous locations and decent online deals.

Bed and breakfasts and Airbnb give you the experience of London with a local: an insider view is a big plus in the big city. The further out you go the better the bargains are and, given the connectedness of the transport system and the hip appeal of some of the outer boroughs, staying away from the centre can be a plus.

WHAT'S ON

Richmond Festival (www.richmond festival.org.uk; ⊙Feb-Mar) Leafy Richmond holds a performing arts festival in early spring.

Hampstead Summer Festival (www. hampsteadsummerfestival.com; ⊙late Jun-early Jul) Head to the heath for events including public drawing and an alfresco painting day.

Kenwood House concerts (www. english-heritage.org.uk/visit/places/ kenwood/events) This grand villa, featured on one of the routes in this chapter, holds major rock, pop and jazz concerts in its grounds.

Notting Hill Carnival (www.thelondon nottinghillcarnival.com; ⊙Aug) Held on the August bank holiday, this is a massive street party – the biggest in Europe – where the city comes together to sing, dance and celebrate Caribbean culture.

Thames Festival (www.totallythames. org; ⊙Sep) An event celebrating mudlarking and the river's wildlife, with local bands plus kayaking, heritage walks and plenty of kid-focussed activities.

41

REGENT'S CANAL

DURATION	DIFFICULTY	DISTANCE	START/END
3½hr	Moderate	9 miles/ 14.5km	Warwick Ave/ Limehouse

TERRAIN	Paved towpaths

Those who are fed up with the busy streets of London should take to this towpath, a meandering watery route which leads all the way across London, from Little Venice in the west to Camden, Kingston and Hackney. The path then curves round past Victoria Park, heading south to spacious Limehouse Basin before joining the mighty River Thames.

GETTING HERE

The starting point for the walk is Warwick Ave tube station on the Bakerloo underground line.

STARTING POINT

From the tube station, head down Warwick Ave to the canal, following signs for Little Venice.

01 **Little Venice** (pictured), where the walk starts, is one of the prettiest spots in the city. The canal basin was once known as Browning's Pool – the poet lived in a house overlooking the basin. The area still has a slightly bohemian and colourful feel, and is surrounded by handsome white regency buildings.

02 The first stretch of the towpath hugs the north bank of the canal along beautiful **Bloomfield Rd**, with bright flower-bedecked houseboats sitting in private moorings.

03 The path joins Aberdeen Place at the point where the canal disappears for a stretch into the narrow 250m **Maida Hill Tunnel**, built in 1812. It was the first of the city's canal tunnels, built because the Portman estate refused to allow permission for an open canal. Beyond this, steep steps lead back to the towpath.

04 From here the path leads past the minarets and bulbous golden dome of London Central Mosque, then skirts the northern boundary of **London Zoo**, the most visible element of which is the soaring Lord Snowdon–designed aviary. The aviary is set to be revamped by architects Foster + Partners and reopen in 2021.

05 Beyond the zoo to the north are the slopes of attractive and village-like **Primrose Hill**, part of a chase (hunting reserve) which was owned by Henry VIII. Despite its historic antecedents Primrose Hill is mostly made up of graceful lines of Victorian terraced houses.

06 Leaving the green embrace of Regent's Park and Primrose Hill, the path then curves round towards Camden. At Oval Rd, where a bridge crosses the canal, there's a diversion in the form of a typically provocative **artwork** by street artist Banksy: it depicts a small girl with a lollipop in one hand, and a missile in a cart in another.

07 Past Kentish Town Lock, the canal continues around to **Camden**, a still slightly scruffy and raffish area with a famous **market** which is well worth a stop – it's also a good point to grab some affordable street food or a coffee. Located in former stable buildings, the market features 200 stalls, and is most famous for selling funky vintage clothes.

08 Under a series of bridges and locks, you continue on the northern bank of the towpath to St Pancras Lock, with its cosy Victorian lock cottage. On the south bank you'll see an old Victorian water tower, and then **Camley Street Natural Park**, a sylvan community space that has been redeveloped and is due to reopen in 2020. Also to either side are the modern developments around King's Cross Station, including a vast new Google building on the

London Canal Museum

The little London Canal Museum (www.canalmuseum.org.uk) explores what life was like for families living and working on Britain's impressively long and historic canal system. The exhibits in the stables upstairs are dedicated to the history of canal transport in Britain, including recent developments such as the clean up of the Lea River for the 2012 Olympic Games. The museum is housed in a warehouse dating from 1858, where ice was once stored in two deep wells. The ice trade was huge in Victorian London, with 35,000 tonnes imported from Norway in 1899 alone, arriving in the city at Regent's Canal Dock before being transported along the canal.

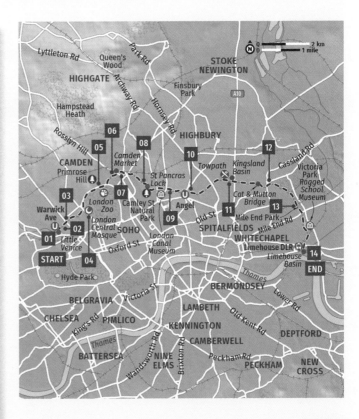

south bank, and the swish campus of Saint Martin's College to the north. Canal aficionados might want to cross the canal at Maiden Lane Bridge to detour to the London Canal Museum, which sits on the basin here (see p167).

09 Where the canal disappears into the Islington tunnel, the route leaves the water for a stretch, and takes to the quiet streets of **Islington**. You head down Duncan St to the north of Angel station, and rejoin the canal just beyond the Duncan Terrace Gardens. This incidentally is where the New River intersects with the Regent's Canal – for more on this other fabled waterway, see p172.

10 From here the towpath takes you on into Hackney – it's a sociable stretch with plenty of walkers and cyclists, and a mix of new developments and characterful warehouses. Immediately beyond the point where the De Beauvoir Rd crosses the canal, the booth-like **Towpath** cafe is an idyllic spot for lunch or cake. You can sit outside, or shelter in a brick alcove.

11 From here you'll see moored boats on the enclave of the Kingsland Basin to the left. The surrounding swish modern apartments belie the fact that the basin was created back in 1822. The next notable stop is the Cat & Mutton Bridge, where you might want to detour left onto **Broadway Market** (pictured). It features a mix of hip and neighbourhood shops, and

on Saturday is taken over by an outstanding food market.

12 Beyond the point where trafficky Mare Street crosses the canal, you curve round to walk past the southern edge of spacious **Victoria Park**. It was opened back in 1845, and became a crucial amenity and leisure space for East Enders in the later 19th century. Beyond the park, the Hertford Union Canal leads off to the left, but you should carry on straight ahead, heading south.

13 To your left is long **Mile End Park**, a new green space with an indoor climbing centre that sits on the spot where WWII bombing ravaged the area. At the southern edge of the park the fascinating Ragged School Museum is testimony to the work of Dr Thomas Barnardo in the East End – he worked to relieve the plight of the destitute, particularly children.

14 From here it's a short stretch south to **Limehouse Basin**, whose rather anodyne modern appearance is at odds with its amazing salty history. Named for lime kilns that sat by the river here in the 14th century, it became an important port from Tudor times. But actually it was the building of the Regent's Canal that made the basin come alive, as goods from ships docked here could be easily transported inland. It has an important part in the history of immigration in the capital too – African and Chinese sailors

disembarked here, and made the area their home. The growth of the railways eventually heralded a decline in canal transport, and the basin was shattered by bombing during the war, leading to the exodus of the Chinese community to Soho. At one point you could apparently cross the basin by stepping from ship to ship. Today, it's a quiet and somewhat bland residential spot, though the crowded yachts add a little life to the scene. You can circle round either side of the basin to emerge at the River Thames, startlingly wide at this point. The nearest transport onwards is the Limehouse DLR station, immediately northwest of the basin.

☕ TAKE A BREAK

Occupying four small units facing Regent's Canal towpath, the simple **Towpath** (☎ 020-7254 7606; rear 42-44 De Beauvoir Cres, N1; mains £8-11; 🕙 9am-5pm Tue & Wed, to 9.30pm Thu-Sun; Ⓤ Haggerston) cafe is a super place to sit in the sun and watch the ducks and narrow boats glide by. The coffee and food are excellent, with delicious cookies and brownies on the counter and cooked dishes chalked up on the blackboard daily.

42

THAMES PATH

DURATION	DIFFICULTY	DISTANCE	START/END
4½hr	Moderate	11 miles/ 17.5km	Tower Bridge/ Thames Barrier

TERRAIN	Paved paths and roads

The Thames Path starts way outside of London, 180 miles away in Kemble in Gloucestershire at the Thames Head. Its end point is the Thames Barrier, the shiny construction that prevents the Thames from flooding. Here we focus on the south bank of the river and the last stage of the walk, starting at Tower Bridge and ending at the barrier.

GETTING HERE

Leave London Bridge station from the Tooley St exit and cross over to Hay's Galleria, once a docking point for 19th-century tea clippers. Once through the gallery, turn right onto the Thames Path, passing HMS Belfast and City Hall to reach the tall pillars of the bridge.

STARTING POINT

This walk starts at Tower Bridge, the late-19th-

century suspension bridge that connects the Tower of London with the south bank of the river.

01 From Tower Bridge, the route runs eastwards along the river, leading along Shad Thames, crisscrossed with high iron bridges. You then cross a muddy inlet at **St Saviour's Dock Footbridge**, the site of Bill Sykes' grisly death in Charles Dickens' *Oliver Twist*.

02 Passing the revitalised wharf buildings of Bermondsey, the path briefly leaves the river, joining it again at the touching memorial to the Salters, a Quaker couple who worked to improve living conditions here in the early 20th century. Beyond you come to Rotherhithe, and the 1716 **Church of St Mary the Virgin**, outside of which sits a memorial honouring the Pilgrim Fathers who left for America from here. Nearby, the 16th-century riverside Mayflower pub looks onto what was the docking point for the Mayflower ship.

Mudlarking

The huge daily surge of the tide disrupts the treasures of the Thames, and lays them on the foreshore for eager mud-larkers to collect. Sadly, the original Victorian mudlarkers were children who scoured the banks of the Thames for sellable items. Today, various tour companies lay on guided mudlarking tours, a safe and fun way to rummage in the mud and occasional filth of the river. In fact, unless you have a Port of London Authority licence, you'll be looking only – you're not permitted to dig or use a metal detector. Visit the Museum of London to see some of the rarer items found on the foreshore. And to see inspiring mudlark finds as they happen, follow @london.mudlark.

ASIASTOCK/SHUTTERSTOCK ©

Best for

A POST-HIKE PINT

03 Just past the pub, the intriguing **Brunel Museum** honours the master engineer's father, who designed the Thames tunnel here at Rotherhithe.

04 Cross the red lift bridge at Surrey Water. The next major landmark is the lovely **Surrey Docks** city farm on the site of an 18th-century shipyard.

05 The river loops south to enter Deptford. You walk through Pepys Park and along some back streets to enter historic Greenwich, where the **Cutty Sark** tea clipper (pictured) is a spectacular and unmissable

sight. Continuing along the river, the Cutty Sark Tavern makes a fine lunch and/or pint stop.

06 The next stretch takes you round a sharp loop in the river, and past the tent-like 02 Arena. From here it's another 3km along the river to the mighty **Thames Barrier**. Since 1982, the glittering gates of the barrier have prevented storm surges from flooding the capital. The nearest transport from here is Charlton Station: to reach it, retrace your steps on the Thames Path, turning left at the Anchor & Hope pub onto Anchor and Hope Lane.

TAKE A BREAK

Housed in a delightful bow-windowed, wood-beamed Georgian building directly on the Thames, the 200-year-old **Cutty Sark Tavern** (☏ 020-8858 3146; www.cutty sarkse10.co.uk; 4-6 Ballast Quay, SE10; ⊙11.30am-11pm Mon-Sat, noon-10.30pm Sun; 🛜; Ⓤ Cutty Sark) is one of the few independent pubs left in Greenwich. Half a dozen cask-conditioned ales on tap line the bar, there's an inviting riverside seating area opposite and the upstairs dining room looks out on to glorious views.

43

NEW RIVER

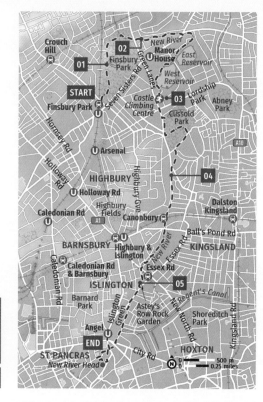

DURATION	DIFFICULTY	DISTANCE	START/END
2hr	Moderate	5.3 miles/ 8.5km	Finsbury Park station/ Angel station

TERRAIN	Tarred paths, some streets

This north London walk follows a now modest waterway with a fascinating place in the social and health history of the capital. It is not in fact a river at all, but a manmade channel which revolutionised London's contaminated water supply when it opened in 1613. The whole walkable route is 62km, but this section follows the last stage, a green ribbon leading into the centre of the city.

GETTING HERE
This north London walk is easily accessible on London's tube system: Finsbury Park is on the Victoria Line, Angel on the Northern Line.

STARTING POINT
Come out of busy Finsbury Park train/tube station, and follow signs for Finsbury Park, entering it through the Stroud Green Gate.

01 Head north through **Finsbury Park**, passing the boating lake to your right, curving to the right, and then taking the little bridge over the water channel. This is your first encounter with the New River. Take the path along the left bank of the channel, cutting through the park and exiting it over Green Lanes road.

02 Go through the green gate to join the scenic raised path along the waterway. Follow the river, leaving it briefly to cross Seven Sisters Rd, until it curves to join the East Reservoir, used for canoeing and boating, and then the wetland of the West Reservoir.

03 The crenellated **Castle Climbing Centre** is an unmissable landmark, and its cafe makes a great spot for lunch or cake. It was built as a water pumping centre, with all the grandeur of the Victorian age. From the centre, turn left onto Green

Creating the New River

The creation of explorer, banker and engineer Sir Hugh Myddelton, the New River replaced the dirty old River Thames as London's water source. Running for 62km from Hertfordshire on a gentle incline, it was so well structured back in 1613 that it still carries water for treatment and, over the centuries, saved thousands from death by cholera. You can veer off the route to see a statue of Sir Hugh, in ruff and baggy pantaloons, which stands on Islington Green flanked by urn-clutching cherubs. At the end of the walk at the New River Head, scant traces of a watermill, engine room and pump house are all that remain to show the spot where water was brought to generations of Londoners.

I WEI HUANG/SHUTTERSTOCK ©

Lanes, cross Lordship Park and head into Clissold Park. The waterway is submerged, but you soon pick it up as it leads through and out of Clissold Park, and onto Church St. Clissold Cres and the New River Path lead to spacious Petherton Rd, where a tree-lined central strip conceals the water below. Go straight ahead up Wallace Rd.

04 The route now follows meandering landscaped areas, created in the mid-20th century to follow the turns of the waterway. The conical brick structure was a watchhouse, built in the 18th century to prevent fishermen and bathers from contaminating the water.

05 Continue to Astey's Row Rock Garden, head south on Essex Rd, then follow the now submerged waterway along Colebrooke Row and Duncan Terrace Gardens. Coming out of the gardens, head up Owen St to Myddelton Sq, named for the creator of the New River. Go up Myddelton Passage to the New River Head. To get from here to the tube, walk north up Arlington Way and then turn left and head up busy St John St, which joins Islington High St; the station is on the right-hand side.

TAKE A BREAK

An utterly unique London experience, **Castle Café** (020-8211 7000; www.castle-climbing.co.uk/the-castle-cafe; The Castle Climbing Centre, Green Lanes; soup £4, cakes £3; noon-9.30pm Mon-Fri, 9am-6.30pm Sat & Sun) is a sustainable social enterprise set within a spacious climbing centre, itself set within a wildly eccentric Baronial-style castle around 45 minutes into the walk. Food is homemade and created with care and flair; they produce their own herbal teas, salads, honey and fruit in the picturesque garden. Daily specials include seasonal stews, soups and curries.

44

HAMPSTEAD HEATH

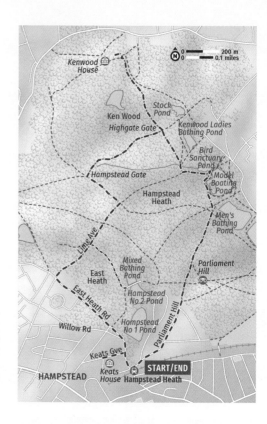

DURATION	DIFFICULTY	DISTANCE	START/END
1½hr	Moderate	3.4 miles/ 5.5km	Hampstead Heath overground

TERRAIN	Some steep paths and woodland

Even hardened Londoners are amazed by the size and wildness of Hampstead Heath. Set on a sandy ridge, it provides sweeping urban views as well as dense ancient and more recent woodland. On a sunny day bring a swimming costume, as the natural ponds provide a gorgeous spot for a dip. Kenwood House is a good stop for art lovers, and Keats House, the poet's home from 1818 to 1820, is a stroll away.

Start from Hampstead Heath station, heading up Parliament Hill towards the Heath. You soon leave the streets behind and ascend the heath itself, climbing uphill for a classic London panorama. Press on and you come to a row of **ponds** with self-explanatory names: the Men's Pond, Model Boating Pond, Bird Sanctuary Pond and Ladies

Bathing Pond. (The Mixed Bathing Pond sits close to the end of the route.)

Beyond, you come to Highgate Gate: go through it to plunge into Ken Wood. After a short stretch the views open up again, with parkland and lovely neoclassical **Kenwood House** (pictured) ahead of you. There's a wonderful art collection here and its **Brew House** cafe is a great lunch or cake stop.

Head back to Highgate Gate, turning right to descend the heath to Hampstead Gate. Follow the wide **Lime Ave** down to the edge of the heath, with a possible detour to the left before you get there to the Mixed Bathing Pond.

Otherwise you come to busy East Heath Road, where you should turn left. Some 600m down the road on the right you'll see Keats Grove, where the short-lived poet's home **Keats House** is well worth a stop.

45

RICHMOND PARK

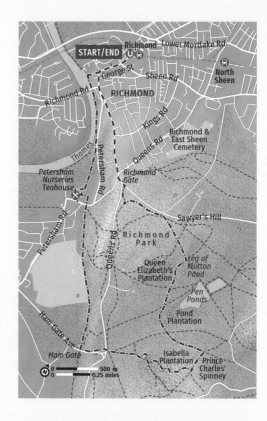

DURATION	DIFFICULTY	DISTANCE	START/END
2¼hr	Easy	6.2 miles/ 10km	Richmond station

TERRAIN	Tarred or grassed paths, some inclines

Richmond Park is London's largest green space, and its wildest. Until you've visited, it's hard to believe that the city limits can encompass such a verdant space, where huge herds of deer roam freely, and where there are more than a thousand 'veteran' trees. From the 13th century this was a royal hunting ground, which was enclosed by a brick wall on the order of Charles I in 1637.

Start from Richmond Station, looking out for River Thames signposts. Turn left at the river, walking past pubs, Georgian villas and houseboats for 1km, and then follow signs across the meadow to **Petersham**. The plant-filled glass houses of Petersham Nurseries Teahouse make a gorgeous food stop.

Retrace your steps from the Nurseries and take the lane towards the church, following a Capital Ring

sign. This will bring you into the park, where you'll see Ham Gate down to your right. Take the network of undulating paths towards the **Isabella Plantation**, with its heather garden and rhododendrons, and Pen Ponds.

Follow the paved curving road and approach **Pond Plantation**, where you turn left, up the horse ride. Ascend the gentle hill with Leg of Mutton Pond to the right, and the dense Queen Elizabeth's Plantation to your left. From the plantation you join a broad track with a Capital Ring sign.

Walk towards the large red-brick building, the former Star and Garter care home, and exit the park at Richmond Gate. Out on the street, head down grand Richmond Hill. At Richmond Bridge go straight ahead on Hill St, which curves right to become George St, to arrive back at Richmond Station.

Also Try...

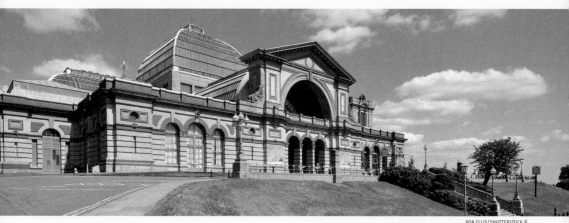

RON ELLIS/SHUTTERSTOCK ©

PARKLAND WAY

This route covers the course of the dismantled Great Northern Railway, which cuts a deep green swathe from Finsbury Park, across Crouch End and into the ancient woodland of Highgate and Queen's Wood, with the option to continue to the parkland that surrounds Alexandra Palace (pictured).

This walk is a revelation in that it shows how much dense woodland survives in a built-up area of London. The trees, a mix of oak and hornbeams, were once part of the huge Forest of Middlesex. Keep your eyes peeled, and you just might see tiny muntjac deer along the route and also, come evening time, foxes and hedgehogs. Other pleasures along the way include the evocative remains of Crouch End Station, a green man sculpture in the old railway arches, magical Queen's Wood cafe hidden among the trees, and the High Victorian grandeur of Alexandra Palace.

DURATION 3hr
DIFFICULTY Moderate
DISTANCE 7.5 miles/12km

THAMES PATH WEST

Affluent Richmond is the starting point for one of London's loveliest walks, a riverside ramble that eventually brings you to mighty Hampton Court Palace.

From Richmond station, head riverward and then begin to follow the curves of the wide Thames River, passing handsome 17th-century Ham House – both it and its orangery tearoom are well worth a stop. Eel Pie Island, accessed via an eccentric river ferry, is also worth exploring. Back on the east bank of the river, the walk continues via the reclaimed Ham Lands to Kingston. Here you cross the river, and continue round Hampton Court Park to access the magnificent palace, built for Cardinal Wolsey in 1516 and subsequently nabbed by Henry VIII.

DURATION 4½hr
DIFFICULTY Moderate
DISTANCE 11 miles/18km

IVANMATEEV/GETTY IMAGES ©

EPPING FOREST

Epping Forest is a wonderful survivor, stretching for around 20km into Essex, and featuring ancient deciduous woodland.

From Chingford Station, the route runs to a fantastical Tudor hunting lodge built for Henry VIII in 1543; close by is one of the last surviving 'forest retreats', refreshment rooms built for late-19th-century day-trippers. From here, a network of paths and 'rides' (wide leafy avenues) takes you across meadows and into dense forest, via a conservation centre and Iron Age Loughton Camp.

DURATION 2½hr
DIFFICULTY Easy
DISTANCE 6 miles/10km

ROYAL PARKS

At the geographical centre of London, you'll find a stretch of greenery that is a place of pleasure, leisure and beauty for tourists and locals alike.

This walk starts at Lancaster Gate tube station, depositing you via three wonderful royal parks at Trafalgar Square. You walk through Hyde Park, past the Serpentine Lake and the memorial to Princess Di and alongside Rotten Row. From here you enter spacious Green Park, renowned for its arching plane trees and magical gas lanterns, then elongated St James' Park (pictured) – home to pelicans, and year-round colourful blooms.

DURATION 1½hr
DIFFICULTY Easy
DISTANCE 3 miles/5km

CAPITAL RING

Often described as the M25 for walkers, the Capital Ring sketches a green circuit around the capital. It covers 126km, and takes in attractions such as Eltham Palace, the Thames Barrier and the Walthamstow Marshes.

The Ring can be broken down into 15 manageable sections. For example, Crystal Palace to Streatham leads you through Biggin Wood and Rookery Gardens and past Norwood Grove Mansion. Go to the Transport for London website to find out about the other routes.

DURATION 1½hr
DIFFICULTY Easy
DISTANCE 4 miles/6.5km

SCOTLAND

Explore
SCOTLAND

Scotland's wild, dramatic scenery and varied landscape have made walking a hugely popular pastime for locals and visitors alike. There really is something for everyone, from easygoing coastal strolls to rugged and remote treks in the hills, and the country is home to the popular sport of Munro bagging (ticking off all the Scottish hills of 3000ft and above).

EDINBURGH

Edinburgh is one of Europe's most beautiful cities, draped across a series of rocky hills overlooking the sea. But it's also a great base for a walking holiday, not least because there's lots of great hiking within the city boundaries – in Holyrood Park, on Blackford Hill, along the Union Canal and along the coast at Cramond and Portobello. And it's within day-trip distance of Fife, Perthshire, the Scottish Borders and even the Northumberland Coast.

FORT WILLIAM

Basking on Loch Linnhe's shores amid magnificent mountain scenery, Fort William has one of the most enviable settings in all of Scotland. The town has carved out a reputation as the 'Outdoor Capital of the UK' (www. outdoorcapital.co.uk), and easy access by rail and bus makes it a good base for exploring the surrounding mountains and glens. Magical Glen Nevis begins near the northern end of the town and wraps itself around the southern flanks of Ben Nevis (1345m) – Britain's highest mountain and a magnet for hikers and climbers.

AVIEMORE

The gateway to the Cairngorms, Aviemore is the region's main centre for transport, accommodation, restaurants and shops. It's not the prettiest town in Scotland by a long stretch – the main attractions are in the surrounding area – but when bad weather puts the hills off limits, Aviemore fills up with hikers, cyclists and climbers (plus skiers and snowboarders in winter) cruising the outdoor-equipment shops or recounting their latest adventures in the cafes and bars.

CALLANDER

Callander, the principal town in the Trossachs, has been pulling in tourists for more than 150 years, and has a laid-back ambience along its main thoroughfare that quickly lulls visitors into lazy pottering. There's an excellent array of accommodation options here, and some intriguing places to eat. Good walking and cycling routes are close at hand.

PORTREE

Portree is Skye's largest and liveliest town. It has a pretty harbour lined with brightly painted houses, and there are great views of the surrounding hills. Portree is well supplied with B&Bs, but accommodation fills up fast from April to October, so be sure to book ahead.

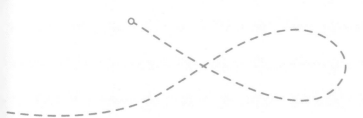

Resources

www.walkhighlands.co.uk Indispensable database of walks all over Scotland.

www.outdooraccess-scotland. scot Information on access rights and responsibilities.

www.mwis.org.uk Specialised weather forecasts for Scottish mountain areas.

www.smidgeup.com/ midge-forecast Useful indication of midge activity across the country.

WHEN TO GO

The best time of year for walking is usually May to September, although snow can fall on the higher summits even in midsummer. Midges – tiny biting flies that can make life a misery – are at their worst from June to August, especially in the western Highlands. Bring insect repellent, antihistamine cream and long-sleeved shirts and trousers.

May, June and September have, statistically, the best chance of dry weather. July and August are warm, but can often be wet. In spring, snow patches linger on the hills, while in autumn the changing of the leaves adds colour to woodland walks.

Winter walking on the hills of Scotland requires an ice axe and crampons and is for experienced mountaineers only. Daylight is in short supply – it's dark by 4pm in December and January.

TRANSPORT

Travelling to Scotland by train is faster and usually more comfortable than the bus, but it's more expensive. There are regular services from London to Scottish cities, including the Caledonian Sleeper, an overnight service connecting London Euston with Edinburgh, Glasgow, Fort William and Inverness.

Train travel within Scotland is relatively expensive, with extensive coverage and frequent departures in central Scotland, but only a few lines in the northern Highlands and southern Scotland. Bus travel is cheaper and slower than trains, but useful for more remote regions that aren't serviced by rail.

WHERE TO STAY

Scotland has a vast range of accommodation, from boutique B&Bs to well-equipped campsites. Free wild camping became a legal right under the Land Reform Bill of 2003. However, campers are obliged to camp on unenclosed land, in small numbers, and away from buildings and roads. Book in advance, especially in summer, at weekends, and on islands (where options are often limited). Recommended places to stay:

Townhouse (www.thetownhouse melrose.co.uk) Boutique hotel in Melrose with excellent restaurant.

Hillstone Lodge (www.hillstonelodge. com) Modern, luxury B&B in the wilds of Skye.

Pennyland House (www.pennyland house.co.uk) Thurso B&B set in lovely 18th-century house with island views.

Callander Hostel (www.callander hostel.co.uk) Top-class hostel in a mock-Tudor building in the Trossachs.

Glenmore Campsite (www.campingin theforest.co.uk) Attractive lochside site amid Scots pines in the heart of the Cairngorms.

WHAT'S ON

UCI Mountain Bike World Cup (www. fortwilliamworldcup.co.uk; ⊙Jun) Fort William pulls in crowds of more than 18,000 spectators.

Highland Games July and August usher in traditional Highland Games across the country.

Edinburgh International Festival (www.eif.co.uk) & **Festival Fringe** (www.edfringe.com) August sees the capital fill to overflowing.

Scottish Borders Walking Festival (www.borderswalking.com; ⊙Sep) Seven days of walks for all abilities.

Ben Nevis Hill Race (www.bennevis race.co.uk; ⊙Sep) Spectators gather for the annual race.

Cowalfest (www.cowalfest.org; ⊙Sep/Oct) Argyll's arts and walking festival.

46

BEN A'AN

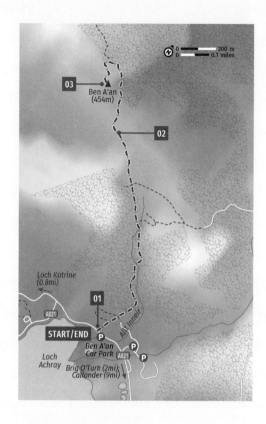

DURATION	DIFFICULTY	DISTANCE	START/END
3hr	Moderate	2.25 miles/ 3.5km	Ben A'an car park

TERRAIN	Good footpath, steep, stony

Although it's only 454m in height, this classic Trossachs hill well deserves its reputation as a 'mountain in miniature'. A conical crag-girt peak with its lower slopes shrouded in woodland, Ben A'an's pointed, rocky summit offers superb views along Loch Katrine and provides many hikers with their first experience of hillwalking.

GETTING HERE

The Ben A'an car park is on the south side of the A821 road, 2 miles west of the village of Brig o'Turk. It's 32 miles north of Glasgow (a one-hour drive), and 60 miles northwest of Edinburgh (1 hour 45 minutes). There is no public transport.

STARTING POINT

The Forestry Commission's Ben A'an car park (£3 per car for all-day parking) has plenty of space, but no facilities. The nearest public toilets are at Trossachs Pier on Loch Katrine, just over a mile to the west.

01 The walk begins along a forestry road opposite the car park, but where this bends to the left after 100m keep straight ahead on a well-made footpath that begins with a flight of steps. The path climbs steadily alongside a burn, through the clear-felled remains of an old **forestry plantation**. This area was originally covered in commercial conifers, but is being replanted with native tree species.

02 Soon after crossing another forestry road the path reaches a level grassy spot among stands of birch, rowan, holly and hazel – a good

Loch Katrine

Ben A'an lies at the heart of the Trossachs, a region of craggy, wooded hills and scenic lochs within Loch Lomond and the Trossachs National Park. The view from the summit is dominated by 8-mile-long Loch Katrine (pictured), whose waters are cruised by the centenarian steamship *Sir Walter Scott* (www.lochkatrine.com). There are various one-hour afternoon sailings, and at 10.30am (plus additional summer departures) there's a trip to Stronachlachar at the other end of the loch. From there you can opt to walk or cycle back to Trossachs Pier via the Great Trossachs Path, an easy, hard-surfaced trail that runs around the north shore of the loch (14 miles).

DAVID C TOMLINSON/GETTY IMAGES ©

spot for a refreshment break. Keep an eye open for roe deer and red squirrels. Ahead you can see the pyramidal peak of Ben A'an towering above – the crags of silvery-grey mica schist here have provided sport for local rock climbers since the 1930s. The path now heads into a gully to the right of the peak and gets steeper, with zigzags and steps fashioned from natural stones. This is the most strenuous part of the climb, but soon levels off before curving around to the left and approaching the summit from behind.

03 The **summit** is a perfectly pointed slab of rock, pro-viding an ideal photo opportunity. You can see now that Ben A'an is actually a minor spur of the higher (but less interesting) hill called Meall Gainmheich, rather than a mountain in its own right. But no matter – provided the weather has been kind, your efforts will be rewarded with a superb view along the wooded shores of Loch Katrine towards the mountains that cluster around the north end of Loch Lomond, known locally as the 'Arrochar Alps'. To the southwest, across the near end of the loch, you can see Ben Venue and, to its right, the more distant peak of Ben Lomond. Once you have had your fill of the scenery,

return to the car park the same way you came up.

TAKE A BREAK

Callander, 9 miles to the east, is famous for its excellent fish and chip shop, **Mhor Fish** (01877-330213; www.mhorfish.net; 75 Main St; mains £9-18; noon-9pm Tue-Sun, closed Tue Nov–mid-Feb;), while Stronachlachar on Loch Katrine has the **Pier Cafe** (01877-386374; www.thepiercafe.com; meals £6-13; 9am-5pm Mon-Thu, to 10pm Fri-Sun Apr-Oct, 10am-4pm Nov-Mar;), which serves tasty breakfasts and lunches in a conservatory seating area overlooking the water.

47

MELROSE

DURATION	DIFFICULTY	DISTANCE	START/END
2hr	Easy	3.5 miles/ 5.5km	Melrose

TERRAIN	Firm level paths, tarred roads

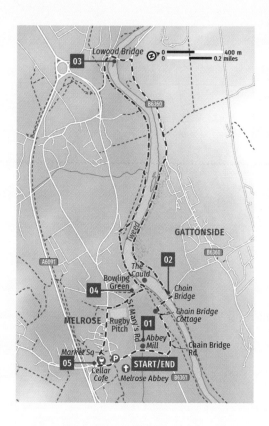

Melrose is one of the prettiest towns in the Scottish Borders, famous for its magnificent ruined abbey and nearby Abbotsford, the former home of Sir Walter Scott. This walk leads along the scenic banks of the River Tweed, one of Scotland's best-known salmon rivers, and returns via the town's picturesque market square.

GETTING HERE

Melrose is 39 miles south of Edinburgh (one hour's drive). There is a pay-and-display car park next to the abbey. Buses run from Edinburgh (2½ hours, half-hourly) Monday to Saturday; on Sundays buses run hourly, and you need to change at Galashiels. The Borders Railway runs from Edinburgh to Tweedbank station (one hour, half-hourly), which is just 500m from Lowood Bridge in the middle of the walk.

STARTING POINT

The impressive ruins of **Melrose Abbey** (pictured) date from the 14th and 15th centuries, and were restored at the instigation of Sir Walter Scott in the 19th century. It's worth taking an hour or so to explore the abbey, famed for its decorative stonework – look out for the pig gargoyle playing the bagpipes – and as the place where Robert the Bruce's heart was buried after his death in 1329.

01 From the entrance to Melrose Abbey head north along Abbey St and Annay Rd past Abbey Mill Woollen Centre, then turn left on Chain Bridge Rd. This leads to **Chain Bridge Cottage**, now used as a motorcycle training facility.

02 The impressive **Chain Bridge** was built in 1826, to connect Melrose with the village of Gattonside on the north side of the River Tweed.

Walks Around Melrose

Melrose is a charming village popular with walkers. There are many attractive walks in the Eildon Hills, just south of town, accessible via a footpath off Dingleton Rd (the B6359). Just west of town is Abbotsford, the former home of Sir Walter Scott, which can be reached via a 4.5-mile walk along the banks of the River Tweed.

The **St Cuthbert's Way** long-distance walking trail starts in Melrose, while the coast-to-coast **Southern Upland Way** passes through town. You can do a day's walk along St Cuthbert's Way as far as Harestanes (16 miles), on the A68 near Jedburgh, and return to Melrose on the hourly Jedburgh–Galashiels bus.

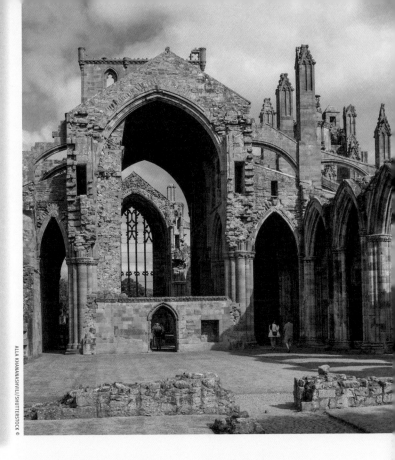

ALLA KHANANASHVILI/SHUTTERSTOCK ©

Originally you had to pay a toll to cross the bridge, and the cottage served as a toll house. Cross over the bridge and turn sharp left on the unsurfaced path that leads along the river bank. Continue along the riverside until the path rises to join the B6360 road, where you turn left. This road leads in 600m to a left turn across a road bridge.

03 The graceful, twin-arched **Lowood Bridge** was built in the 1760s; as with the Chain Bridge, travellers originally had to pay a toll to cross – the little cottage on the north side was the toll house. Turn left at the far end of the bridge and con-

tinue along the road for 100m, where you will find a Southern Upland Way marker post – take the footpath on the left and follow the riverside walk for almost a mile.

04 As you reach the bowling green, you will see a weir on the river to your left. Known as **the Cauld**, this was built in medieval times to divert water to the mills operated by the monks of Melrose Abbey. Turn right along a good path, cross St Mary's Rd and continue past the rugby pitch (home of the famous Melrose Sevens rugby tournament), then turn left along High St.

05 You soon arrive at Melrose's attractive **Market Square**, with its restored 16th-century market cross topped by a unicorn bearing a shield. Turn left on Abbey St to return to your starting point.

🍵 TAKE A BREAK

Drop into the **Cellar Cafe** (Abbey Fine Wines, Rhymer's Fayre; ☎ 01896-823224; www.abbeyfinewines.co.uk; 17 Market Sq; mains £5-8; ⏱ 9.30am-4.30pm Mon-Sat Apr-Oct, 10am-4pm Mon-Sat Nov-Mar) for a caffeine hit or to enjoy a glass of wine on the market square accompanied by speciality cheeses.

48

LOCH AFFRIC CIRCUIT

DURATION	DIFFICULTY	DISTANCE	START/END
5-7hr	Hard	11.5 miles/ 18.5km	River Affric car park

TERRAIN	Good paths, forest roads

Glen Affric – Gaelic for 'valley of the dappled woods' – is a scenic wonderland of shimmering lochs, rugged mountains and mist-shrouded forests of native Scots pine, home to a treasure trove of iconic Scottish wildlife including ospreys and golden eagles, wildcats and otters, red squirrels and pine martens. The upper reaches of the glen are designated as the Glen Affric National Nature Reserve (www.nnr.scot).

GETTING HERE

The start of this walk is at the end of a narrow, single-track road that leads 10 miles southwest from the village of Cannich, which is itself 28 miles southwest of Inverness. The nearest you can get by public transport is Cannich village.

STARTING POINT

The Forestry Commission's River Affric car park provides plenty of spaces (£2 for all-day parking), though it can fill up quickly on summer weekends. There are toilets (summer only), picnic tables and information boards describing short waymarked hiking trails in the vicinity. This walk is not waymarked, and there can be some boggy sections and tricky stream crossings after heavy rain. Be prepared to turn back if a stream looks as if it can't be crossed safely.

01 From the entrance to the car park the route heads west along the unsurfaced continuation of the approach road, taking the righthand fork (the small No Entry signs apply to motorised vehicles only). The road follows the north shore of the eastern part of Loch Affric, where you are immediately surrounded by the beauty of birch and pine woods reflected in dark peaty waters. From the access gate to private Affric Lodge a path, signposted to Kintail and Glen Affric SYHA Hostel, continues straight ahead and then skirts around to the right of some estate buildings. A few hundred metres along, a single, creaky plank crosses a small stream and from here you can get a view south to the impressive Affric Lodge, backed by tall Scots pines, gazing down the loch.

02 **Affric Lodge** was built in 1872 as a hunting and fishing retreat for Lord Tweedmouth, who developed the breed of dog known as the golden retriever in his kennels

at Guisachan Lodge, east of Glen Affric. His son married Fanny Spencer-Churchill, a wealthy socialite who entertained top politicians and members of the royal family at the lodge. She was the aunt of former British prime minister Winston Churchill, who visited the lodge in 1901, and is said to have learned to drive a motor car here on the estate's private roads. The current owner is David Matthews, father-in-law of Pippa Middleton (the sister of the Duchess of Cambridge, who is married to HRH Prince William). If you have the cash to spare, you can rent the eight-bedroom lodge for the

princely sum of around £12,000 for three nights.

03 The trail now runs along the upper edge of a fenced area of protected woodland – some of the Scots pines here are more than 200 years old. Even in the relatively short time since the nature reserve was established in 2002, it's easy to see the positive impact of the fencing that keeps grazing deer at bay, in the proliferation of regenerating Scots pine and birch across the hillside. The path maintains a good height above the loch and reveals wonderful views west to the mountains around the upper reaches of

 ## Caledonian Pine Forest

When you realise that 8000 years ago, thousands of square kilometres of the Highlands were covered with natural Caledonian pine forest, and that the area has since shrunk to a mere 180 sq km, the vital significance of forest reserves hits home. The 17,466-hectare Glen Affric National Nature Reserve, the largest in northern Scotland, protects a diverse community of Scots pine, birch, aspen, rowan and willow, many shrubs and wildflowers, mammals (including red deer, pine marten and red squirrel) and about 100 species of bird, notably Scottish crossbill and golden eagle. Some of the Scots pines are more than 300 years old.

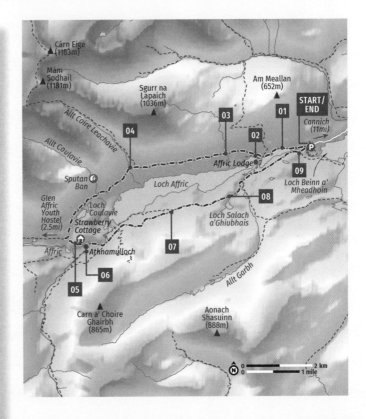

Glen Affric. There are many Munros (Scottish mountains whose height exceeds 3000ft) here, including the peaks of Mám Sodhail and Cárn Eighe rising steeply above the path to your right (their summits hidden by the lower slopes), and Mullach Fraoch-choire and An Socach framing the entrance to the upper glen ahead of you. Successive streams are crossed on stepping stones and occasional footbridges as the path traverses across the steep slope, passing vigorously regenerating clumps of birch and scattered remains of stone buildings.

MUNRO/GETTY IMAGES ©

04 A substantial bridge takes you across Allt Coire Leachavie (a short distance before reaching the bridge, a prominent path leads north into the corrie – the route to Mám Sodhail and other nearby Munros) then it's gently downhill towards little **Loch Coulavie**. On the way, the crossing of the Allt Coulavie, which tumbles down through the fine waterfall of Sputan Ban, can be difficult after heavy rain. The path, here rather boggy and eroded, curves around Loch Coulavie, climbs slightly and then descends to join a 4WD track.

05 Turn left at the T-junction. The main track here is part of the **Affric-Kintail Way**, which runs between Loch Ness and the west coast – a right turn would lead in 3 miles to the remote Glen Affric youth hostel. It is also the route followed by the annual Highland Cross charity race (www.highlandcross.co.uk), held every June since 1989,

where competitors run 20 miles cross-country from Morvich in Kintail to the west end of Loch Beinn a' Mheadhoin, then cycle another 30 miles to the finish line in Inverness.

06 About 600m after the junction you reach **Strawberry Cottage**, a remote mountaineering club hut, and cross the wooden bridge over the River Affric to reach the abandoned croft buildings of **Athnamulloch**. This ancient farming settlement was inhabited until the 1950s, and cattle were still grazed here until the 1970s. One of the old cottages was restored in 2016 by the charity Trees For Life, and now serves as a base for forest restoration workers, and as accommodation for hikers (it must be booked in advance). Turn

left after the bridge and follow the Affric-Kintail Way signposts along a forestry road that climbs gradually up the south side of Loch Affric into beautiful open pine forest.

07 The scattered Scots pines here and throughout Glen Affric constitute one of the largest remaining areas of ancient pinewoods in the country. Studies of tree pollen found in local lake bed mud cores show that Scots pines have been growing here for at least 8300 years, having colonised the area as the glaciers retreated at the end of the last Ice Age. The Glen Affric forest is particularly important, as it straddles the divide between the drier and colder climate of the eastern Highlands, where native woodland is dom-

The Affric-Kintail Way

It's possible to walk all the way from Cannich to Glen Shiel on the west coast (35 miles) in two days, spending the night at the remote and rustic **Glen Affric SYHA Hostel** (SYHA; ☎ bookings 0845 293 7373; www.syha.org.uk; Allt Beithe; dm £24.50; ☉Apr–mid-Sep). Facilities are basic – there is no phone, internet or mobile phone signal – and you'll need to take all supplies with you (and all litter away). The route is now part of the waymarked Affric-Kintail Way (www.affrickintailway.com), a 44-mile walking or mountain-biking trail leading from Drumnadrochit to Morvich in Kintail.

inated by Scots pine, and the wetter and milder west, where birch, rowan, alder, willow, holly and hazel predominate.

08 About 3 miles east of the bridge you reach a high point just north of **Loch Salach a'Ghiubhais**, where you can pause to take in the stupendous view across the loch to the lofty summits of An Tudair, Sgurr na Lapaich and Mám Sodhail (1181m), and back west towards the pass that leads to Kintail. On a calm, clear day these are among the most beautiful mountain views in Scotland. The way ahead now descends to a bridge over the Allt Garbh (ignore paths to right and left here and keep straight ahead on the main track).

09 Where the road forks, go left through a gate and across a bridge over the Garbh Uisge (Gaelic for 'rough water'), the stretch of river that connects Loch Affric to its neighbour Loch Beinn a' Mheadhoin. From here it's a mere 50m uphill to the car park where you started. If you're still feeling energetic, a short (500m) hike up to the little hillock of **Am Meallan** (follow the white-waymarked trail opposite the car park entrance) provides a glorious view back up Glen Affric.

TAKE A BREAK

Cannich village is the nearest spot where you can find something to eat or drink; there are two cafes (one of them in the camping ground) and a small grocery store.

Seven miles further along the A831 road towards Beauly, in the heart of lovely Strathglass, the Victorian **Struy Inn** (☎ 01463-761308; www.thestruy.co.uk; Struy Village; mains £18-27; ☉5.30-9.30pm Wed-Sun Apr-Oct, Thu-Sat Nov-Mar; 🅿 🛜) is a haven of old-fashioned charm with a top-quality restaurant serving the finest Scottish cuisine; booking is essential.

49

STEALL WATERFALL

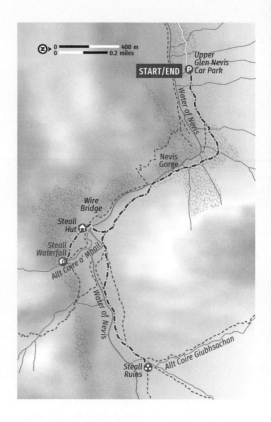

DURATION	DIFFICULTY	DISTANCE	START/END
2hr	Moderate	2.5 miles/4km	Upper Glen Nevis car park

TERRAIN	Rough, stony path, occasional steps

Set in the shadow of Ben Nevis, Britain's highest peak, this walk packs a huge variety of scenery into a relatively short route. The rocky slot cut through the hillside by the Water of Nevis has been likened to a miniature Himalayan gorge, while the spectacular 120m-high Steall Waterfall in the upper valley is the second highest in Britain, and has appeared as backdrop in a couple of Harry Potter films.

From the far end of the car park, follow the obvious path winding through the trees across the hillside high above the Water of Nevis. The woods thicken as the route bends to the right and enters the **Nevis Gorge**, a narrow rocky defile. The path winds among huge boulders, often on the edge of scary drops above the cascading river, eased here and there by steps and protected by wooden handrails.

Suddenly, you emerge from the gorge into a wide grassy amphitheatre. The broad, flat expanse of Steall Meadow offers a grand view ahead to the white bridal veil of **Steall Waterfall**, draped across the mountain slope. A short distance further on the path branches. Brave hikers can take the righthand branch and cross the river via the notorious **Wire Bridge** (one cable for your feet and one for each hand) then scramble up to the foot of the waterfall.

Alternatively, the lefthand branch leads easily along the wide valley floor to the **Steall ruins**, the remains of an 18th-century crofting settlement (an extra 1.4 miles/2.2km in total). Return by the same path.

50

STACKS OF DUNCANSBY

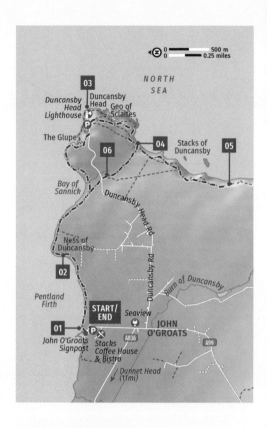

DURATION	DIFFICULTY	DISTANCE	START/END
2-3hr	Easy	5.5 miles/ 9km	John O'Groats car park
TERRAIN	Grassy footpaths, some wet spots		

Although John O'Groats gets all the attention for being the northernmost extreme of the British mainland, the sea cliffs of Duncansby Head, less than 2 miles to the east, beat it hands down for scenic splendour. A series of pyramidal rock pinnacles – the Stacks of Duncansby – lie just offshore, offering stunning coastal scenery and, in summer, the spectacle of thousands of nesting seabirds.

GETTING HERE

John O'Groats is 120 miles north of Inverness, a drive of just under three hours, and 20 miles east of Thurso. It's possible to take a bus from Inverness to Wick (three hours, five daily), from where you can get a bus to John O'Groats (30 minutes, four to five a day Monday to Saturday).

STARTING POINT

The huge car park at John O'Groats is often crowded with coach tours; try to get here early or late in the day to avoid the crowds. Facilities include public toilets, a tourist information office, cafes, snack bars and gift shops.

01 The famous **signpost** – the traditional end point for Land's End to John O'Groats journeys – overlooks the harbour behind the tourist information office. From here, descend the steps towards the harbour and continue past it. A pair of pointed stone slabs marks the start of the coastal path, which follows the turf just above the high water line.

02 An information board and a bench mark the **Ness of Duncansby**, a good place to pause and look out over the Pentland Firth, whose fierce tidal currents make it one of Britain's most dangerous stretches of water. The beaches on either side are

Dunnet Head

Eleven miles west of John O'Groats a minor road leads to dramatic Dunnet Head, the most northerly point on the British mainland. There are majestic cliffs dropping into the turbulent Pentland Firth, dramatic views of the Orkney Islands, and a lighthouse built by the grandfather of Robert Louis Stevenson (author of *Treasure Island* and *Kidnapped*). The headland is an RSPB reserve, and a short walk from the car park at the road end leads to a superb viewpoint above sea cliffs where thousands of seabirds nest in summer, including puffins, razorbills, guillemots, fulmars and kittiwakes.

Best for

COASTAL SCENERY

good places to search for 'groatie buckies', tiny white cowrie shells that were once used as a local currency. The way now runs along the dunes above the Bay of Sannick, crosses the burn at the far end, and climbs steeply up to pass the Glupe, a natural arch in the cliffs, before reaching a car park.

03 **Duncansby Head Lighthouse** (pictured) dates from 1924. A good path leads south from here over close-cropped grass, past the end of a deep ravine in the cliffs known as the Geo of Sclaites – in spring and early summer this area is alive with nesting seabirds.

04 As you descend to the lowest point of the clifftop, you get some good views of the sea stacks ahead, as well as the natural arch called Thirle Door.

05 Continue along the rising clifftops towards the **Hill of Crogodale**, where keen photographers will get the best views of the Stacks, looking back north along the coastline. Return to point 04 and take an occasionally boggy path that cuts left across country.

06 This path reaches the lighthouse road opposite a gate. From here you can take a

path bearing left across the field to rejoin the coastal path leading back to John O'Groats, or turn left and take the road back (half a mile longer).

TAKE A BREAK

There's excellent eating at **Stacks Coffee House & Bistro** (☏01955-611582; www.facebook.com/stacks bistro; mains £10-13; 🕙10am-4pm Tue-Sun), while the pub at the **Seaview** (☏01955-611220; www. seaviewjohnogroats.co.uk; County Rd; dm £25, pods £50, s/d £75/95; 🅿🛜), near the junction of the southbound and westbound roads, does simple bar meals and pizzas.

51

SANDWOOD BAY

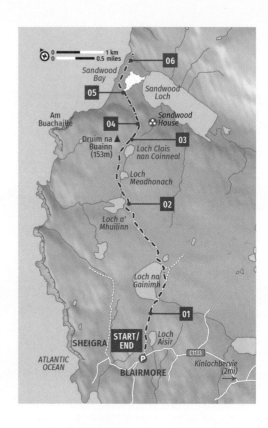

DURATION	DIFFICULTY	DISTANCE	START/END
4-5hr	Moderate	9 miles/ 14.5km	Blairmore car park

TERRAIN	Mostly firm path, wet patches

Scotland's coast is strewn with wild beaches, but few are as wild, or as remote, as Sandwood Bay. This walk follows a former peat track across bleak moorland, puddled with lochans, before arriving, almost unexpectedly, at this coastal jewel. Few people walk all the way to the beach's northern end, so if you've packed a picnic, that's the spot to aim for.

GETTING HERE

Kinlochbervie is a 95-mile (2½-hour) drive northwest of Inverness, or 250 miles (5½ hours) from Edinburgh or Glasgow. On Saturdays year-round, and Monday to Saturday in July and August, a minibus service (www.thedurnessbus.com) links Inverness to Kinlochbervie.

STARTING POINT

The car park at Blairmore is 3½ miles northwest of Kinlochbervie, and has toilets and a public telephone box. All the land that the walk crosses belongs to the John Muir Trust, a charity devoted to preserving wild land in Scotland.

01 From the east end of the car park, an unsealed road signposted to Sandwood forks left between two houses and passes through a gate. It leads across moorland along the shore of Loch na Gainimh; keep left as you round the loch and continue on the road, now heading north.

02 As you pass little **Loch a' Mhuilinn** the peat road deteriorates into a footpath, crossing the outflow from the loch via stepping stones. The way ahead now curves rightwards along the lower slopes of Druim na Buainn. There is no view of the sea yet – it is part of Sandwood's charm that there is

Cape Wrath Trail

This walk is part of a long-distance hiking route called the Cape Wrath Trail (www.capewrathtrail.org.uk), which runs from Fort William to the cape (200 miles). Unofficial and unwaymarked, it travels through some of the roughest and wildest terrain in Scotland and is considered to be the toughest and most challenging backpacking trail in all of Britain. Although going the full distance is for fit and experienced hikers only, there are many short sections like this that make for a good day walk. See *The Cape Wrath Trail* by Iain Harper (www.cicerone.co.uk) for more details.

JUSTINA SMILE/SHUTTERSTOCK ©

no hint of its existence until you are almost upon it.

03 Where the path passes between old wooden gateposts, freshwater Sandwood Loch comes into view ahead, and far to the north (in clear weather) you might be able to see Cape Wrath lighthouse poking above the skyline. To the right of the path lie the ruins of **Sandwood House**, built as a farmhouse in the second half of the 19th century.

04 The trail now dips into a small valley, affording the first glimpse of the beach at Sandwood Bay. Here, peat bog gives way to bright green machair. The final stretch leads down through grass-covered dunes to the beach.

05 Exit from the dunes into **Sandwood Bay** (pictured), a 2-mile-long sweep of pinkish sand bounded to the north by outcrops of Lewisian gneiss (at three billion years old, one of the oldest rocks in the world), and to the south by the 60m-tall sea stack of Am Buachaille (Gaelic for 'the herdsman').

06 Stroll along the sand to the north end of the beach, and find a way across the small river that flows out of Sandwood Loch. The ridge of rock that marks the end of the beach provides a grandstand view back across the bay to Am Buachaille. Return via the outward path.

TAKE A BREAK

The small fishing port of Kinlochbervie is the nearest place where you can get something to eat. **The Old School** (☏ 01971-521383; www.old schoolklb.co.uk; B801, Inshegra; dinner mains £10-16; ⊗ noon-2.30pm & 5-7pm Feb-Apr & Nov-Dec, 8am-9pm May-Oct; 🛜 🍴), 2 miles east of the village, has outdoor tables with views and serves local haddock and chips, plus salmon steaks, crab sandwiches and venison pie. There's also an inexpensive takeaway menu.

52

ARTHUR'S SEAT

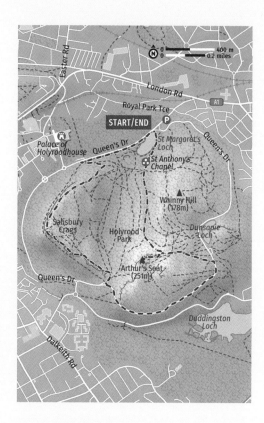

DURATION	DIFFICULTY	DISTANCE	START/END
2-3hr	Moderate	3.5 miles/ 5.7km	St Margaret's Loch

TERRAIN	Good paths, some steep sections

The rocky peak of Arthur's Seat (251m), carved by ice sheets from the deeply eroded stump of a long-extinct volcano, is a distinctive feature of Edinburgh's skyline. The view from the summit is well worth the climb, extending from the Forth Bridges in the west to the distant conical hill of North Berwick Law in the east, with the Ochil Hills and the Highlands on the northwestern horizon.

Begin at St Margaret's Loch – there's a convenient car park nearby, and buses stop on London Rd, a five-minute walk to the northeast. Take the path around the south side of the loch, slanting up towards the ruins of **St Anthony's Chapel**, then continue south on a rough path that follows the floor of a shallow dip before curving around to the left across the hillside and rising more steeply to a saddle; turn right here and follow the obvious path to the rocky summit of Arthur's Seat.

Descend eastwards all the way to the road (Queen's Dr) and follow it around to the right for 0.75 miles, with good views across the city to the Pentland Hills. Look out for an obvious path (opposite a litter bin) slanting back up rightwards towards the southern end of **Salisbury Crags**.

Head up this path past the rocky outcrops and, when you can, make your way up left via a path along the top of the crags (but not too near the edge!) with superb views across the city. At the far end, descend to the road near the Palace of Holyroodhouse and turn right to return to your starting point.

53

THE UATH LOCHANS

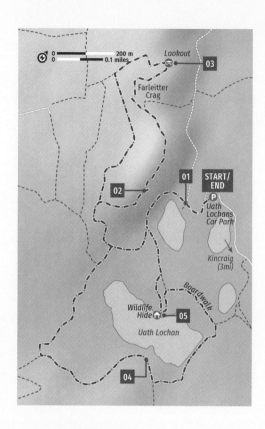

DURATION	DIFFICULTY	DISTANCE	START/END
2hr	Easy	4 miles/ 6.5km	Uath Lochans car park

TERRAIN	Forestry road, paths, boardwalks

Cairngorms National Park is the largest national park in the UK. The wild mountain landscape of granite and heather provides a challenge for experienced hillwalkers, but this short, low-level hike through some of the park's prettiest woodland offers an excellent introduction to the scenery of the Cairngorms.

GETTING HERE

The Uath Lochans are 10 miles southwest of Aviemore. Drive south on the B9152 to Kincraig and turn left (signposted Feshiebridge and Inshriach). After crossing a bridge over the River Spey and passing Loch Insh water sports centre, turn right on the B970 for half a mile and then left along a minor road (signposted Glenfeshie); the Uath Lochans car park is signposted on the right.

STARTING POINT

The Forestry Commission's Uath Lochans car park (free parking) has picnic tables and an information board. Two waymarked hiking trails start from here, one marked in red and one in white.

01 The walk sets out along a forest road that runs between a lochan and the steep, moss-draped rocks of Farleitter Crag. At the first junction (a red-waymarked trail on your right), keep straight on. Ignore the next two junctions (white-marked trails leading off to the left) and continue uphill on the red-marked trail.

02 Turn right opposite a green marker post and follow the red-marked trail as it winds up through forests of birch and Scots pine (look out for red squirrels!) to the crest of **Farleitter Crag**. A small clearing with a rock outcrop offers a gorgeous view (pictured) across the Uath Lochans

Legacy of the Ice Age

Cairngorms National Park is famous for its glacial landforms, a legacy of the last Ice Age. These include kettle hole lakes, of which the Uath Lochans are a prime example.

Around 15,000 years ago, the area around the Uath Lochans (Gaelic for 'small lakes of the hawthorn trees') lay at the foot of the huge Strathspey glacier. As the climate warmed and the glacier began to melt, four huge blocks of ice were left stranded in a plain of sand and gravel washed down by the meltwater from the glacier. When these blocks finally melted away they left oval-shaped hollows ('kettle holes') in the outwash plain that filled with water to form the four lochans.

DGDIMAGES/ALAMY STOCK PHOTO ©

to the humped, heather-clad hills of Sgòr Gaoith and Cárn Bán Mor.

03 The trail continues along the top of the crag to a wooden bench beside a large granite boulder, the highest point of the walk. The view here extends northeast across miles of uninterrupted forest to the hill of Meall a' Bhuachaille, not far from Aviemore. As the path heads downhill from here, go left at the first junction to regain your outward path at the green post. At the next junction, turn right on the white-marked trail which leads to a gravel road. Turn left here and follow the road.

04 About 100m after passing a wooden bench with a view across the lochan, turn left between two large rocks and follow the path along the lake shore. Soon a **boardwalk** leads across open bog – wildlife to look out for here includes frogs, damselflies, and the rare northern emerald dragonfly. As you head back into the woods, turn left at the white marker post.

05 The path leads to a wildlife hide on the north shore of **Uath Lochan**. Goldeneye ducks and greylag geese nest here in spring and early summer, while in October and November the trees put on a spectacular display of autumn colours. Follow the path leading directly away from the lochan to rejoin the white-marked trail and return to the car park.

 **TAKE A BREAK**

The nearest places to eat include the cafe at **Loch Insh Outdoor Centre** (01540-651272; www.lochinsh.com; Kincraig; day ticket incl all activities adult/child £35/25; 8.30am-5.30pm;), and the delightful **Old Post Office Cafe** (01540-651779; www.facebook.com/kincraigartcafe; The Brae, Kincraig; mains £5-11; 9.30am-5pm Mon-Sat, 10.30am-5pm Sun, closed Wed Apr-Sep, closed Mon & Tue Oct-Mar; P   ).

54

THE QUIRAING

Best for

WILD VIEWS

DURATION	DIFFICULTY	DISTANCE	START/END
2-3hr	Hard	4 miles/ 6.5km	Uig–Staffin road

TERRAIN	Rough paths, some steep ground

The spectacular cliffs and pinnacles of the Quiraing are a compact and easily explored example of the dramatic landscape features that make Trotternish – the Isle of Skye's northern peninsula – unique. Rough hill paths give access to the summit plateau of Meall na Suiramach (543m), with fine views of the surrounding islands, the Applecross hills on the mainland and the towering cliffs of the Trotternish escarpment itself, before returning through the heart of the Quiraing.

GETTING HERE

A narrow singletrack road cuts across the northern part of the Trotternish peninsula, connecting the ferry port of Uig on the west side with the village of Staffin on the east. The walk starts at a parking area at the highest point of this road (not suitable for caravans or large vehicles), 1.8 miles west of its junction with the A855 at Brogaig, which is about 1 mile northwest of the straggling village of Staffin. There is no public transport – the nearest you can get by bus is Staffin.

STARTING POINT

The unofficial parking area at the start of the walk is uneven and unsurfaced, with no facilities except a snack bar that sets up here in July and August. It's best to plan your walk for early or late in the day, or in spring or autumn, as the parking area can get very busy from mid-morning to late afternoon during the summer.

01 Set out along a well-worn path on the north side of the road, signposted to Flodigarry. (Flodigarry, a tiny hamlet with a hotel and a youth hostel, is an alternative starting point for a hike to the Quiraing.) Follow this path for 200m to where it crosses a stream, then strike uphill in a northerly direction across heathery slopes (there is a faint but muddy and meandering path) to a grassy stone wall. As you gain height the views open up eastwards to the island of Raasay and the mainland mountains of Applecross, Torridon and Fisherfield.

02 Follow the stone wall rightwards (northeast) for a few hundred metres until it disappears, then zigzag up the steep slope (again, there is only a faint path here) to find a much clearer trail leading northeast

across the hillside. Wet in places, it leads into a wide, shallow and grassy depression in the hillside. You are now climbing onto the **Trotternish Ridge**, a designated Site of Special Scientific Interest for its unusual geology and rare, nonvascular plants known as bryophytes. The ridge has the longest continuous cliff line in Britain, and offers a challenging 23-mile hike from Flodigarry to Torvaig, just north of Portree.

03 Go through a gate in the fence here and continue northeast up the slope. About 400m further on, the path swings north to parallel the cliff edge, offering stupendous views

across the jumbled pinnacles of the Quiraing. The rocks of the Trotternish peninsula consist mainly of basalt lavas that were erupted 50 to 60 million years ago as the Atlantic Ocean began to open up. The horizontal lava flows were cut into by the glaciers of the last Ice Age, and when the glaciers melted the now-unsupported edges of the glacial valleys began to slump and slide, causing the distinctive, landslip-block landscape of northern Skye. The village of Staffin down below takes its name from the characteristic columnar form of the lava cliffs along the coast (from the Old Norse meaning 'pillar').

Skye Dinosaurs

The occasional dinosaur bone has been turning up in the Jurassic rocks of the Trotternish peninsula since 1982. More recently following a storm in 2002, a set of fossilised dinosaur footprints was exposed in Staffin Bay. Their interest piqued, geologists began taking a closer interest in the Trotternish rocks and, in 2015, a major discovery was made near Duntulm Castle – a 170-million-year-old trackway of footprints left by a group of sauropods. Skye is now a major focus for research into dinosaur evolution. It's an easy walk to the footprints in Staffin Bay – for more info visit the nearby **Staffin Dinosaur Museum** (www. staffindinosaurmuseum.com; 3 Ellishadder, Staffin; adult/child £2/1; ⊙9.30am-5pm; P).

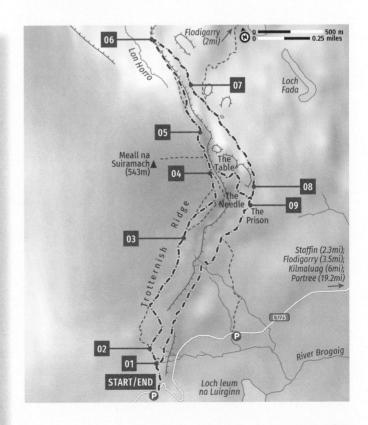

04 As you follow the edge of the cliffs northward there's a fantastic view down into the heart of the Quiraing (an old Gaelic/Norse name meaning 'round enclosure'). A series of flat-topped grassy plateaus lies between the cliffs and a row of massive basalt bluffs and pinnacles. The largest of these plateaus is an uncannily smooth grass-topped block called the Table, which can only be reached from below (described later under stop number 8).

05 Continue past a cairn (not a summit – the true summit of Meall na Suiramach, marked by a trig point, is 400m to the west) with fine views north across the Minch to the distant hills of the Outer Hebrides. Keeping close to the edge, start to descend more steeply (400m beyond the cairn) and you'll soon reach another large **cairn**. A clear path descends north from here near the edge of the outer cliff line on your right, down to a small saddle and a break in the cliffs.

06 Climb over a stile and go down a steep, deeply eroded zigzag path into a green valley with the dramatic, jagged pinnacles of Fir Bhreugach rising to the north. You now begin the passage back south through the **Quiraing** itself. The trail leads through chaotic, hummocky terrain with towering black cliffs on the one hand and a jumble of crags and pinnacles on the other.

07 As you cross a stone wall, suddenly there's wide open space and a steep, airy drop on your left! After a short descent, the path from Flodigarry joins from the left, and soon there's easier going as the path leads along a valley, past a small lochan and up to a little saddle, where the path squeezes beneath the highest part of the cliffs. Here, flat-topped **Dun Caan** on Raasay off to your left and the Trotternish ridge ahead come into view. (Dun Caan is itself a superb viewpoint, and makes a great walk from the ferry pier on Raasay; 10 miles, allow five to six hours.)

08 Cross another fence at a stile and descend steeply into the heart of the Quiraing. To your left is **the Prison**, a jumble of towers, blocks and pinnacles. High up to the right is **the Needle** (pictured), a huge, lopsided pinnacle. The adventurous (and sure-footed) can scramble up to the left of the Needle, and continue rightwards through a narrow slot in the cliffs to find the hidden, grass-topped plateau known as **the Table**. Legend has it that stolen cattle were once hidden here, and a shinty match was played on the level turf to celebrate the end of WWI. Retrace your steps to the main path.

09 Pass a large cairn and make your way carefully down a scree slope and through a jumble of boulders. From here on, the well-used path contours across the steep slope, winding up and down and in and out of a series of gullies for a mile or so. Some of these are wet and rocky, and can be awkward to cross – take your time and be careful.

Trotternish Walks

The Trotternish peninsula has many excellent short walks. The 50m-high, basalt pinnacle known as the **Old Man of Storr** is prominent above the road 6 miles north of Portree. Walk up to its foot from the car park at the northern end of Loch Leathan (a 2-mile round trip). Just south of the ferry port of Uig, a minor road (signposted 'Sheader and Balnaknock') leads a mile or so to the **Fairy Glen**, a strange and enchanting landscape of miniature conical hills and rocky towers. And from the red telephone box 800m east of Duntulm Castle, a path leads north for 1.5 miles to **Rubha Hunish coastguard lookout**, now restored as a tiny bothy overlooking the northernmost point of Skye.

TAKE A BREAK

Five miles north of Staffin, the turf-roofed, timber-clad art gallery and espresso bar **Single Track** (www. facebook.com/singletrackskye; Kilmaluag; snacks £3-4; ⏰10.30am-5pm Sun-Thu mid-May–late Oct; P 📶) has been featured on British TV's *Grand Designs*. The coffee is seriously good, as are the accompanying cakes and scones. Art by the owners and other Skye artists is on display, and for sale. Portree, 17 miles south of Staffin, has a good range of cafes, including the **Isle of Skye Baking Co** (www.isleofskyebakingco. co.uk; Old Woollen Mill, Dunvegan Rd; mains £4-9; ⏰10am-5pm Mon-Sat; P 👶).

Also Try...

APOSTOLIS GIONTZIS/SHUTTERSTOCK ©

THE HERMITAGE

Set on the banks of the River Tay, Dunkeld is one of Scotland's prettiest villages. As well as its ancient cathedral, there's much walking to be done in this area of magnificent forested hills.

One of the most popular walks is the Hermitage, where a well-marked trail follows the River Braan upstream through a forest of giant Douglas fir trees to Ossian's Hall, a quaint folly built by the Duke of Atholl in 1758. It overlooks the spectacular Black Linn waterfall where you can see salmon leaping, especially in September and October. The walk begins from the National Trust for Scotland's Hermitage car park, signposted off the A9 just west of the village. You can extend the walk to more waterfalls at Rumbling Bridge (total 3 miles round trip).

DURATION 1hr
DIFFICULTY Easy
DISTANCE 1 mile/1.6km

BEN NEVIS

As the highest peak in the British Isles, Ben Nevis (1345m; pictured) attracts many would-be summiteers who would not normally think of climbing a Scottish mountain.

A staggering (often literally) 100,000 people try to reach the top each year. Although anyone who is reasonably fit should have no problem climbing Ben Nevis on a fine summer's day, an ascent should not be undertaken lightly; every year people have to be rescued from the mountain. You will need proper walking boots (the path is rough and stony, and there may be snow on the summit), warm clothing, waterproofs, a map and compass, and plenty of food and water. And don't forget to check the weather forecast (www.bennevisweather.co.uk). Start and finish at Glen Nevis Visitor Centre.

DURATION 8hr
DIFFICULTY Challenging
DISTANCE 8 miles/13km

LOCH CLAIR

Set in the heart of the Torridon hills, this walk leads to one of the classic Scottish mountain views.

Beginning from a parking area on the A896 (signposted Public Footpath to Glen Carron by the Coulin Pass), a 4WD track leads south along the eastern shore of Loch Clair, where – if the weather is kind – you will see the picture-postcard view of Liathach reflected in the waters of the loch. The track continues to Coulin Lodge, allowing you to make a circuit of Loch Coulin, with stunning views of Beinn Eighe.

DURATION 3hr
DIFFICULTY Easy
DISTANCE 5.5 miles/9km

BEN LOMOND

Ben Lomond (974m), Scotland's most southerly Munro, is one of the country's most popular climbs.

Most hikers follow the Tourist Route up and down from Rowardennan car park; it's a straightforward ascent on a well-used and maintained path. The Ptarmigan Route is less crowded and has better views, following a narrow but clearly defined path up the western flank, directly overlooking the loch, to a curving ridge leading to the summit. You can then descend via the Tourist Route.

DURATION 5hr
DIFFICULTY Challenging
DISTANCE 7 miles/11km

GLENFINNAN VIADUCT TRAIL

Glenfinnan is hallowed ground for fans of Bonnie Prince Charlie.

The monument here marks where he raised his Highland army. It's also a place of pilgrimage for steam train enthusiasts and Harry Potter fans – the famous railway viaduct (pictured) features in the Potter films, and is regularly traversed by the Jacobite Steam Train. A pleasant and easy walk of around 0.75 miles east from Glenfinnan train station (signposted) leads to a viewpoint for the viaduct and for Loch Shiel.

DURATION 1hr
DIFFICULTY Easy
DISTANCE 1.5 miles/2.5km

WALES

Explore
WALES

Rolling hills, wild mountains, windswept clifftops and green, green valleys – few corners of Britain can match Wales in terms of walking scenery. The three national parks are the main draw for walkers: in the southeast, the Brecon Beacons are all about stark, sheep-grazed hills; in the west, the Pembrokeshire Coast boasts Wales' most stirring clifftop views; and way up north, the snow-dusted mountains of Snowdonia are home to the most challenging peaks. But wherever you are, Wales is a walkers' paradise, with big-sky scenery that never fails to inspire. Just don't expect to get away without some wet weather – there's a reason those hills and valleys stay so green, you know.

CARDIFF

Wales' capital since 1955, Cardiff is also its most dynamic city. It brims with bistros, bars and boutique B&Bs, and makes an excellent base for day trips to the surrounding valleys and coast, where you'll find castles, beaches, interesting industrial sites and ancient monuments. The Brecon Beacons are just over an hour's drive north.

SWANSEA

Wales' second city has long lagged behind the capital Cardiff in terms of culture, clout and style, but the drab post-war centre is gradually undergoing regeneration more suited to its setting on the 5-mile sweep of Swansea Bay. It has a good range of hotels, B&Bs and restaurants, especially around The Mumbles. It's well placed for the Gower Peninsula and the southern Welsh coast, and is within an hour's drive of the Brecon Beacons.

LLANGOLLEN

Set on the tumbling River Dee (Afon Dyfrdwy), pretty little Llangollen (khlan-*goth*-len) makes a logical launchpad for jaunts into Snowdonia – it's about an hour's drive west of the main hiking base of Betws-y-Coed. It has some decidedly upper-scale guesthouses, as well as hostels and B&Bs for those on a budget.

Book well ahead during the International Eisteddfod in July.

ST DAVIDS

Britain's smallest city is best known for its 12th-century cathedral, devoted to Wales' patron saint. It's perfectly positioned for exploring the Pembrokeshire Coast. The city centre has a range of B&Bs, pub accommodation and boutique hotels, and there are some good campsites and a hostel nearby.

BETWYS-Y-COED

Betws-y-Coed (*bet*-us-ee-*coyd*) sits at the junction of three river valleys (the Llugwy, the Conwy and the Lledr) and on the verge

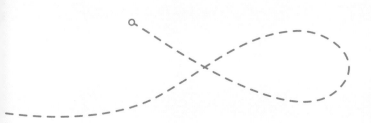

Resources

www.walking.visitwales.com
Useful first-stop site with hiking suggestions across Wales.

www.breconbeacons. org/walking Hiking advice for the Brecons.

www.snowdonia.gov.wales/ visiting/walking Good range of walks for all abilities.

of the Gwydyr Forest. With outdoor-gear shops appearing to outnumber pubs, walking trails leaving right from the centre and guesthouses occupying a fair proportion of its slate Victorian buildings, it's the perfect base for exploring Snowdonia.

WHEN TO GO

The Welsh weather is nothing if not unpredictable: it's not unusual to get a dose of all four seasons, even in summer. Good waterproof gear is essential at all times of year. Summer and Easter can be busy in many areas, especially during school holidays, and many popular trails such as Snowdon and Pen y Fan can be uncomfortably crowded. It's definitely worth saving these for shoulder seasons, outside the school holidays, half-terms and summer weekends – early spring and late autumn are the ideal times.

Snow usually descends on the hills and peaks of the Brecon Beacons and Snowdonia by November, and lingers well into April, occasionally even longer. Welsh winters can be very severe, with sub-zero temper-atures, fierce winds and heavy rainfall or snowfall lasting several months. Only the hardiest hikers tramp the hills at these times.

TRANSPORT

Bus is by far the most useful form of public transport, with routes connecting most towns and villages (although many services don't run on Sunday). Services such as the Snowdon Sherpa bus are very useful for hikers – this network of five bus lines links trailheads and principal towns in the Snowdon area. The rail network isn't extensive, but is handy for towns connected to it. As always, driving allows you to access the more remote corners.

For up-to-date information and a journey planner, visit **Traveline Cymru** (📞0300 200 22 33; www.traveline-cymru.org.uk).

WHERE TO STAY

Wales has a wide range of accommodation, from basic bunk-barns and campsites to farmhouse B&Bs, country inns and swanky hotels. Hostels (both YHA-affiliated and independent) can be very useful for walkers; some are located in seriously remote areas that allow you to explore the Welsh wilderness in all its green glory.

Country pubs are often a good fallback bet: nearly every village has one, and most have a couple of rooms available for overnight stays.

WHAT'S ON

Hay Festival (www.hayfestival.com; 🕐May & Jun) Lively festival of literature and the arts.

International Musical Eisteddfod (www.international-eisteddfod. co.uk; day/festival ticket £12/230; 🕐Jul) Llangollen's annual cultural party.

National Eisteddfod (www.eisteddfod.cymru; 🕐Aug) Wales' biggest celebration of music and culture.

Brecon Fringe Festival (www.brecon fringe.co.uk; 🕐Aug) Live music in pubs around Brecon.

Abergavenny Food Festival (www. abergavennyfoodfestival.co.uk; 🕐mid-Sep) The mother of Welsh food fests.

55

TINTERN ABBEY & DEVIL'S PULPIT

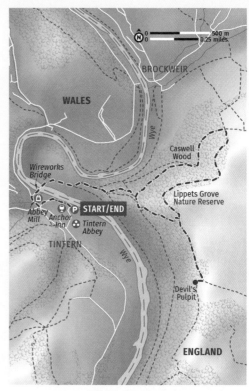

DURATION	DIFFICULTY	DISTANCE	START/END
2hr	Easy	4 miles/6.5km	Tintern Abbey car park

TERRAIN	Riverside and woodland

Popular since the days of the Romantic poets, this short walk takes in a stretch of the River Wye, an area of lovely Welsh woodland and a famous viewpoint over the dramatic ruins of Tintern Abbey.

William Wordsworth penned a famous ode to **Tintern Abbey** (Cadw; www.cadw.gov.wales; Tintern; adult/child £6.90/4.10; ⏱9.30am-5pm Mar-Jun, Sep & Oct, to 6pm Jul & Aug, 10am-4pm Mon-Sat, 11am-4pm Sun Nov-Feb; P), torn down during the dissolution under Henry VIII. It's remained a romantic ruin ever since, picturesquely framed against the River Wye. Park in the car park next to the abbey, then walk along the river past the Anchor Inn, then along the road to Abbey Mill. Cross over the Wireworks Bridge behind the mill; congratulations, you're now in England.

Walk up towards the trees, following signs to Devil's Pulpit, climbing through glorious groves of oak, beech and ash (the walk's particularly photogenic in autumn). Keep following signs; eventually you'll reach a fork onto **Offa's Dyke**. Turn right to reach the **Devil's Pulpit**, a rocky outcrop with a grandstand view over Tintern Abbey and the Wye (legend has it the devil preached here to try and tempt the monks from their faith). Just behind the pulpit, steps lead down to a clearing where a yew tree has sprouted from a rock – all very pagan.

On the return leg, retrace your steps to the fork, but this time stay on Offa's Dyke north into **Caswell Wood**, past Lippets Grove Nature Reserve (a haven for the endangered dormouse). Past the gate for Beeches Farm, turn left downhill through the woods, over the Wireworks Bridge and into Tintern.

56

ST DAVIDS HEAD

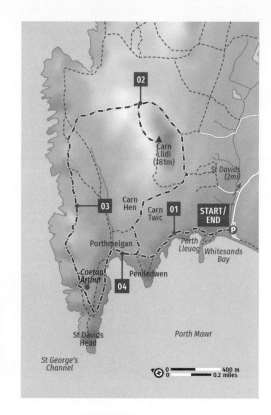

A short coastal walk that encapsulates all that's special about the Pembrokeshire Coast: wild seas, craggy cliffs, booming surf and widescreen skies.

DURATION	DIFFICULTY	DISTANCE	START/END
1½ -2hr	Easy	3.8 miles/6km	Whitesands Bay

TERRAIN	Grassy cliffs with some rocks

GETTING HERE

Whitesands Bay is 2 miles northwest of St Davids. From 25 March to 25 September the Celtic Coaster bus circles between St Davids, St Non's Bay, St Justinian and Whitesands. For destinations further afield, up to nine 411 buses per day go to/from Solva, Newgale and Haverfordwest. Public transport is limited, especially on Sunday and in winter.

STARTING POINT

The large public car park at Whitesands Bay is a dramatic spot, with wild views of the rolling sea and sandy beach.

01 This walk doesn't cover a great amount of distance, but it really excels in terms of coastal views. If you have the energy, it's definitely worth hiking to the rocky top of **Carn Llidi**, the looming hill to the northeast of the beach. From the Whitesands Bay car park, head north along the coast on an easy-to-follow clifftop trail. You'll pass the cove of Porth Lleuog, then the small headland of Penlledwen. Here you want to turn right off the coast path, climbing up between the small hillocks of Carn Hen and Carn Twic. When you reach a drystone wall, follow it round as it turns southeast, then skirts the southern edge of Carn Llidi.

02 The Ordnance Survey map indicates a trail leading to the summit of Carn Llidi here. You can follow this path if you wish, but it's actually easier to climb the east side. Continue to follow the wall round; on the hill's east side, a side-track leads

Old Time Rock

The rocks around St Davids Head are some of the oldest in Britain, dating back to the Pre-Cambrian era, a mind-boggling 600 million years ago. These layers of rock were originally formed by layers of sediment created by ancient volcanoes – once upon a time, the whole landscape here would have been covered in liquid magma.

CHRISTOPHER NICHOLSON/ALAMY STOCK PHOTO ©

away from the wall, then turns west, and continues up the rocky **east flank** of the carn. It's a fantastic 360-degree view at the top, stretching right over Whitesands Bay to Ramsey island, south over St Davids and east towards the pyramidal peaks of Carn Pefedd and Carn Penberry in the far distance.

03 Backtrack down the path, and follow it northwest until it joins up with the coast path. The trail heads up and around the downs, bearing southwest all the way to St Davids Head. Nearby is an impressive, partially collapsed Neolithic dolmen called **Coetan Arthur**, or Arthur's Quoit; the capstone measures a mighty 6m by 2.5m. The monument is believed to date from around 4000 BC, and was probably a burial chamber. There are also the remains of an Iron Age hill fort from around 2000 BC near the point. If you look carefully, you can just about make out where the defensive ramparts would once have stood.

04 From St Davids Head, the trail continues south along the coast path past the little cove of **Porthmelgan**, then returns to Whitesands Bay car park.

TAKE A BREAK

St Davids has plenty of options for lunch. For something quick, you can't beat an oggie from **Original St Davids Oggie** (☎ 01437-720632; www. facebook.com/stdavidsoggies; 15 High St; oggies £3-5; ☺ 9am-5.30pm) – a pastry-wrapped parcel similar to a Cornish pasty.

57

THE FOUR FALLS WALK

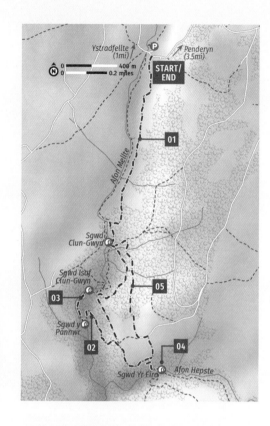

DURATION	DIFFICULTY	DISTANCE	START/END
2-3hr	Moderate	4 miles/ 6.5km	Cwm Porth car park

TERRAIN	Forest trail with rocky steps

The Brecon Beacons aren't all about hills, you know. This is also waterfall country, and this well-trodden path takes in four of the very finest, along with some of the best-preserved areas of woodland in southeast Wales.

GETTING HERE

The falls are near the village of Ystradfellte, about 13 miles from Merthyr Tydfil. There is no useful public transport.

STARTING POINT

There is a small visitor centre and car park at Cwm Porth, where you can pick up trail maps and souvenirs. The car park costs £7 per day.

01 The **Four Falls Trail** explores a series of cascades created where the Rivers Mellte,

Hepste and Pyrddin pass through steep, wooded gorges. It's a Tolkienesque landscape that would feel right at home to the Elves and Ents – it's also popular, so it's probably best avoided in high summer. It's a good option for a rainy day, when the waterfalls really thunder. The path is well maintained, but it traverses several steep, stepped sections, which are rocky and rooty, and can be extremely slippery when wet. Wear good waterproof boots, and perhaps bring walking poles as a back-up. Avoid stepping on tree roots.

Park up at Cwm Porth car park (there's a back-up car park nearby at Gwaun Hepste if it's full). Take the trail across the road, and follow the lane south along a drystone wall. After just over a kilometre, you'll enter the woods, and soon a short side-path descends to the first waterfall: **Sgwd Clun-Gwyn** (Fall of the White Meadow), tumbling over a ridge into the valley below.

DAVIDALTONPHOTOGRAPHY.COM/ALAMY STOCK PHOTO ©

Fforest Fawr Geopark

Established in 2005, the Fforest Fawr ('Great Forest' in English) covers more than 300 square miles of upland in the heart of Brecon Beacons National Park. The varied habitat includes mountain, moorland, lakes, rivers and some of the oldest forests in southeast Wales. Find out more at www.fforestfawr geopark.org.uk.

02 A precarious path leads along the edge of the gorge to the next fall, but it's extremely exposed – we really don't recommend it. It's much safer to rejoin the main trail, and follow it south. The path zigzags under overhanging oak trees covered with moss. After another kilometre or so, you'll reach a right-hand turn down to the next two waterfalls. The path gets very rocky here, so watch your step. First comes **Sgwd y Pannwr** (Fall of the Cloth Washer), a low, wide waterfall tumbling over a rock shelf. Presumably, this was where local people once came to wash their togs.

03 From here, a boardwalk leads along the boggy banks to **Sgwd Isaf Clun-Gwyn** (Fall of the Lower White Meadow), a multi-levelled fall crashing over a series of rock terraces.

04 Retrace your steps back to Sgwd y Pannwr, then back up the steep path to the main trail. From here, the path winds south around a bend in the river, then down a stone staircase to the final and most impressive waterfall of all: **Sgwd Yr Eira** (Fall of the Snow; pictured), framed at the end of a lichen-cloaked gorge. Excitingly, a hidden path leads right behind the waterfall – but be prepared to get wet. Very wet.

05 Head back up the staircase, then follow the main trail north out of the forest and back to Cwm Porth, following the same trail you took in – an easy, level stroll of about 1.7 miles.

☕ TAKE A BREAK

The **Red Lion** (☎01685-811914; www. redlionpenderyn.com) in Penderyn, 4 miles south of Cwm Porth, serves decent pub grub, while for a quick snack, **Laura's Diner** (☎07807 726326; ⊙10am-4pm Mon, Tue & Thu-Sun) is a popular food van serving both meat and vegan options from a layby on the A4059, next to the turn-off to Ystradfellte.

58

RHOSSILI BAY

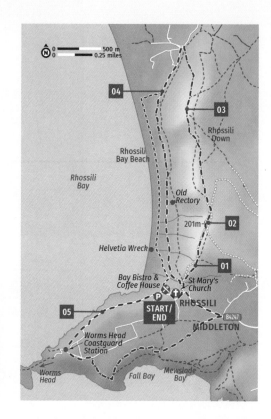

DURATION	DIFFICULTY	DISTANCE	START/END
2½-3hr	Moderate	6.5 miles/ 10.5km	Rhossili visitor centre
TERRAIN	Grass downs and beach		

Pembrokehire is home to some fabulous beaches, but there aren't very many that can match the golden sweep of Rhossili, a shining, sandy crescent backed by a steep heather-covered hill dotted with Neolithic remains.

GETTING HERE

Rhossili is 19 miles west of Swansea. The 118/119 bus (one to 1¼ hours, up to 11 daily) runs regularly, stopping at Parkmill and Port Eynon on the way.

STARTING POINT

There's a National Trust **visitor centre** (☎ 01792-390707; www.nationaltrust.org.uk/gower; Coastguard Cottages; ⏰ 10.30am-4.30pm) and car park above the beach. Members park for free.

01 This loop around Rhossili is best done on a clear, blue-sky day, when the coastal views shine – the beach gets busy in summer, so consider hiking it in early autumn for the heather, or on a moody winter's day. The walk begins with a steep slog on the southern side of Rhossili Down. Walk along the main road; just past the church, turn onto a minor road, follow the path into the fields and take the well-defined path up the hillside through bracken and ferns (it can be quite boggy after heavy rain, so wear good boots).

02 After the stiff climb, you'll top out on **Rhossili Down**. A path leads along the ridge, passing rocky cairns littered with Neolithic remains, most probably burial sites. From the top of the down, you'll have a widescreen view right along the Pembrokeshire Coast. In late summer and autumn, the top of the down is ablaze with heather.

Worms Head

The unmistakeable, serpent-like profile of Worms Head (pictured) is one of the most distinctive sights on the Pembrokeshire Coast. The mile-long headland gets its name from the Old English word *wurm*, meaning dragon or serpent, and it does indeed look uncannily like a sea monster emerging from the ocean. It's possible to cross over to the island for 2½ hours either side of low tide; crossing and return times are posted at the visitor centre and the coastguard lookout station, but keep a close eye on your watch and make sure you factor in ample time for the return walk.

Best for

COASTAL SCENERY

03 Continue along the ridge, passing more rocky cairns along the way; you might spy wild Welsh ponies up here too. Eventually the path leads down the north flank of the down; watch your footing on the way down, as the slope is quite steep. When you reach the caravan park at the bottom, turn left, heading downhill towards the beach.

04 You've got a choice for the next stage. One path leads through the grassy bluffs above the beach, past the whitewashed old rectory that stands in glorious isolation above the sands. Alternatively, you can head down onto the beach itself, take off your boots and feel the sand between your toes. At low tide the stark, ghostly ribs of the *Helvetia*, a Norwegian barque wrecked in a storm in 1887, protrude from the sand. Whichever path you choose, the walking is easy; after half an hour or so you'll reach the incline up to Rhossili car park.

05 The final section loops west around the point to a coastguard lookout station overlooking Worms Head. You can stop in at the station, chat to the coastguards there and maybe pick up a souvenir fridge magnet. From here, a clear path circles round the coast, tracking above Fall Bay and Mewslade Bay before leading back across the fields to the NT visitor centre and car park.

 ### TAKE A BREAK

Bay Bistro & Coffee House (☏01792-390519; www.thebaybistro.co.uk; mains £6-12; ⏰10am-5pm daily plus 6.30-9pm Thu-Sun in high season; 🍴) has by far and away the best beach view, and serves a light menu of baguettes, paninis and cakes, plus more substantial salads and burgers. Big picture windows frame the view, and if it's sunny, there are outside tables too. On summer evenings it opens for alfresco meals.

59

PEN Y FAN, CORN DU & CRIBYN

DURATION	DIFFICULTY	DISTANCE	START/END
4hr	Moderate	8.2 miles/ 13.2km	Neuadd car park

TERRAIN	Rocky mountain, exposed edges

At 886m above sea level, Pen y Fan is southern Wales' highest mountain – which means *everyone* wants to climb it. Tackle it from the less-trodden southern side to avoid most of the crowds.

GETTING HERE

There is no public transport to the Neuadd reservoirs, so you'll either need your own car to get here, or potentially hire a bike. Merthyr Tydfil is 9 miles to the south, accessed by winding minor roads.

STARTING POINT

The Neuadd car park usually has plenty of spaces, but can get full at particularly busy times. There's an alternative car park at Pont Cwmfedwen about half a mile south.

01 The most popular route up Pen y Fan (pronounced *van*, not *fan*) is an up-and-down slog from the Storey Arms outdoor centre. But it's both busy (locals refer to it as 'the motorway') and a little boring; on a summer weekend you'll be sharing it with hundreds of other walkers. As such, this is definitely a spring or autumn walk, especially since route-finding can be tricky in bad weather. Make no mistake: despite its popularity, this is a proper mountain walk, so pack appropriately.

Our favourite route climbs up from the valley to the south, and factors in two other summits – a boon for peak-baggers. The route begins at the car park near the Upper Neuadd Reservoir. Take the trail up through the woods and into the wide, grassy valley, where you'll have a clear view up to the ridge – it looks formidable from this angle, but it's more straightforward than you might initially think.

02 The trail climbs gently for a while, then abruptly switchbacks up the west slope: leg-testingly steep, but mercifully short. You should reach the ridge in under half an hour. From here, the trail leads north along the ridgeline, with increasingly airy drops on the right. If it's sunny, you'll have a clear perspective on Corn Du and Pen y Fan; if not, they'll probably be obscured by cloud.

03 Follow the ridge onwards, drinking in the wonderful views. The ridge ascent is surprisingly gentle, so you'll barely even notice you're climbing. After about an hour, you'll reach the hill of **Craig-Gwaun-Taf**, from where you should see the side-by-side summits of Corn Du (on the left) and the flat table of Pen y Fan (on the right).

04 Bear right along the **Corn Du** (left-hand) trail. The summit of 'The Black Horn' is reached at 873m. From here, you can follow the rocky ridgeline along to **Pen y Fan** at 886m. In good weather the views are glorious: north across green valleys, south across the reservoirs. Unfortunately, you're extremely unlikely to have the summits to yourself – the crowds can be overwhelming on summer weekends – which is why this walk is best reserved for quieter times of year. The name of Pen y Fan roughly translates as 'top of the mountain', and there's no doubting that this is a truly sky-topping view: no other mountain in the Brecon Beacons commands such an eagle's-eye perspective. When the weather is clear, you can see all the way to the coast, including the Bristol Channel, Carmarthen Bay, Swansea Bay and the Gower Peninsula; the Black Mountains extend to the northeast, the Preseli Hills far off to the west. It also gives you a great perspective on the glacial landscape of this part of the Brecon Beacons; even to

The Neuadd Reservoirs

Since the late 19th century, the Upper and Lower Neuadd Reservoirs provided water for the residents of nearby Methyr Tydfil (and a popular location for photographers; the Victorian dam is a Grade II–listed monument). However, the reservoirs have recently been drained with a long-term aim to rewild the valley and restore the original river course; you may still see earthworks in progress.

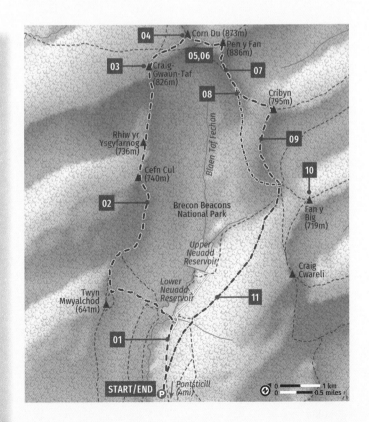

non-geologists, it's fairly obvious how the massive glaciers must have sculpted the dramatic array of ridges, slopes, cwms and corries.

05 Don't be surprised if you feel a little tired by the time you reach the **summit**. The mountain is used by the army as part of the gruelling selection process for the SAS. To candidates the ordeal is known, with characteristically grim squaddie humour, as the 'Fan Dance'; it involves hiking 15 miles loaded down with 25kg of kit and a 4.5kg rifle. To pass, the march must be completed in under four hours in favourable weather conditions, making it much closer to a run than a hike. Various trail-running events are held throughout the year that seek to emulate the ordeal for average walkers.

06 Both the Corn Du and Pen y Fan summits also mark the sites of **Bronze Age cairns**, centring on a central stone cist that would once have been used as a burial tomb. It would probably also have contained burial goods such as pottery, tools and funerary herbs or flowers. It's worth spending some time at the summit: peregrine falcons, buzzards and red kites can often be seen surfing the updrafts. Unfortunately, even when the surrounding valleys seem still, the top of Pen y Fan is usually extremely windy – sometimes brutally so. As such, it's not always that pleasant a place to sit down and ponder the landscape, but if you happen to be up here on that rare no-wind

ATTILIO PREGNOLATO/SHUTTERSTOCK ©

day, make the most of it, and consider yourself extremely fortunate indeed.

07 Snap the obligatory selfie next to the summit cairn, then continue east down a steep path that leads into the gully below Cribyn. The approach down into the gully, with a steep drop on your left and a clear view along the sharp, crescent-shaped **escarpment**, is arguably one of the most dramatic anywhere in Wales. Slate stones have been embedded into the hillside to make the descent easier, but take care, as these can ironically be even slippier in the wet. Try to stick to the main trail as much as you can: the pressure of all those feet has led to the development of multiple braided paths,

exacerbating erosion of the peat surface. Every year, National Trust rangers and teams of volunteers spend countless hours repairing the degraded trails around the Pen y Fan massif, so try and do your best not to give them more work than they already have.

08 Once you've reached the gully, an exit trail turns right (south) along the valley here; if you're too tired to face a third summit of the day (particularly given that it's the steepest climb of them all), then you can follow this trail all the way back down to the reservoirs. However, if you still have the legs, it's absolutely worth climbing the steep slope to **Cribyn**. A well-maintained stone staircase

 The Beacons Way

The ridge route between Corn Du, Pen y Fan and Cribyn is just a short section of the Beacons Way (www.breconbeacons.org/beacons-way), a linear long-distance route established in 2005 by local walker John Sansom. It covers 99 miles, with stops along the way including Carreg Cennen Castle near Llandeilo.

leads straight up the hillside all the way to the summit at 795m, which feels gloriously, blissfully quiet after the crush of Pen y Fan. A rocky platform makes a perfect place to rest and contemplate the view, and if the wind is really howling, a circular cairn has been fashioned out of discarded slate to provide at least a smidgen of shelter.

09 From Cribyn, a clear trail leads south along the hilltop of Craig Cwn Cynwyn from the peak, descending into another gully and rejoining the main trail to the east of Upper Neuadd Reservoir along Tor Glas. This gully is known as **Bwlch ar y Fan**, and is crossed by a very ancient trail, sometimes known locally as 'The Gap Road', that is thought to have been in use since prehistoric times, as it's the easiest route across the Pen y Fan massif.

10 If you're feeling really hardcore, you could even add in a fourth peak at this point – another 120m of sheer hillside ascent will carry you to the top of nearby **Fan y Big** at 719m – but it's completely optional, and by now, your thighs are probably feeling the strain, so there's no shame in missing it. It'll always be there for another day, after all. All four summits feature as part of the walk along the Beacons Way.

11 Follow Tor Glas along the east side of the reservoir, joining a rocky access path that leads back to the reservoir car park.

TAKE A BREAK

The **Red Cow Inn** (www.redcow.wales) in Pontsticill, a couple of miles south of the reservoirs, serves no-nonsense pub grub and a good range of local ales, including Wye Valley Bitter and Butty Bach Ale.

60

SNOWDON RANGER

DURATION	DIFFICULTY	DISTANCE 8	START/END
6hr	Hard	miles/ 13km	YHA Snowdon Ranger/Rhyd Ddu station

TERRAIN	Steep, exposed mountain path

You might be able to summit Wales' highest mountain by train, but you'll be missing out on one of Britain's great walks if you do. On a clear day the views stretch to Ireland and the Isle of Man.

GETTING HERE

It's well worth considering public transport if you're planning on taking on Snowdon: car parks can fill up quickly and the Pen-y-Pass car park costs £10 per day.

The **Welsh Highland Railway** (📞01766-516000; www.festrail.co.uk; ⏰Easter-Oct, limited service winter) stops at the trailhead of the Rhyd Ddu Path, and there is a request stop (Snowdon Ranger Halt) where you can alight for the Snowdon Ranger Path. Snowdon Sherpa buses and trains also run to Caernarfon, Beddgelert and Porthmadog.

STARTING POINT

The walk begins, rather conveniently, at the **YHA Snowdon Ranger** (📞0845 3719 659; www.yha.org.uk; Rhyd Ddu; dm/tw from £23/50; 🅿🛜), a handy place to overnight for an early start on the mountain, and ends just as conveniently at the Rhyd Ddu train station.

01 There are seven possible paths to Snowdon's summit, all taking around six hours return. We've chosen two of the quieter routes, combining them to make a memorable mountain circuit that presents the very best side of the king of Welsh mountains. The Snowdon Ranger path is reasonably straightforward and quiet, and it doesn't involve difficult scrambles. The suggested descent via the Rhyd Ddu Path can be difficult and sometimes dangerous in wet, windy or foggy conditions – so if the weather doesn't look favourable, you're best to err on the side of caution and double back down the Snowdon

Ranger Path. Either way, this is a proper mountain walk, involving around 970m of ascent – so don't underestimate it, and make sure you're properly equipped before you set out. Whichever path you choose, be prepared for crowds at the top. Every year more than 400,000 people walk, climb or take the train to the 1085m summit of Snowdon, and the crush at the top on midsummer days can be disheartening. Save Snowdon for a crisp, clear day in spring or early autumn – you might not quite have the mountain to yourself, but at the very least you won't feel like you're in the middle of a festival.

02 The Snowdon Ranger YHA sits on the site of a 19th-century inn built by John Morton, an English mountain guide who used to lead guests to the summit on this track; he's the original 'Snowdon Ranger' after whom it's named. He was one of the early guides who pioneered walking and climbing routes around Snowdon.

03 The path climbs gently for roughly 1.2 miles along the lower slopes of Moel Cynghorion to Bwlch Cwm Brwynog, where you'll see the lake of **Llyn Ffynnon-y-gwas** on your right. Here the path starts

to get steep and hard-going, so take it slow and steady. You'll climb up onto the shoulder of Clogwyn Du'r Arddu (the Black Cliff), following the zig-zag path up the mountainside. It's tough work, but thankfully the sweeping views over the glacial valley of Cwm Clogwyn are inspiring; you can see right across the valley to the Bwlch Main and Llechog ridges you'll be descending later.

04 Follow the cairns along the path as it flattens out slightly, then draws parallel with the **Snowdon Mountain Railway**. The path crosses the tracks at a

Snowdon Mountain Railway

Opened in 1896, the **Snowdon Mountain Railway** (☏01286-870223; www.snowdonrailway. co.uk; adult/child return diesel £29/20, steam £37/27; ◷9am-5pm mid-Mar–Oct) is the UK's highest rack-and-pinion railway. Vintage steam and modern diesel locomotives haul carriages from Llanberis up to the summit in just an hour, with half an hour at the top before heading back down again. Single tickets can only be booked for the journey up; if you want to walk up and ride down, you'll have to hope there's space. From March to May (or during high winds) the trains only head as far Clogwyn Station, at 779m.

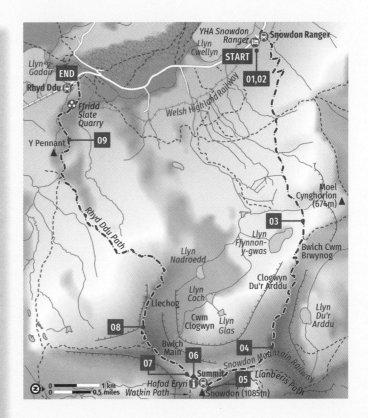

standing stone, turns right and merges with the Llanberis Path for the final approach to the summit.

05 At 1085m, **Snowdon** is the highest mountain in Wales, but it's actually only the 61st highest in Britain (the top 60 are all in Scotland). To the Welsh, the mountain is known as 'Yr Wyddfa' (pronounced uhr-with-vuh, meaning 'the Tomb'); an alternative name for the mountain is Carnedd y Cawr ('Cairn of the Giant'). Legend has it that it's the mythical resting place of the giant Rhita Gawr, who had the unpleasant habit of taking his victim's beards to add to his great cape; he met his match in King Arthur, who supposedly slew the giant and buried his body beneath the Snowdon cairn. The English name of Snowdon comes from the Saxon 'Snaw Dun', roughly translating as the 'Hill of Snow'.

There are stunning views over Snowdon's fine jagged ridges, which drop away in great swoops to sheltered cwms (valleys) and deep lakes. Even on a gloomy day you could well find yourself above the clouds – but if the weather's nice, you definitely won't have the summit to yourself. On the very clearest of days, it's said that you can see Ireland, England, the Isle of Man and Scotland, along with more than 20 counties – although in practice the view is rarely quite as all-encompassing.

06 Take a breather at the striking **Hafod Eryri** (www.snowdonrailway.co.uk; ⊙10am-20min before last train departure Easter-Oct; 🛜) visitor centre. Clad in granite and curved to blend into the mountain, the centre houses a cafe, toilets and interpretive elements built into the structure itself. A wall of picture windows gazes down towards the west, while a small row faces the cairn. Closed in winter or if the weather's terrible, it's open whenever the train is running. It's hard to imagine nowadays, but at the end of the 19th century the summit of Snowdon was actually once home to two hotels. The mountain also has an extremely

rare flower named after it, the Snowdon Lily, a delicate alpine plant with white flowers that has never been found anywhere else in Britain. Needless to say, it's protected by law – so if you're fortunate enough to see one, do not pick it.

07 When you're ready to descend, pick up the **Rhyd Ddu Path** below the visitor centre. After 200m a standing stone marks the point where the Watkin Path veers off; continue straight ahead.

08 The next section along **Bwlch Main** (meaning 'Slender Path') is a narrow track

Snowdonia National Park

Wales' best-known slice of nature, **Snowdonia** (☎ 01690-710426; www.eryri-npa.gov.uk; Royal Oak Stables , Betws-y-Coed; ⏰ 9.30am-5.30pm Easter-Oct, to 4pm rest of year) became the country's first national park in 1951. Its 823 sq miles embrace coastline, forests, valleys, rivers, bird-filled estuaries and Wales' biggest natural lake. Like Wales' other national parks, this one is lived in, with sizeable towns at Bala, Dolgellau, Harlech and Betws-y-Coed, and a population touching 26,000. Two-thirds of Snowdonia is privately owned, with more than three-quarters used for raising sheep and cattle. The Welsh for Snowdonia is Eryri (eh-ruh-ree) – 'highlands'.

with steep slopes on either side: this is the bit that you want to avoid in wind and bad weather, as it is extremely exposed. Near the end of this stretch the path splits into two; keep on the right-hand track. From here the path broadens as it zigzags down and then edges along the barren Llechog ridge. Here you'll have an impressive outlook to the north over Cwm Clogwyn and its three little lakes, Llyn Nadroedd (Lake of the Snakes), Llyn Coch (Red Lake) and Llyn Glas (Blue Lake). The path starts to flatten out after it passes the ruins of an old refreshment hut.

09 The final stretch continues alongside the abandoned **Ffridd Slate Quarry** – slate-mining was once a massive industry on the slopes of Snowdon, and Welsh slate continues to be highly prized as a building material. The path comes to an end near the Rhyd Ddu train station, where you can catch a train on the Welsh Highland Railway back to Blaenau-Ffestiniog and Caernarfon.

☕ TAKE A BREAK

The eccentric **Pen-y-Gwryd** (☎ 01286-870211; www.pyg. co.uk; Nant Gwynant; s/d £58/115; P 🛜 🐾) coaching inn is familiar to many a Snowdon walker – including the 1953 Everest team, who used it as a training base. TV, wi-fi and mobile-phone signals don't penetrate here; instead, there's a comfy games room, a sauna, and a lake for those hardy enough to swim. Meals and packed lunches are available. You'll find the hotel below Pen-y-Pass, at the junction of the A498 and A4086.

Also Try...

TAPPIX/SHUTTERSTOCK ©

CARREG CENNEN

Photogenically perched on the top of a black limestone crag, high above the River Cennen, the part-ruined castle of Carreg Cennen (pictured) is many people's idea of the classic storybook fortress.

Originally a Welsh castle, the current structure dates back to Edward I's conquest of Wales in the late 13th century. It was partially dismantled in 1462 during the War of the Roses. An easy 1½-hour loop takes in both the castle itself and the surrounding countryside, including a section of the Beacons Way. You'll get brilliant views of the castle for much of the way: on a moody Welsh day under glowering grey skies, it really does look like something out of *Game of Thrones*.

DURATION 1½hr
DIFFICULTY Easy
DISTANCE 3.1 miles/5.5km

CADER IDRIS

Cader Idris (893m; Cadair Idris in Welsh) is a menacing-looking mountain with all kinds of mythology swirling round it. Its Welsh name means the 'Seat of Idris', who was either a mythological giant or a 7th-century Welsh prince (or possibly both: the historical Idris was apparently a big fella).

Legend has it the hounds of the underworld fly around its peaks, and strange lights are often sighted; it's said anyone who spends the night on the summit will awaken either mad or a poet. The usual route is the 'Tŷ Nant' or Pony Path, which begins from the Tŷ Nant car park, 3 miles southwest of Dolgellau. It's rocky but straightforward – but this is still a mountain, so wear proper clothing and double-check weather conditions.

DURATION 5hr
DIFFICULTY Hard
DISTANCE 6 miles/10km

IANWOOL/GETTY IMAGES ©

PRESELI HILLS

The only upland area in Pembrokeshire Coast National Park, these hills rise to a height of 536m at Foel Cwmcerwyn.

They encompass a fascinating prehistoric landscape, scattered with hill forts, standing stones and burial chambers, and are famous as the source of the mysterious bluestones of Stonehenge. The ancient Golden Road track, part of a 5000-year-old trade route between Wessex and Ireland, runs along the crest of the hills.

DURATION 3hr
DIFFICULTY Moderate
DISTANCE 6 miles/9.7km

SUGAR LOAF

The cone-shaped pinnacle of Sugar Loaf (596m) is one of the best-known hills in the Black Mountains, the largely uninhabited hills stretching northward from Abergavenny to Hay-on-Wye.

The middle track from the Mynydd Llanwenarth viewpoint car park follows a stone wall, skirts a wood and climbs steeply uphill, turning right to bisect a grassy ridge before a final steep summit scramble. The descent route flanks the head of the valley.

DURATION 2½-3hr
DIFFICULTY Moderate
DISTANCE 4.5 miles/7.2km

LAUGHARNE

Laugharne (pronounced 'larn') sits above the tidal Taf Estuary and a Norman castle (pictured).

Dylan Thomas spent the last four years of his life here: the town was the model for Llareggub in *Under Milk Wood*. A lovely walk takes in the boathouse where Thomas worked, preserved as though he's just popped out for a pint, and the poet's grave in the churchyard of St Martin's Church.

DURATION 1½hr
DIFFICULTY Easy
DISTANCE 3.1 miles/5.5km

Behind the Scenes

Send us your feedback

We love to hear from travellers – your comments help make our books better. We read every word, and we guarantee that your feedback goes straight to the authors. Visit **lonelyplanet.com/ contact** to submit your updates and suggestions.

Note: We may edit, reproduce and incorporate your comments in Lonely Planet products such as guidebooks,websites and digital products, so let us know if you don't want your comments reproduced or your name acknowledged. For a copy of our privacy policy visit lonelyplanet. com/privacy.

WRITERS' THANKS

OLIVER BERRY

Many thanks to all the people who helped me with my research out on Britain's footpaths, but especially to Rosie Hiller, Justin Foulkes and Susie Berry. Special mentions for my co-authors Neil Wilson and Helena Smith, to Anne Mason for the gig, and to all the fantastic team at Lonely Planet who have helped put the book together.

HELENA SMITH

Thanks to everyone who came walking with me, with an especially loud shout-out to Suzanne Hill, who generously shared her expert knowledge of the Peak District with me.

NEIL WILSON

Thanks to Carol Downie, Steven Fallon, Keith Jeffrey and Charlie the dog for keeping me company (and on the right track) while researching some of these walks.

ACKNOWLEDGMENTS

Digital Model Elevation Data
Contains public sector information licensed under the Open Government Licence v3.0 website http://www.nationalarchives .gov.uk/doc/open-government- licence/version/3/

Cover photograph Hadrian's Wall, daverhead/Getty Images ©

Photographs pp6–11: Alex Treadway/Getty Images ©; Kevin Standage/Shutterstock ©; Ian Woolcock/Shutterstock ©; David Lyons/Alamy Stock Photo ©; Lilly Trott/Shutterstock ©; Oliver Strewe/Getty Images ©; Dan Tucker/Alamy Stock Photo ©; Linda Lyon/ Getty Images ©; Oliver Berry/ Lonely Planet ©; Harry Green/ Shutterstock ©

THIS BOOK

This book was researched and written by Oliver Berry, Helena Smith and Neil Wilson. It was produced by the following:

Product Editor Kate James

Book Designer & Design Development Virginia Moreno

Cartographers Hunor Csutoros, Alison Lyall

Cover Design & Researcher Ania Bartoszek

Assisting Editors James Bainbridge, Melanie Dankel, Andrea Dobbin

Product Development Imogen Bannister, Liz Heynes, Anne Mason, Dianne Schallmeiner, John Taufa, Juan Winata

Cartographic Series Designer Wayne Murphy

Thanks to Dave Connolly, Piotr Czajkowski, Barbara Di Castro, Daniel Di Paolo, Tina Garcia, Shona Gray, Martin Heng, Chris LeeAck, Jennifer McDonagh, Campbell McKenzie, Darren O'Connell, Katerina Pavkova, Piers Pickard, Rachel Rawling, Wibowo Rusli, Kate Sullivan, Glenn van der Knijff, Steve Waters

By Difficulty

EASY

MODERATE

HARD

Index

Notes

HELENA SMITH

Helena is an award-winning writer and photographer covering travel, outdoors and food – she has written guidebooks on destinations from Fiji to northern Norway. Helena is from Scotland but was partly brought up in Malawi, so Africa always feels like home. She also enjoys global travel in her multicultural home area of Hackney and wrote, photographed and published *Inside Hackney,* the first guide to the borough (https://insidehackney.com). Her 1000-word autobiography won Vogue's annual writing contest, and she's a winner of the *Independent on Sunday*'s travel-writing competition.

My favourite walk is the Seven Sisters, which I have been walking since I was a small child and love for its wonderful roller-coaster cliff ride, crashing seas and secluded villages.

NEIL WILSON

Neil was born in Scotland and has lived there most of his life. Based in Perthshire, he has been a full-time writer since 1988, working on more than 80 guidebooks for various publishers, including the Lonely Planet guides to Scotland, England and Ireland. An outdoors enthusiast since childhood, he has explored every corner of Great Britain and is an active hiker, mountain-biker, sailor, snowboarder and rock-climber, and a qualified fly-fishing guide and instructor.

My favourite walk is the circuit of Loch Affric. Not only is this one of the most beautiful parts of Scotland – the perfect juxtaposition of mountain, lake and forest – but it offers the chance of spotting iconic Scottish wildlife including red squirrels, red deer and golden eagles.

Our Story

A beat-up old car, a few dollars in the pocket and a sense of adventure. In 1972 that's all Tony and Maureen Wheeler needed for the trip of a lifetime – across Europe and Asia overland to Australia. It took several months, and at the end – broke but inspired – they sat at their kitchen table writing and stapling together their first travel guide, Across Asia on the Cheap. Within a week they'd sold 1500 copies. Lonely Planet was born.

Today, Lonely Planet has offices in Tennessee, Dublin, Beijing and Delhi, with a network of over 2000 contributors in every corner of the globe. We share Tony's belief that 'a great guidebook should do three things: inform, educate and amuse'.

Our Writers

OLIVER BERRY

Oliver Berry is a writer, photographer and filmmaker, specialising in travel, nature and the great outdoors. He has travelled to 69 countries and five continents, and his work has been published by some of the world's leading media organisations, including Lonely Planet, the BBC, Immediate Media, John Brown Media, the *Guardian* and the *Telegraph*. You can follow his latest work at www.oliverberry.com.

My favourite walk is Haystacks and Fleetwith Pike in Buttermere, which is in my opinion the most beautiful of all the lovely Lakeland valleys. It also allows you to pay your respects at the last resting place of the late, great Alfred Wainwright – the patron saint of British hillwalkers, and a personal hero of mine.

← MORE WRITERS ─○

STAY IN TOUCH LONELYPLANET.COM/CONTACT

IRELAND Digital Depot, Roe Lane (off Thomas St), Digital Hub, Dublin 8, D08 TCV4

USA 230 Franklin Road, Building 2B, Franklin, TN 37064
✆ 615 988 9713

 twitter.com/ lonelyplanet

 facebook.com/ lonelyplanet

 instagram.com/ lonelyplanet

 youtube.com/ lonelyplanet

 lonelyplanet.com/ newsletter